Shaunti has brought into biblical perspective the "Y2K Problem." As Senator Robert Bennett, chairman of the Senate Year 2000 Committee said, "I think that civilization as we know it is not going to come to an end [in 2000]...[But] if Y2K were this weekend...it would." Fortunately, it will not occur until January 1, 2000. I pray we will not be caught unaware.

Larry Burkett
Founder and CEO
Christian Financial Concepts

This moment is creating the occasion for God's people to seriously question whether the Y2K computer glitch may be a judgment of God. Is God using this to drive his people and the nation back to himself?

Henry T. Blackaby
author of *Experiencing God*

Shaunti Feldhahn is a uniquely qualified person to address the question of what could happen as a result of the millennium bug. She not only has identified the potential problem but, more importantly, she challenges the Christian community to take the proper leadership role in responding to the considerable fear that is very likely to result over the next several months or possibly years. It is a privilege for me to recommend this book.

Ron Blue
Ronald Blue & Company, LLC
Atlanta, GA

Whatever confusion befalls, the "Y2K" question challenges our modern dependencies and idols. With credibility and moderation, Shaunti Feldhahn gathers the facts and envisions possible real-world outcomes.

Kelly K. Monroe
editor of *Finding God at Harvard: Spiritual Journeys of Thinking Christians*

In an engaging, accessible, and evidence-driven manner, Shaunti answers timely questions about Y2K and proposes an important response for the global Christian community. Just as Joseph prepared for the coming famine—and was able to not only save Egypt but bless the surrounding areas—Christians must take the lead in preparing for a great opportunity of ministry and service. I enthusiastically recommend that you read this book.

Dr. William M. Hinson
President, Haggai Institute
Atlanta, GA

Y2K

The Millennium Bug

A BALANCED CHRISTIAN RESPONSE

Shaunti Christine Feldhahn

Multnomah Publishers *Sisters, Oregon*

The fictional chapters' characters, incidents, and dialogues, unless otherwise noted, are products of the author's imagination. Any resemblance to actual events or persons, living or dead, is entirely coincidental.

Y2K: The Millennium Bug
published by Multnomah Publishers, Inc.

International Standard Book Number: 1-57673-470-6
Printed in the United States of America

Design by Kirk DouPonce
Cover illustration by Henk Dawson/Dawson 3-D, Inc.

A NOTE FROM THE PUBLISHER

This book is designed to provide competent and reliable information in regard to the subject matter covered. However, it is sold with the understanding that neither the author nor the publisher is engaged in rendering legal, tax, investment, accounting, or other professional advice or services. Laws and practices vary from state to state, and because every reader's personal and financial situation is unique, and financial products, market conditions, and laws or interpretations of laws are subject to change, if legal or other expert advice is needed, the services of a professional should be sought. The publisher and author specifically disclaim any liability that is incurred from the use or application of the contents of this book.

For information:
Multnomah Publishers, Inc.•Post Office Box 1720•Sisters, Oregon 97759

Cataloging-in-Publication Data

Feldhahn, Shaunti Christine.
Y2K : the millennium bug / Shaunti Christine Feldhahn.
p. cm.
ISBN 1-57673-470-6 (alk. paper)
1. Year 2000 date conversion (Computer systems)—United States.
I. Title.
QA76.76.S64F46 1998 98–30853
005.1'6—dc21 CIP

99 00 01 02 03 04 05 — 10 9 8 7 6 5 4

This book is joyfully dedicated
to Jeff,
my beloved, my friend.

A special message to
the Joseph Project 2000 team,
especially Kate and Greg Allen and Mel and Harriett Guinn,
the hands and feet and heart who brought the Project
from concept to reality;
and to all of God's shepherds:

May you gain strength and joy as you join him and watch a God-sized work unfold.

FOREWORD

Will We Be Ready?

Several years ago I wrote a book entitled *Storm Shelter,* the gist of which was that by following certain financial principles, you could thrive—regardless of what the economy does. At the time, the stock market hit new highs with astounding regularity, inflation was at an ebb, and unemployment numbers were dropping. The few voices warning of an economic downturn were drowned out by a chorus of bullish investors and optimistic analysts.

What a difference a few years make! As I write this, dramatic market swings, international financial crises, and threats of an impending global crash elbow each other for front page coverage in news reports almost every day. And the looming specter of Y2K grabs the headlines more often than not.

We know that Year 2000 will occur. What we do not know is how bad the computer-generated problems will be. Some experts predict a complete and global gridlock through inaccessible bank accounts, dead phone lines, and widespread power outages, while others maintain that the millennium will waltz in amid balloons, champagne, and little more than a flip of the calendar.

If you are a Y2K skeptic, expecting the computer glitch to be a "non-event," I hope the fact that you are reading this book means you are at least willing to take an objective look at the potential risks associated with the Millennium Bug. If, on the other hand, you count yourself among those who are convinced that the problems are both real and likely to occur, this book may be just one more piece of evidence in the case for being prepared.

But regardless of our personal perspectives, none of us can ignore what may be the greatest risk factor of all: namely, *the fear and panic that the Millennium Bug is already generating.* In my profession as a financial and investment counselor, I have witnessed all manner of panic-driven behavior—from wholesale stock selloffs to the hoarding of food, gold, and even the purchase of guns for self-protection. Yet when we respond to uncertainty like this, letting panic and worry dictate our behavior, we put ourselves in the greatest possible danger.

From an economic standpoint, fear-based decisions are rarely wise. Anxiety can cripple the best-laid financial strategies, creating a "hoarding" mentality in place of a purposeful, steady approach to financial security. If you fear a loss of wealth, you will do anything to protect yourself—and more often than not, the fear-driven decision is the wrong one.

Spiritually, the risks are no less significant. We think that with enough money we will have freedom from fear, but in reality, just the opposite occurs. Grasping our wealth in a tightly clenched fist, we become enslaved to it. And as Eugene Peterson recounts Matthew 6:24 in *The Message,* "You can't worship two gods at once. Loving one god, you'll end up hating the other. Adoration of one feeds contempt for the other. You can't worship God and Money both." When we become preoccupied with stockpiling and hoarding, we cannot help but turn our backs on God. The fear of loss always leads to a loss of faith.

To guard against succumbing to financial and spiritual danger, we must take a thoughtful, alert, faith-based approach to uncertainty. To this end, this book is an invaluable tool. Shaunti Feldhahn does not employ scare tactics or extremist language; rather, she presents a balanced, carefully researched case for being prepared. In her easy-to-read, vividly illustrated style, Shaunti both informs and challenges—enabling us to spot and correct vulnerabilities in our churches, our communities, and our homes.

Again, the economic uncertainty we face today is very real. It is not, however, unique. We have only to look back through the pages of history to find equally unsettling times, from the Great Depression of the 1930s right on through to the nuclear fears of the '60s, the oil crisis of the '70s, and the runaway inflation of the '80s. Uncertainty will always be with us; what matters is how we respond to it.

As Christians, our response to the Y2K situation must be one of faith, not fear. After all, God is not worried about the problem, nor is he surprised by it. As individuals, we must pray that God will use the questions surrounding the Millennium Bug to draw people to Jesus Christ. And as a church, we must be ready to respond to those who are looking for answers in the face of doubt and uncertainty. Far from being a reason to worry or panic, the new millennium represents an unprecedented opportunity to share the gospel with a solution-hungry world.

The only question is, will we be ready?

RON BLUE
NOVEMBER, 1998

CONTENTS

JANUARY 2000

SUN	MON	TUE	WED	THU	FRI	SAT
						1
2	3	4	5	6	7	8
9	10	11	12	13	14	15
16	17	18	19	20	21	22
23	24	25	26	27	28	29
30	31					

PROLOGUE

The Millennium Bug

"It will be good for those servants whose master finds them ready."
Luke 12:38, NIV

As you read this, technology all over the world is ticking toward an event unprecedented in human history. Computers are about to encounter a year that does not begin with the number 19, and many will stop functioning normally as a result. Because of our heavy reliance on computer technology, this Year 2000 glitch (also known as "Y2K" or the "Millennium Bug") may soon create some unusual, unpredictable, and potentially serious disruptions in our lives....

Manhattan, February 4, A.D. 2000—8:20 A.M.

Julia Ashford hurried west on 27th Street, trying to ignore—or at least try to look like she was ignoring—the sights and smells that assailed her senses. Manhattan used to be such a fun place to live, and she had loved the frenetic pace, high salary, and prestige of her position as a vice president of a large investment bank downtown. She even used to love her morning commute, walking to the subway that would speed her to the Fulton Street stop in less than fifteen minutes. But that was before the crash, and everything was different now.

She continued her brisk pace down the crowded sidewalk, pushing her way past slower pedestrians, narrowly avoiding piles of smelly garbage and discarded furniture, and skirting the dozens of shivering panhandlers with signs and cups asking for change.

Crash? Was that what she should call the events of the past year? That word was used daily in news reports, but it hardly seemed appropriate. A crash, though disastrous, implies a finite event, on a particular day or maybe within a particular month, with an easily defined beginning and ending. The dive of the stock market in October of 1987 had been a crash. The last year had actually been more of a transition—a major, foreseeable change over a period of time for which the world could and should have been better prepared. Living through it had been like suddenly finding yourself in a suspense movie—you didn't know exactly how or when it began, you sure don't know how it is going to end, and in between you're subject to gut-wrenching shocks and insecurity.

She smiled grimly at this melodramatic thought. A movie would be a blessing. This was real life and *this* epic couldn't be escaped by shutting your eyes.

Well, she thought, she actually did know the *real* beginning of the story. The real genesis of the current economic recession and social unrest wasn't that one-day 780-point drop in the stock market last spring or even the eventual loss of 57 percent of the market's value from its earlier high. This real-life horror story began way back in the 1960s, when mainframe computers were invented and computers were wired for date "shortcuts"—to assume that a '99 date meant the year 1999. How could such a ridiculously simple thing lead to such distress? At the time, she guessed, the shortcut had made sense—but why had the moronic computer nerds of the last two decades not foreseen that they were creating a time bomb that would explode like a nuclear holocaust in so many countries around the world? During the 1990s so many people had claimed that the whole thing would be fixed by the last day of the century, but she had somehow known that when that clock hit midnight there would be some pretty serious repercussions. Boy, had she been right.

Julia darted around a "temporary" scaffolding wall—which had been there for well over two years—only to collide with a discarded air conditioner. Her briefcase flew from her hand and landed in a trail of gunk that leaked from the garbage bags stacked fifteen feet high across the street. Ugh. She fervently wished the city would resume regular garbage pickup, but under the circumstances she knew she should be grateful for once or twice a month. She picked up her briefcase at arm's length and headed toward a corner store for some napkins to wipe it down.

She stopped when she remembered that both stores on that corner had gone out of business in the last few weeks. They had hung on for a while, but how could they resist the economic tidal wave that was claiming even some large department stores, banks, and factories across the country? The Korean family and the Indian shopkeeper hadn't had a chance, particularly in *this* city. Just yesterday a government economist had announced that in this year alone, 7 percent of midsized businesses would close or were in danger of bankruptcy. One of every fifteen.

She found a Kleenex and wiped the worst of the sludge from her briefcase, then turned onto Park Avenue and began impatiently striding the thirteen blocks south. She was still annoyed at having to walk so far to a subway when she could see the sign for the Local 6 Train a few yards away. But it wasn't just businesses that were finding it difficult to resume normal operations. The Metropolitan Transit Authority had been forced to shut down most local subway service, leaving only the express trains in continuous operation. Under normal circumstances the resulting overcrowding would have been horrendous, but so many people had left Manhattan or were on "temporary leave" since the rollover that the congestion was gradually becoming more tolerable.

At the big intersection of 23rd and Park, she passed the long Contingency Services table manned by people with clipboards and pens. She had vaguely noticed the variety of workers in the past few weeks: government services, telephone and utility companies, the Salvation Army, and a bunch of religious groups. Julia didn't pause. She didn't need help. Manhattan no longer was a playground for her and her affluent friends, but she was self-sufficient and proud of it.

The Bronx

Marvin Rogers, M.D., watched the morning breakfast rush with satisfaction. The buzz of conversation, the sounds of upbeat rap music, and the smells of hash browns and eggs filled the Bronx Good Shepherd Center. Four hundred men, women, and children filled the sprawling, warm room of the old warehouse to capacity, finding sanctuary against the raw winter outside. There would be another group of four hundred coming through in about an hour, mostly the elderly, those "on leave," and others who didn't need to hurry off to work or daycare.

Across the room, eight other volunteers broke off to meet the truck arriving with perishable food donated for the second shift. Right on time. Again. Tears sprang to Marvin's eyes as he observed the reality of God's tender care for his people. It had been just a month since the rollover, and he had wondered how these people were going to make it. But God had been so faithful. Marvin was sobered with the awareness that there were others around the world, and even in this city, who were still struggling for their daily existence. He found himself praying silently for them as he continued clearing dirty dishes.

He was jerked back to the moment by an exuberant little girl who was trying to dance to the rap song. Her chubby four-year-old cheeks, laughing eyes, and bristling cornrowed hair spoke of an impish nature unquenched by the chaos of the last month. Marvin bent down to hug her, then impulsively scooped her up for an impromptu groove around the table, dancing and posing to the beat.

The other diners turned and watched, smiles erupting on their faces. Some started clapping in time. "You go, boy!" someone shouted. Others joined in with shouts of encouragement. When the song ended, Marvin propped the girl in his arms and took a deep, melodramatic bow to their audience, who immediately broke out in whoops of laughter and applause.

Outside the warehouse, a few hardy people waiting in line for the second shift looked at each other curiously, grinned, and shrugged their shoulders.

THE MILLENNIUM BUG...AND YOU

The previous stories illustrate a few potential Y2K disruptions. *Y2K: The Millennium Bug* demonstrates why these problems are likely to occur, explains what they might look like, and outlines how you can personally be ready for them. That, however, is not the core reason I have prepared this book for you. As Year 2000 approaches, information on personal preparedness will be available in every newspaper and on every television network...and it is hardly unique to Christians. What *is* distinctive in the Christian community is our charge to emulate the sacrificial love and servant leadership of Jesus, and our devotion to God above all else.

Thus, my threefold purpose is to call Christians to: (1) personal preparation, (2) immediate and dynamic Year 2000 leadership and service in our communities, ministries, and businesses; and (3) personal reflection on God's message to us through this unique event in history.

Many of you will be skeptical that this issue is cause for attention or concern, and that is understandable. There are a great many Year 2000 doomsday opinions proliferating in the public arena, and it is often difficult to separate fact from fiction. However, the evidence that we will encounter Year 2000 problems is powerful, and we should neither scoff at nor exaggerate the possibly unpleasant implications.

Biblically, it is not our responsibility to precisely predict the future but to be "servants whose master finds them ready" (Luke 12:38). Proverbs 22:3 (TLB) advises, "A prudent man foresees the difficulties ahead and prepares for them; the simpleton goes blindly on and suffers the consequences." In response to the Year 2000 threat, we must be neither panic-stricken nor complacent; we must be ready. This issue is important, difficult, and at times even intimidating—but we can lean on God's saving grace and on his very practical promises.

ABOUT THE STRUCTURE AND USE OF THIS BOOK

I've chosen to provide companion chapters to illustrate Year 2000 facts with stories, all of which are based on the concrete evidence currently available. Research indicates that the impact of the Millennium Bug may vary substantially among different age groups, socioeconomic strata, industries, and even geographic locations. Therefore, odd-numbered chapters follow a few fictional, diverse characters as they encounter Y2K disruptions. These stories are set in Champaign-Urbana, Illinois; Austin, Texas; and New York City, to represent small, medium, and large cities. The evidence for the disruptions encountered by our fictional characters will be laid out in the even-numbered chapters that follow each series of vignettes. (Please note that I chose these cities only for geographic purposes and did not intend to suggest anything about the cities' readiness for Y2K.)

This book is evidence-driven. The only conclusions offered are those supported by credible evidence and data currently available. To the extent possible, the fictional character vignettes employ only illustrations supported by the Y2K facts outlined in subsequent "technical" chapters. The prologue that you have already read provided a good example of this: The character of Julia Ashford remembers a government announcement that 7 percent of midsize businesses were in danger of bankruptcy. That figure was not simply picked out of thin air; I incorporated it because a leading Y2K expert, Capers Jones, currently estimates that Y2K problems will bankrupt 5 to 7 percent of medium-sized companies. (Other independent research firms believe bankruptcies could be as high as triple that rate.)

This book should be used as a launching pad for further personal investigation and action. I have sought to provide the Christian community—individuals, churches, nonprofit groups—with practical and hopefully useful initial information about the Year 2000 problem and how it can be addressed. The book will provide as many examples of potential impact as possible and is written to be accessible for the nontechnical layperson. While I do go into depth in some areas (for example, with a unique nonprofit case study to help ministries examine their potential vulnerabilities), there are over forty books on the market addressing various technical aspects of the Year 2000 problem in great detail, and I do not intend to reinvent the wheel. Further resources are included in the appendix at the back of the book. My hope is that you will immediately begin to consider and prepare for the ramifications that will affect you and the people the Lord has placed in your path. Please also commit to intercessory prayer and personal reflection on what God desires to reveal to you through the coming Y2K event.

I do not pretend to predict the future with certainty. But I do wish to spark awareness, leadership, and reflection in the Christian community, as well as propose a Christian response. The Year 2000 quandary stems from a complex set of voluminous and interconnected problems, and it is confounding even the most knowledgeable experts in government and business worldwide. No one but God knows exactly what is going to happen when the clock strikes midnight on the new millennium. Therefore, there is no way that any book can predict precisely what will happen as A.D. 2000 approaches.

Furthermore, because Millennium Bug information is added or changed daily, the issues discussed are as current as possible based on information and data available at the time of writing. I have attempted to use only the most credible sources, but the opaque nature of the Y2K problem frequently demands that these be secondary sources. Thus, while I have made significant effort to verify both the accuracy and timeliness of data, I cannot guarantee the reliability of all information presented. I encourage readers to stay apprised of developments through news sources, the resources I list in the book, and/or through my organization, Joseph Project 2000.

Finally, readers should be aware that the flow of the vignettes is based on the assumption that many Y2K problems will not occur until the year 2000, enabling some people to remain unaffected by the problem—and even somewhat uninterested in it—until that time. It is, however, entirely possible that the opposite will be true: if pre-2000 disruptions are significant, there will be very, very few people who aren't fully attuned to the issue by the end of 1999.

Y2K is a global concern, not just an American one. Year 2000 disruptions will probably affect every country in the world, to a greater or lesser extent. Since it seems that business and government in the United States and Great Britain (recognized as global Y2K leaders) will not be fully prepared for Year 2000, the readiness level in other developed countries will almost certainly be lower, leading to greater disruptions. Although this book focuses on the United States and cannot provide detailed information regarding other countries, most Y2K risk factors—and the need for a Christ-centered response—are universal. The characters of New York, Texas, or Illinois could just as easily be set in South Korea, Germany, or Brazil.

ABOUT THE INTERVIEWS WITH CHRISTIAN LEADERS

A number of respected leaders in the Christian arena graciously consented to interviews for this book, and their insight and wisdom have been included throughout. You may assume that, in most cases where direct quotes are not further attributed via the notes section, I am quoting directly from these personal interviews. Please keep in mind, however, that these leaders would not always necessarily agree with all of the points made by each other or by me, although the book was written largely to focus on those areas where the Y2K evidence, the interviewees, and the judgments of outside experts *are* in agreement.

ABOUT MY BACKGROUND AND EXPERIENCE

It may be perfectly natural at this point for you to ask, "How can I be comfortable with what you are saying on a technical level?" Many Y2K books are written by either former programmers or professional authors, and I am neither. My experience has revolved around identifying risk factors in the business and government sectors (particularly in the financial arena), and Y2K is without question the most important "risk factor" I have ever seen.

I hold a master of public policy (an analytical degree) from the John F. Kennedy School at Harvard University. In addition to experience on Capitol Hill and as the director of a business program to China, for three years I was a financial analyst at the Federal Reserve Bank of New York, analyzing and briefing senior officials on the status of Asian financial markets and institutions. Recently, I have been focused entirely on readying the Christian community for action on Y2K as the founder and president of the Joseph Project 2000.

As you read through the facts on Y2K, I don't want you to take my word for it. You need to read and listen to what others are saying, and investigate the issues for yourself. I have simply used my experience and training to identify what I think are the most important starting points for your personal investigation and preparation.

PART ONE

YEAR 2000

CHAPTER ONE

December 31, 1999

Champaign-Urbana, Illinois, near midnight

"Five! Four! Three! Two! ONE!"

As the room erupted in cheers and shouts, Johnny Barry took his wife into his arms. Anne returned the kiss, then turned her head to look out the window. She dropped her head to his chest, her arms tight against her body. Johnny could feel her leaning into him, trembling, seeking protection within his embrace. As he smoothed her hair, he followed her gaze. A major intersection was visible down the road in the swirling snow, and its stoplights had suddenly darkened. *Oh, dear God,* Johnny prayed silently. *It's real, isn't it? Be with us.*

This historic night was suddenly a time of both rejoicing and trepidation. It was the start of a new millennium—and, he was now sure, a new challenge for the people of God. Now that the long anticipation had given way to reality, he felt suddenly bereft and insecure. He took a deep breath, not willing to release Anne yet.

A sudden clout on his shoulder threw him off balance. "Happy millennium, Pastor!" Patrick O'Neill's smile beamed from a ruddy face under a shock of thick red hair.

Johnny and Anne stepped apart, smiles on their faces. Johnny hugged Patrick while Anne brushed cheeks with Cindy O'Neill. "Happy New Year to you, too! And blessings on you both." For some reason, Johnny knew, people always liked to receive a blessing from their pastor at the New Year. But he wasn't done yet. "And may you have love and strength for the year ahead."

Patrick looked at him with a quizzical smile as he turned to slap backs with the next partygoer. Johnny sighed. Patrick had been in services nearly every Sunday as all the practical advice and spiritual admonition had been forthrightly discussed. How many others hadn't listened? Hadn't *heard,* he corrected himself.

Anne cupped his cheek with her hand, gently turning his face toward her. "'He who has ears to hear, let him hear.' You've done as much as you can to get people ready, hon. Some people just won't hear, no matter how hard you try. We knew that would happen."

Johnny sighed again. "I know. It just makes—"

"Makes you sad. I know. But you know what?" Her voice rose with indignation as her dark eyes flashed. "It doesn't make me sad, it makes me mad. Because I know perfectly well who'll have to carry the brunt of everything, now that it's finally here." She made an exasperated noise through her teeth. "If they just would have listened!"

Johnny was uncomfortable. In any other situation he would have gestured for her to lower her voice. But in this din, he had to admit that Anne could have shouted and not been overheard. And they were off in a corner anyway. She shrugged, reaching for the glass of Coca-Cola she'd set on a table. "But the human tendency to ignore consequences is what got us into this mess in the first place, isn't it?"

"Look here, guys." The soft voice made them both turn. They smiled as Becky Lee snapped a picture.

Johnny and Anne hugged her in turn, both feeling they might break the diminutive Korean. Johnny took a quick snapshot of Becky and Anne toasting the New Year with their beverage glasses. "Happy New Year, Becky," he said as he handed back her camera.

Becky rested her hand on Anne's arm. "I hope you are having fun tonight." The party was at her brother's simple but spacious house. "I just wanted to let you know that I'll be praying for you and Grace Chapel over the next few weeks."

Their thanks were interrupted by a barrage of good wishes from other friends and a horde of scampering, wound-up children in pajamas, all of whom seemed to have found their corner at the same time. As he passed from person to person through the festive room, shaking hands and receiving bear hugs, Johnny did begin to relax. He decided to enjoy the rest of this evening. "Let tomorrow take care of itself…."

Five miles away, Don Kramer, Alex Marchani, and Travis Pitt sped to their third party of the night, headlights cutting a path through the light snow. The digital readout on the car's dashboard read *12:28*. They had some female friends waiting at Design, the cool new restaurant right outside town, and they didn't want to be too late. These friends were, after all, quite cool themselves.

The car slowed as Alex turned into the parking lot of Illinois OneBank. "I need to get some cash. I'm a little low," he explained. He pulled up to the drive-up ATM, swiped his card, and started punching buttons. He raised his eyebrows at his old college buddies. "And we don't want the ladies to think we're losers, do we?"

Don shoved him roughly, laughing. "I don't know about you. No woman would ever make that mistake with me." He flashed his own wallet, opening it enough so the others could see all the cash inside. "Besides, I'm packin'."

Travis whistled from the backseat. "Man! Did you rob your bank or something?"

Alex grabbed his cash from the machine and drove away, rolling up the window against the cold. "No problem whatsoever. Okay, Travis, what were all those jerks talking about, anyway?"

Don was concentrating on slotting the money into Alex's wallet. "What do you mean?" he asked before Travis could answer.

Alex grunted. "All those scare-mongers, like Travis and those guys at work trying to convince me that I wouldn't be able to use the ATM after midnight. C'mon, Don, you know what I mean. You're a banker. I forgot to get cash earlier and just about had a heart attack when I realized it. Those idiots had practically convinced me to buy survival gear, they made such a fuss. But look!" Alex grabbed his wallet from Don. "Everything's working fine."

Don glanced sideways out his passenger window. "Yeah. It was all overblown. Some people just can't live without a crisis to worry about." He ignored the weak protest from the backseat. Despite Travis's insufferable efforts to "set him straight," Don hadn't really paid much attention to the issue. He knew that his employer, Midwest Bankcorp, had spent over eighty million dollars to fix their computer systems. Just a few months ago he had read assurances that the bank's operations in all seven states "would be completely Year 2000-compliant," so he had stopped worrying about it at that point.

Alex still sounded irritated. "This whole Year 2000 scare was nothing but a huge opportunity for newspapers and consultants to make money. Just because the Dow takes a big dive, people think it's doomsday or something. What a joke." Alex was a T-bills man himself and had been feeling quite superior during the past year as his coworkers moaned about their mutual funds. He hoped Travis would shut up about the whole thing now.

Don laughed as they pulled up to the warm lights of the restaurant. "People will play it to the hilt to take advantage of any opportunity they can find." The irony of that statement hit him as he walked through the doors and searched the crowd. He chuckled. He hoped Jennifer hadn't been waiting too long. He checked his digital watch.

12:00:00.

Huh?

New York City—12:07 A.M.

The high-pitched squeal of a monitor filled the hallway as Dr. Marvin Rogers raced toward room 203. "What've we got?" he asked the senior nurse, Lena Bridinski, as she met him halfway.

"Code blue, cardiac arrest. No warning." She shouted ahead as they approached the nurses station. "Crash cart, stat!"

Two nurses had already grabbed a trolley of medical equipment and were on the doctor's heels as he rounded the corner. The heart patient, William Temple, was lying unconscious on the floor as two nurses performed CPR.

Marvin bent to check the patient's vitals. Probable massive myocardial infarction. No breath, no pulse. Marvin glanced up at the monitor. The patient was flatlined. How could this have happened without warning? He looked out to the vacated nurses station and exclaimed under his breath. The large heart monitor was completely dark.

Nurse Bridinski noticed at the same time. "Oh no."

Marvin swiftly pulled the half curtain, blocking the view of the hallway. "We'll worry about that later. Full ACLS protocol, stat!" They lifted the patient to the bed and Marvin pulled on latex gloves. He watched, tense, as a nurse injected epinephrine into the IV line. Time was running out. *This isn't working...*

"No response. Defib!" Marvin exposed the patient's chest, positioned the paddles on bare skin, and prepared for the electric shock. This was the third time tonight he'd had to use this defibrillator to restart a patient's heart.

"CLEAR!" He pressed the button. Nothing happened. No shock, no convulsive movement. A chill passed down his spine. Nurse Bridinski shot him a look of pure consternation. He tried not to let his voice betray the stress he felt inside. "Quickly, check that cord in back of the machine." *Please, let it be that.*

She swiftly bent down, pushing connections tighter, probing and checking. "I can't find anything wrong!"

Marvin clutched the paddles tighter. "Try it again. CLEAR!" Again, nothing. One of the nurses cursed. Marvin knew how she felt. "It's not compliant! Prepare for an emergency chest crack and direct cardiac stimulation. No time to get him to surgery. Scalpel, spreader, plasma. NOW." *Oh, Lord, I haven't done many of these procedures. Help me. Don't take him yet!*

For several frantic minutes, Marvin wasn't sure of the outcome. Then he felt a flutter under his taut fingers. He hardly dared breathe. *Oh, God, restore life to this man.* He massaged gently, gradually lessening tension as the heart began a weak but steady beat. Marvin carefully withdrew his hand, watching the heart muscle, counting the beats. *Thank you, Lord. Thank you!*

Once the heartbeat stabilized, he began the process of closing the patient and preparing him for transfer to ICU. He steeled himself against the fatigue that always swamped him after an emergency. He could feel his own heart thudding. When he finished, he told the nurses he was going for coffee and would be back in five minutes.

He walked down the stairs and toward the 24-hour coffee shop in Lobby B, off the cardiac and maternity wards. That was one good thing about working for a well-known, prestigious hospital. The hospital had enough money to support these conveniences. Both staff and visitors could get pretty much anything to eat at odd hours.

As he retraced his steps with a steaming cup in his hands, he noticed a young couple at the check-in desk. The woman was obviously far along in labor. Marvin watched as she was placed in a wheelchair and wheeled toward the doors to the ward. She was looking back over her shoulder, teeth clenched in pain, calling out, "Mike? MIKE!" Her husband wanted to follow her, but the hospital administrator stood in his way.

The administrator was a small woman but was feeling her authority. "I'm sorry, Mr. Houston, but you have to complete this paperwork first."

"Why do I have to do this again?" The young husband was clearly frustrated and angry. Marvin was close enough by this time to see that he was almost crying with the urgency of getting to his wife. "Sue and I filled out every single one of these forms two weeks ago so that we *wouldn't* have to do them when we came in. And now you're telling me you don't have any record of us? Not Sue's blood type, or the medical history on the baby, or the doctor's requested medicines?"

The administrator folded her arms. "I'm terribly sorry." She didn't sound sorry. "But we're having some computer problems, and the keypad on the door to our records room is jammed somehow, so we can't retrieve your paper copies either. For liability reasons, we simply cannot permit your wife to be treated until we have this information. You don't want something to go wrong with the baby now, do you?"

Curious, Marvin approached the pair and looked over a partition into the administration station. There were about ten computers on the desks and sideboards, and the screens of most of them were dark. A few displayed gobbledygook. Another chill ran down his spine, and Marvin shivered reflexively despite the warmth cupped in his hands.

The administrator's last comment had taken some wind out of the young man's sails. He grabbed the offered clipboard from her hands. "Okay. I'll fill this out. But please, please let me work on it while I'm with my wife. This is our first baby." He started tearing up. "She's scared and she needs me. And I'm not going to miss the birth of my first child."

The woman pursed her lips in irritation and was clearly going to refuse. Marvin decided it was time to speak up. "I'm sorry to have eavesdropped on your conversation," he said. "But I believe you should get this man back to maternity at once. If the OB doesn't have the computer record of the mother's blood type or drug interactions, it could lead to some serious complications."

The husband looked even more desperate at that information. Marvin sighed internally. He was, after all, a doctor. He was also trying to help. He clarified, "This gentleman can at least verbally provide those details to the physician while he completes this backup information you've requested. It's your call, of course."

Ten seconds later, Marvin watched the husband disappear through the doors to the maternity ward. He smiled an apology to the administrator and continued back to his domain.

As he walked, he thought about the events of the evening and their potential ramifications. *Thank God for that prayer group at Good Shepherd right now.*

Victor and Teresa Luccio sat facing each other in a wooden pew, holding hands, heads bowed. A few feet in front of them, a male voice was urgent in prayer. "Your eye roams to and fro across the earth, searching for a place you can prove yourself strong. Prove yourself strong in our world tonight, Lord Jesus."

A smattering of amens and other encouraging words echoed through the darkened sanctuary of the Bronx Good Shepherd Church. A woman kneeling at the altar steps began weeping, pleading with the Lord. "Oh, Jesus, protect your people tonight. Help your children bless others in your name during the coming weeks, that your glory might be revealed throughout the earth. Lord, forgive the sins of our country and our world, in Jesus' precious name. Turn our hearts back to you." She fell silent, tears still flowing.

Victor roused himself and glanced at his watch. *12:43.* They'd been here for more than two hours and had committed to staying until 2 A.M. He heard the doors at the back of the sanctuary creak and turned to see the Eagles family quietly leave, David hugging a limp child against his shoulder. Nancy followed her husband slowly out the door, her pregnant body stiff from sitting for three hours.

Tears stung Victor's eyes. He knew that Nancy had insisted on participating in the marathon prayer watch, even though she'd had a perfectly good excuse for staying home. *Thank you, Lord, for your faithful saints.*

Another group entered and walked halfway down the aisle—eight teenagers in sloppy jeans and long shirts. Some slid into a pew, while others dropped to their knees on the old carpet. Victor wiped away fresh tears and smiled in the dim light. *And thank you, Lord, for a new generation of saints.*

Teresa silently rose and went to the media station at the back of the sanctuary. The big video screen over the altar briefly flickered and then the view of the map changed. New names appeared. *Wisconsin, Illinois, Alabama. Honduras, Belize, Guatemala.* Heads throughout the sanctuary came up as the people read down the list silently. It would be midnight in those places in a few minutes.

The Millennium Prayer Watch had started more than twelve hours earlier. It would continue in shifts as each country around the world passed through midnight into the next century. Victor knew these prayer services were being held all over the world. Right now there were people in Singapore praying for the United States, although in Singapore it was already past noon on January 1. What an odd thought.

He looked around the sanctuary as voices began lifting up the new states and countries listed, asking God's protection over businesses, churches, hospitals, homes, and schools. Everyone here was passionate, pleading with God for mercy and protection. Many of these people had been given a foretaste of the coming afflictions. The need for prayer was very real to them.

Victor reached for Teresa's hand as she slid back into the pew beside him. Despite the difficulties ahead, Victor felt peace wash over him. *You will supply all our needs in Christ Jesus. Thank you, Lord.*

"Of course I'm all right!" High above 57th Street in Manhattan, Julia Ashford impatiently twitched her arm out of Brad's grasp and continued down the stairs. He followed her, saying nothing more. She was exasperated and hot in this concrete stairwell. It wasn't as if she hadn't walked down stairs before. *Just not so many of them at once.*

She peered at the marker on the next landing. Fortieth Floor. *Well, that's halfway there.* It wouldn't be so bad if she were completely clearheaded. *Maybe I shouldn't have had that last shot of Cuervo,* she thought. Every now and then the stairwell would weave a bit, and she'd have to rest her hand on the banister and wait. The walls were a dreadful slate color. But then, how many people used the stairwells in a luxury high-rise?

She wished Brad weren't following her. But they had to get down, and the stupid elevators were stuck at the first floor. She was mad at having to walk down from the party, and she was taking it out on him. That he was being so nice about it only made her more angry. All day, she and her banking colleagues had closely watched the news wires, dispassionately observing the incoming reports of water utility shutdowns in New Zealand, power outages in Singapore, riots in Indonesia. They had even snickered at one story about top central bank officials being stuck in an elevator in Germany. She had heard all the reports, but somehow she hadn't really considered that she might encounter the same predicament. This was, after all, *New York.*

In another ten minutes they reached the street. Carolyn Hendricks and her husband were waiting for them on the sidewalk. Julia tried to shrug off her irritation, forcing a smile for her former roommate. She took her coat back from Brad, who had carried it all the way down the stairs. *What a way to ring in a new century.*

Austin, Texas—1:40 A.M.

Billy Phillips drummed his fingers on the steering wheel, staring at the yellow-and-white-striped parking barrier. It refused to open and let him out of the parking lot. He swiped his parking pass again. No movement. *Give me a break.* This was one problem he hadn't anticipated. He reparked his car and jogged back to the restaurant. He caught Jim and Courtney Thicke just as they were leaving. Jim was buckling himself into their Jeep Grand Cherokee. "Hey, can I get a ride with you guys?" He explained what had happened.

Jim chuckled. "The parking garage is holding you hostage, eh? Sure, hop in."

As they sped down LBJ Highway, Billy got an idea. "Hey—you were going to that Promise Keepers thing tomorrow, weren't you?" Jim nodded. "Well, would you mind carpooling? The Capitol building isn't too far away from my parking garage. I'm sure whatever's wrong will be fixed by then, and I can drive my car home."

Jim was glad to oblige. Billy had been a huge help ever since they moved to Austin two years ago, when Jim and Courtney didn't know anyone. Not five minutes after he met them at Community Church that first Sunday, Billy had offered to help them unload their moving truck. Billy was a good Texan—the sort who thought most problems could be fixed by a little old-fashioned elbow grease. Jim smiled to himself. He knew Billy was somewhat naive, but at least he got things done.

Suddenly, Jim sat up straight. "Wow, Billy. I'm glad you reminded me about Promise Keepers. I promised to bring drinks and stuff, and I completely forgot."

Courtney flashed him a sardonic grin, and snorted.

"Oh, you be quiet. I remembered this time, didn't I?" They found a huge twenty-four-hour supermarket and the men hustled inside, on a mission for Cheetos and Pepsi.

As the guys brought their treasures to the checkout lane, Billy pointed to a sign. *NO CHARGE CARDS. CASH ONLY.* "I hope you weren't planning on using your credit card."

Jim frowned. "Actually, I was." He turned to the elderly clerk, who was ringing up another customer's purchases. "Why can't I use my credit card?"

The clerk shrugged as he tapped information into the cash register. "The phone lines aren't working. We can't get confirmation from the credit card companies. My manager is having to use cell phones to call outside, and we're using our old walkie-talkies instead of the intercom system. Good thing we have plenty of batteries around." He began bagging up the other customer's groceries.

Billy whistled under his breath. "I was wondering if this would happen."

Jim didn't look up. "Pardon me?"

Billy leaned against a rack of candy bars. "The telecommunications managers in some areas were concerned that their network conversions wouldn't be completely tested by midnight tonight. Last night, that is. The folks at the budget office have been talking about it all month."

Jim didn't know what Billy was talking about. He watched as the clerk started ringing up his purchases. The clerk searched a liter of soda and typed in a number. A price popped up on the screen. "Our bar code system isn't working, either," he explained, as he began to repeat the process. "Broke down about two hours ago. My manager is having fits. And one of my customers just had to put back her groceries because our ATM isn't working either." The clerk gestured toward the mini-ATM near the doors. He didn't seem overly concerned.

Billy shook his head. "The Millennium Bug. It was bound to happen. It affects so many things—bar codes, elevators, accounting systems, utilities, even common

PBX phone systems." He nodded at the clerk, who was rechecking his work. "One of the news shows even said that some cars might not start after midnight tonight, if you can believe it. Didn't you see that government announcement yesterday, that one out of fifteen businesses might not survive the year?"

Jim wasn't paying much attention. He watched the final price on the screen. "That'll be $28.08, please." Billy handed over a ten-dollar bill, and Jim pulled the last twenty from his wallet. He had paid cash at the restaurant party tonight and was out of money already.

Well, Jim wasn't worried. He had a hundred dollars stashed away at home.

Deborah Carey buckled her twins into the back of her battered minivan, taking care not to wake them. She was glad her shift was over; now she could get them into their own beds. Not that her mom minded keeping them when she worked late, but her mom was unreliable and thoughtless—even when sober—and Deborah's preschoolers were a handful.

She smoothed back Gary's hair and propped Gail into a more comfortable position, careful to avoid the rough edges on the old car seats. Well, these car seats might not look all fancy, but they were clean and they would keep her babies safe.

She quickly walked around to the driver's seat, mindful of the dark street and sketchy surroundings. She saw a group of men casually sauntering down the sidewalk across the street. It took just seconds to jump in and lock the doors. The men turned and looked in her direction. She fumbled with the key ring, rapidly sorting through the jingling mass. *Restaurant, deadbolt, mailbox, Mom's apartment, supply cabinet...*

The group across the street stopped and watched her intently through the window. Three men? Four? She tried to appear unconcerned, but her heart started racing. She caught a glimpse of movement out of the corner of her eye. No. No!

She finally grasped the right key and inserted it in the ignition. *Phew.* She turned the key. Nothing. The motor didn't even turn over. She tried again, pumping on the gas pedal. What was going on?

A loud knock on her window made her jump, and she stifled a cry. A shadowy face leered at her through the glass.

Mustering years of street smarts, Deborah gathered her courage and put on an exasperated air. She cranked down her window and put her finger over her lips in an admonishing gesture, clearly surprising the street tough. "*Shhhhh!* Can't you see they're sleeping?" She gestured to the little children asleep in the backseat, praying that this tough guy actually had some sense of decency.

She sat still, her heart pounding in her ears, as he backed off and sauntered toward his friends. They slipped away into the darkness. Deborah sucked in a deep breath and exhaled slowly, trying to calm the pounding in her chest. She would have to take the kids back inside her mom's place for the night. But she fought back a deep despair. She had to work. What was she going to do without her car?

CHAPTER TWO

HOW DID THIS HAPPEN?

What deserves your attention most is the last thing to get it.
Epictetus

In the calendar of the average computer's brain, 98 means 1998, 99 means 1999. This is the same shorthand we humans have used naturally for decades, and we have programmed it into our technology.

Since the dawn of the computer era in the 1960s, many timekeepers inside computer-related technology—everything from the tiny chip embedded in your VCR to the vast network of global telecommunications—have operated under the assumption that years have only two digits. Thus, when January 1, 2000, rolls around, many computers will blithely continue as they have been programmed to do and will assume the date is January 1, 1900. And in calculations, 99 + 1 will equal 00, a mathematical impossibility.

Although this technicality seems inconsequential and even a bit absurd, it has the potential to be extremely serious. This apparently simple problem is expected to cause some portion of the world's computer technology to function poorly or stop functioning altogether—including many cases in which the year wouldn't seem to matter. While many forward-looking governments, organizations, and individuals around the world are devoting substantial resources to fixing this problem, many others are doing little or nothing. Unfortunately, many in the Christian community are not thinking about, much less preparing for, the possible consequences of the Millennium Bug.

While we have become accustomed to computer-aided functions in our individual professions, most of us don't realize just how fundamental computer technology is to the smooth functioning of our entire society. The United States houses nearly half of the computer capacity in the world. And it's not just our millions of computers and computer systems that are cause for concern; an estimated 25 to 70 billion microprocessors (computer "chips") are embedded in everything from pacemakers to nuclear missiles. With such immense volume, even a tiny percentage of chip malfunctions could have grave consequences.

The task of resolving the Year 2000 problem is enormous, involving millions of man-hours, billions of lines of code, and trillions of dollars worldwide. Because of this overwhelming magnitude, a shortage of time and resources, and a host of other interconnected factors, it is widely acknowledged that the job will not be fully completed in time and that some disruptions to business and society are unavoidable. Senator Robert Bennett, chairman of the Special Senate Committee on the Year 2000 Technology Problem, reported in July 1998: "We have reached the point where we cannot solve the whole problem. That is very clear. As a nation, as a government, we cannot get this problem solved."[1] An official government Y2K study by the General Accounting Office (GAO)—which usually avoids taking strong positions—stated in April 1998: "At the current pace, it is clear that not all mission critical systems will be fixed in time.... The public faces a high risk that critical services provided by the government and the private sector could be severely disrupted by the Year 2000 computing crisis.[2]

Peter de Jager, widely regarded as the world's foremost expert on Y2K, said recently on *The 700 Club*, "We've prided ourselves on being a technologically advanced civilization. The bottom line is that technology has got a flaw. And unless we fix it, we will lose the benefits of that technology. There is no way to sugarcoat that message."

It is important to remember that the extent and impact of potential Y2K disruptions is unknown and will depend largely on how intensely we focus on fixing our most important systems and preparing for contingencies in the time remaining.

CAUSE: SAVING SPACE

During the first few computer decades, a basic computer would fill a room or two and disk space was limited and expensive. Those walls of whirring, ceiling-high computers in the TV shows of the late 1970s (think *The Six Million Dollar Man*) had less computing power than today's typical desktop PC. At that time, one megabyte of computer disk space—which today costs around ten cents—cost over half a million dollars. To save expensive space, computer programs had to be as compact as possible. One easy shortcut was to assume that all years began with 19, thus shortening all dates to just six spaces: month month/day day/year year, for example. Under this method, September 20, 1975, became 09/20/75. These truncated dates became entrenched in millions upon millions of lines of computer code and burned into vast volumes of computer chips.

Of course, everyone knew at the time that this date convention was temporary and would only work until December 31, 1999. After that time, the computer would not know that 00 meant A.D. 2000 unless the date field was expanded from two to four spaces. However, no one was overly worried because astonishing advancements were being made yearly in computer technology. Everyone figured that (1) the old programs would no longer be in use decades later, or (2) the problem was so simple that it would be easy to fix when the time came. Unfortunately, these assumptions lasted well into the 1990s, when people began hoping someone might invent a "magic bullet" to find and convert those year fields to four spaces at the touch of a button. Over the last few years, we have come to the sober realization that many of the old shortcut programs are just as heavily used today as back then, that no magic bullet will be possible, and that fixing this "easy" problem will be greatly hindered by the fact that we have waited too long.

A SNAPSHOT OF THE PROBLEM

Jim Lord, a former technical expert in the government and defense industry and now a nationally recognized Y2K expert, has written a book called *A Survival Guide for the Year 2000 Problem*. He also publishes a monthly newsletter. Much of what follows comes from Jim's research into the Y2K situation, information he has graciously shared in interviews and discussions with me.

In general, computers can be divided into four different categories:

Mainframes. These are mostly older systems and are used predominantly by government and large corporations.

Midrange computers. These are common business systems, in use by the entire spectrum of business (particularly small and medium-sized enterprises) and non-profit organizations.

Personal computers. These are the desktop and laptop computers used in everyday professional and personal life. This category includes not only the hardware but also software applications and files, network equipment, servers, and the Internet.

Embedded systems. These are the chips (essentially, tiny computers) that are incorporated into and control or assist much of our modern technology—everything from automobiles to digital watches to X-ray machines.

It is important to understand that *all* computers are potentially vulnerable to Year 2000 problems, but it is sometimes difficult to tell which ones. While it is appealing to accept the popular myth that only 1970s-vintage mainframes are riddled with Y2K bugs, the reality is that, unfortunately, each category of computer is susceptible to Year 2000 problems (although the likelihood and potential severity of Y2K problems vary widely among computers). Even the tiny computer chips that run items with no seeming awareness of the date are sometimes vulnerable. Of course, not every individual computer will have Y2K problems; there will be many millions that keep humming along just fine. The trick is to figure out which are which.

Why Don't They Just Fix It?

You may be asking yourself, "Changing a date code sounds like it should be relatively simple; why don't they just fix it?" The simple answer is, they *are* fixing it. Hundreds of thousands of computer programmers and managers all over the world are spending days, nights, and weekends doing literally nothing but scanning and fixing lines of code.

In a nutshell, the Year 2000 quandary is this: it's a relatively simple problem, with a relatively easy fix but an overwhelming magnitude. Fixing the Year 2000 problem is no longer a technical problem; it's a resource problem. And that is precisely why it has become a problem of such intense concern.

Jim Lord provides a good analogy:

> Imagine that under your sink you have two straight pipes that are connected by a simple joint, and the pipes are leaking because the joint is broken. You call a plumber or buy a joint and a wrench, and replace the defective part. Simple problem; easy solution. This in many ways is like Y2K; it's a simple problem, easy solution. It really is.
>
> But now imagine that you find out that there is something wrong with some percentage of *all* plumbing joints that have ever been manufactured, all over the world. And most of these defects will cause leaks or breaks in the plumbing to which they are attached. Problem is, you don't know *which ones* are defective; you have to examine every pipe joint in the world, fix the ones that are defective, and then test the plumbing to make sure you fixed it right. Suddenly, you don't have a plumbing problem; you have a resource problem. There just aren't enough plumbers or wrenches to go around, and there is an enormous backlog on replacement parts, of course.
>
> Not to mention that many of these pipe joints are hard to find, and in obscure places. You can't just stop with your sink; there's a pipe in your furnace, in the back of your refrigerator, and in your car. They are embedded in the walls of skyscrapers, hidden on locomotives, buried deep under the sea in oil pumps, and up in space on satellites.
>
> Now you see—simple problem, relatively easy fix, overwhelming magnitude. And we just don't have the resources or the time to get it done.

This analogy should actually be carried further. Imagine that after much aggravation, many months, and lots of money, you've found all these hidden pipes in your house and your car, figured out which ones will break, waited months for the replacement parts, and fixed the defective joints. You dust off your hands and congratulate yourself that *you* are finally finished. Then you turn on the tap to get a drink...and no water comes out. Not only that, but suddenly your lights go dark. What's happening?

Well, *you* may have been finished with your repairs, but the water utility up the street wasn't. They had too many pipes and not enough repairmen, so there was a break in the plumbing a couple of miles upstream from your house. And because of a similar break in the plumbing at the hydroelectric station, there was no longer water-generated electricity for your town and your house.

Now you're starting to see why fixing this seemingly simple problem isn't so simple. It can be quite difficult and expensive to find and fix all of your own vulnerabilities; and then you could still be affected because other people haven't done their part. The Year 2000 issue is more complex because of the *volume* of potential defects than their inherent intricacy (although computer intricacy does sometimes impede progress). Furthermore, you could fix all of the Year 2000 bugs you can think of in your business, your church, your home—and still encounter difficulties because others are not as ready. A common sentiment among those addressing the problem is "You are only as ready as those you do business with." That concept can be applied to your personal life as well.

Now that you're more nervous than when you started this book, please keep in mind the *very important* mitigating factor to this uncomfortable scenario: just as, in the above example, only a small percentage of all pipes had defects, not all computer technology is date-sensitive. In other words, there will be vast volumes of computerized functions that will be completely unaffected by the fact that the clock is rolling over to the year 2000. Further, even some of the functions that *are* date-sensitive may not be mission-critical. They may be relatively unimportant to you or your organization (you won't care much if your fifteen-dollar digital watch stops) or may not prevent core technology from operating after the rollover (your car still runs, but its diagnostic software says it is ninety-nine years past due for a tuneup).

The challenge, of course, lies in the need to examine every single computerized function, identify which mission-critical and important functions are date-sensitive (it is less obvious than it seems), and fix them in the little time we have left. Unfortunately, there are millions of date-sensitive systems that *are* extremely critical for business, government, and personal functions. You will very likely care if your bank cannot release funds for your paycheck, your lights go off, or if food distribution breakdowns temporarily cut off the supply of food to your city. These are not far-fetched concerns. The April 1998 GAO report noted a *"high risk* that…financial transactions could be delayed, flights grounded, power lost and national defense affected" (emphasis added).[3]

INSUFFICIENT RESOURCES

Shortage of Time

In our race to fix the Millennium Bug, our most severe resource deficiency—by far—is lack of time. Those working on the problem have described the rollover to January 1, 2000, as "the biggest nonnegotiable deadline in history."

As a wealthy and innovative society, we are used to being able to creatively solve every problem that comes our way—and we have become especially accustomed to the particular brand of magic that our Information Technology (IT) departments somehow wield over seemingly grumpy and uncooperative computers. Pat Robertson notes that "[Everyone] thinks Y2K is just some technical problem, that those guys that always make the computers work are going to come and do it again." Unfortunately, we have finally snagged a problem that cannot be solved easily by massive amounts of money, labor, or ingenuity: a rigid deadline. There is literally nothing we can do to alter the fact that, when clocks tick to January 1, 2000, many unfixed date-sensitive systems will stop working properly.

You are likely asking, "Why didn't they see this coming?" The simple answer is, they did—they just didn't do much about it. Unfortunately, given human nature, if the deadline were still ten years hence we probably would procrastinate right up to the point where the new deadline is just as impossible as the one we are now facing. The following factors contribute to our procrastination:

- *Greed/Self-concern.* During the greatest economic expansion in history, few business managers wanted to spend big money to fix an obscure computer problem that seemed years away. Thus it was easy to ignore. No CEO or president wants to see the shareholder value of their company drop because they spent $10 million to fix a poorly understood, "trivial" problem. Many CEOs, realizing they weren't going to be around in a few years, were more than willing to pass the buck to their successors. Others repeatedly said, "We'll spend the money next year." This critically delayed the start of the fix.
- *Denial.* It truly has seemed impossible to many—in fact, probably to many of you reading this—that such a simple thing could really be that big of a deal. And with many issues competing for valuable money and time, any business or government entity will attend only to the issues they consider most critical. While the average programmer may have tried to alert management that the problem could threaten future profitability, if the average manager or government official did not understand or want to believe it, money was never allocated.
- *Assuming a magic bullet.* Finally, nontechnical managers assumed that, with the astounding advances in computer technology (the power of which doubles every eighteen months), someone would eventually invent a quick cure—a magic bullet that would fix all the code problems at the touch of a button. Even today, people outside the Y2K arena tend to think of the problem as "something Bill Gates will fix." Unfortunately, computers operate in more than five hundred completely different computer languages, many of which have then been custom-programmed for the operations of a particular organization. Therefore, no one uniform fix is possible.

Shortage of "Repairmen"

As in the plumbing analogy above, the worldwide shortage of computer programmers and other technical personnel has become critical. Without sufficient experts to fix and test their computer technology, any computer-dependent organization—which could be anything from Fortune 500 businesses to community churches—might be vulnerable to significant disruptions as the rollover approaches. Unfortunately, the supply of programmers is lagging far, far behind the current demand—and the gap is only expected to worsen in the coming months. A March 1998 study by the Information Technology Association of America revealed that the U.S. *alone* already had 350,000 unfilled job vacancies for computer scientists and programmers.

Why are so many programmers needed? The process of individually investigating every single computer system, embedded chip, and desktop PC is mind-bogglingly time-intensive. Particularly vexing is the challenge of examining and fixing heavily used mainframe computer systems, as it involves individually scanning millions upon millions of lines of code in *each system*. Unfortunately, the documentation for many of the older computer languages has disappeared and many of the programmers familiar with those systems have since died.

While the layman may perceive computer programming to be a highly standardized and technical science, it is actually more like an art in some ways. And it may require an enormous effort for a programmer today to understand and fix the quirks of a single line of code written by someone else thirty years ago. Programmers at a typical medium-sized business may easily face *five million* such lines in their main system. Therefore, although hundreds of vendors have crafted new programs that help automate the process of finding and fixing older code, it remains an extremely labor-intensive task.

In addition, the programmer shortage also creates several key side effects. One is that the government's chances of readiness are rapidly diminishing as high-paying businesses offer enormous salaries and perks that the public sector cannot hope to match. Similarly, foreign countries are facing an increased risk of critical economic and social disruptions as the U.S. and other wealthy western nations lure away massive numbers of their poorly paid but talented programmers, particularly as these other countries are already considered to be seriously lagging behind the U.S. in their Y2K preparations.

Shortage of Money

Largely because of this labor shortage, the already high costs of fixing the problem will only escalate as the rollover approaches.

The rising cost estimates of the Gartner Group, a technology think tank that is widely regarded as a pioneer in the Y2K field, provide an illustration. In 1995 and 1996, the Gartner Group found that it was costing companies around $1.00–$1.10 per line of code to fix the Year 2000 problem. In 1997, that cost was raised to $1.40, then again to $2.40 in early 1998—but with common spikes into the $4.00, $5.00, and even $8.00 range. By late 1998, Gartner estimated that the minimum cost had risen to $3.60, and both they and other industry observers anticipate that costs could easily spike past $10.00 per line by mid-1999.[4]

With these prices, a medium-sized business with five million lines of code could easily take a $10 million hit in just one year. Obviously, many businesses and governments will not be able to afford such a costly fix. Luckily, in some cases a corrupted system is not mission-critical, or its records and functions can be reproduced on paper and completed by hand. However, where the very survival of their business is on the line and cannot be done by hand, an organization that does not fix its corrupted systems may be forced to close its doors.

As noted earlier, the real problem for some businesses is not lack of money but the incorrect expectation that enough money will solve their Y2K dilemma. Simply buying the services of massive numbers of programmers will not necessarily accelerate the complicated, highly personalized, and time-intensive process of fixing code. Ed Yourdon, coauthor of the bestselling book *TimeBomb 2000* and a longtime giant in the programming arena, explains that programming by its very nature is a lengthy effort, regardless of the number of people devoted to it. In his book, he explains that many managers who don't understand this think they can speed up the fix simply by hiring extra programmers. But, "like trying to produce a baby in one month by assigning nine women to the task, there are some things you just can't speed up."[5]

Shortage of Replacement Parts

As A.D. 2000 approaches, replacing noncompliant technology will be increasingly difficult if new parts cannot be manufactured quickly enough to meet demand. Where computer technology breaks down or works incorrectly after the rollover, it may simply have to be abandoned until sufficient replacements are manufactured. The benefit of a market economy, however, is that intense demand will generate intense efforts to meet it—although likely at a high price. The primary problem with meeting demand will arise when the manufacturing cycle for replacement parts is simply too long or too inflexible to allow a massive increase in production. For example, in mid-1998 a senior executive at a top U.S. automobile manufacturer confidentially stated that the company expects one-third of its 40,000 robots to encounter problems in the year 2000 due to embedded chip problems. Unfortunately, the replacement parts have an eighteen-month manufacturing cycle, so the company reportedly isn't sure if these robots will be fixed in time.

Tangentially (and more important for individuals to be aware of), the shortage doesn't just apply to replacement computer parts. It also affects those devices that can temporarily *substitute* for potentially suspect functions. For example, thousands of extra businesses and individuals are expected to buy electric generators to ensure an emergency power supply if their local power grid is temporarily disrupted. At some point, manufacturers simply may not have the ability to make enough generators to meet this increased demand. This shortage may begin to apply to any substitute item. In an interview with me in June 1998, Christian financial counselor Larry Burkett illustrated how this problem is already being encountered:

> I recently called an Amish supply company to order a couple of their coal oil lamps, since they make the best in the world. The person there said, "I can't give you any delivery time on these. We may never be able to deliver them, and if we can, it may be six months." He said, "If you had called me two months ago, I would have shipped you some; if you had called me a month ago, I would have told you it would be two weeks late. Today I must tell you that we are so swamped with orders that we don't know that we'll ever get to them all. We just aren't equipped to manufacture them all." And that is what will be happening...the longer we wait.

EXACERBATING THE Y2K PROBLEM

As if the resource shortages themselves weren't enough, other difficulties exacerbate the severity of the Millennium Bug problem and hinder our ability to solve it. Again, I am grateful to Y2K expert Jim Lord for many of the key points we will highlight here.

Interconnectedness

The extreme interconnectedness of our world has allowed great leaps forward in economics and society but has also magnified the scope of the Y2K problem. A small problem in one system somewhere has the potential to spread—through transmission of corrupt data—to dozens or hundreds of others to which it is connected. Jim Lord illustrates: "In today's economy, from your home computer, you can buy Japanese stocks from a broker in Germany and denominate the transaction in Swiss francs. You can see how one problem somewhere could interrupt the chain." Both personally and professionally, we are extremely dependent on each other. The April 1998 GAO report notes that "a high degree of information and systems interdependence exists among various levels of government and the private sector in each of these sectors. These interdependencies increase the risk that a cascading wave of failures or interruptions of essential services could occur." Christian commentator and evangelist Pat Robertson told me:

> We are terribly interdependent in our society. Terribly. We're dependent on the power grid, on aircraft...on communications. Look what happened just the other day when a communications satellite [Galaxy 4] went on the fritz for twenty-four hours, and all the pagers went down of doctors all across the country. They couldn't deliver medical services, the druggists couldn't service the prescriptions they needed to write, supermarket suppliers [couldn't] get their orders filled. The whole chain goes throughout our society. It's wonderful to have it, but it's also a risk. There was a book written years ago called *Brittle Power,* and it was the idea that this society is so brittle because it has so little flexibility. It's all interdependent. Just think about the electricity we use for heat, cooking, air conditioning. We run our media with electricity. If one electric power grid goes down because of a Y2K-type problem, you could wipe out the grid on a whole quadrant of states. It's...very serious.

Another sobering example further illustrates this point. Millions of diabetics around the world are dependent on whether a municipal power plant in Denmark will be ready for Y2K. Why? Roughly 70 percent of the world's insulin comes from one company, Novo, in Denmark. If you or a loved one is diabetic, you can imagine how a moderate power disruption in a faraway country could have serious personal ramifications.

"Just in Time" Inventory Systems

The insulin example illustrates another disturbing facet of this problem: the businesses that sell products today no longer have weeks of extra inventory lying in a back room. Instead, they order inventory "just in time"—just as it is needed. So when a hospital, for example, knows it is about to run out of insulin, it simply places an order and insulin is shipped within hours from a central warehouse somewhere else in the country or the world. This same procedure is mirrored at most businesses in the country, whether it's a supermarket, a clothing store, or an automobile manufacturer. Probably the most crucial example of this is that most cities in the U.S. have only a seventy-two-hour supply of food on grocery store shelves. Rather than being stored "out back," replacement foodstuffs are delivered daily via train and truck to the supermarket's loading dock. Similarly, an auto manufacturer doesn't keep inventories of car oil pumps on site; they are shipped from suppliers via boat or rail to be slotted "just in time" into cars being built.

If Y2K disrupts some of these distribution systems for even a small time—if a train switching system is shut down, for example, or an inventory tracking system malfunctions—the consequences could be enormous; store shelves could quickly be picked clean and assembly lines could be forced to stop production. The recent strikes at UPS and General Motors provide telling examples of how a Y2K-like breakdown in the supply system can quickly spread and multiply; in the GM case, although Flint workers went on strike, plants all over the country had to shut down within days for lack of parts—costing GM roughly $75 million *per day* in lost revenues. Although hospitals usually keep more extras of life-and-death items around than would a normal business, at some point those stores would also run out. These consequences are one reason why companies are sometimes reluctant to conduct full-scale live tests of their systems once they conduct a Y2K "fix": they can't *afford* a disruption if the fix didn't quite work right.

"Fly By Wire" Economy

Many businesses in today's economy are vulnerable to Y2K not because of an inventory problem or because their customer accounts might be garbled, but because they literally cannot function without computer technology. For many businesses, Y2K system disruptions will cause weeks or months of frustrations and even lost or reduced revenues, but the core business can be sustained by reverting to old-fashioned manpower and paper and pencil if necessary. However, as we have grown increasingly sophisticated, we have created a whole sector of our economy that will have to shut its doors within two or three days if its computers stop working.

The concept of "fly by wire" comes from high-performance jet aircraft, which are so complicated technologically that human beings can no longer fly them without the aid of computers. Obviously, these jets have pilots, but the minute and precise adjustments in flight surfaces that must be made instantaneously many times a second cannot possibly be made by a human—and so are left to a computer. In some jets, if every on-board computer system is switched off, the plane will drop out of the sky like a rock; it simply cannot be flown manually. The same concept applies to many businesses that will be particularly vulnerable to Y2K. One easy example would be the online stores that have sprung up in recent years—if their system goes down, no business is conducted. Similarly, although an insurance company or an accounting firm might, in theory, be able to conduct their business manually, in practice they are fully automated and no longer have the staff to do manual work.

Legal Liability

Most Y2K watchers agree that two of the most important elements in a speedy resolution of the problem are communication and cooperation. Companies willing to open their processes and share ideas and mistakes will help each other proceed much faster along this tricky ground. Unfortunately, as you might imagine, the legal industry is gearing up for a whole new practice area revolving around Y2K lawsuits—and many lawsuits are already being filed as Y2K disruptions occur in advance of the year 2000. Y2K experts estimate that the cost of litigation worldwide could exceed $1 *trillion*—which roughly equals the entire federal government's annual budget. Although the need for redress against negligent companies is clear, the unfortunate effect of the specter of litigation is that companies are afraid to talk about their state of Y2K readiness and are therefore less willing to cooperate in fixing the problem.

As one example, banks have been unable to determine the readiness of their most important supplier—telecommunications companies. Without working phone connections to allow wire transfers, conduct trading activities, or clear and settle interbank transfers, most banking institutions will be dead in the water within minutes. Governor Edward Kelley of the Federal Reserve testified before Congress that, since the major phone companies were so critical to the banking system, he had officially asked the major phone companies about their state of readiness but was unable to get that information. Reportedly, the phone company lawyers would not allow it to be released; thus, even the central bank of the United States could not get the information it so desperately and legitimately needed. While the telecommunications sector has reportedly begun to work more fully with the banking sector, this illustrates the difficulties inherent in our interdependent economy.

Denial of Tragedy

As Christians, the idea of human sinfulness is less of a surprise to us than to most Y2K experts, who bemusedly wonder how people could have been so blind to procrastinate for so long. One fundamental, overwhelming problem with readying for Y2K is that so many people just refuse to believe the issue could possibly be that serious, all evidence to the contrary. Just as people diagnosed with terminal illnesses deny that it could happen to them, many people, when confronted with Y2K, refuse to consider that it could truly be real and serious and require action on their part.

Political Scandals

Given the potential scope and severity of the crisis, Y2K should have officially been the top and overwhelming priority of the U.S. government (as it is for Great Britain) for the last year or two. Instead, Washington has been sidetracked and weakened by scandal after scandal, and top government leaders have not focused on truly leading our country to prepare for this critical event. While fighting for integrity in governmental leaders is important, it pales in comparison with the need to ensure that the country is secure and that we will *have* a properly working government come January 1, 2000.

Truly, the situation would be farcical if it weren't so horribly serious. It is almost as if we were standing directly in the path of a devastating, advancing forest fire, quarreling about how to confront the cohabitating couple in the next tent.

Ed Yardeni, chief economist at Deutsche Morgen Grenfell, said in July 1998 that the Y2K situation had become grave enough that we no longer need a "national leader" on the subject...we need someone to come in and "break kneecaps."[6] Both Republicans and Democrats share the blame for not dropping nearly everything else and focusing on this critical issue; the only exceptions are two committees in the Senate and House of Representatives that have focused on Y2K and called for concerted government action for some time. Those working on Y2K are concerned that by the time the full Congress and executive branch truly get behind this issue it may be too late to actually accomplish very much. Therefore, their leadership will be largely symbolic. It will be much too little, far too late.

CHAPTER THREE

Flashbacks: 1998-1999

New York City, February 1998—1:14 A.M.

"What did you say?" Keith Hendricks sat bolt upright in bed, holding the receiver to his ear, eyes stretched wide in disbelief. Before the agitated voice on the other end had finished talking, he was out of bed, grabbing a pen and writing furiously in his Franklin Planner.

"Nineteen *million?* Oh no—we never should have done it live. Tell me the exact specs!" His hands were trembling as he forced himself to take careful notes of the conversation. He was going to have to repeat this to Tom in a few minutes, and he had to get it right. Despite the chilly morning air, he was perspiring. Heads were going to roll—and one of them might be his own.

After a few more minutes Keith slammed down the phone and ran to pull on his khakis. He changed his mind the second he opened the closet doors and saw the meticulously arranged line of Hugo Boss suits. He would be at the office a long, long time today, and under the circumstances he had better look every bit his role of executive vice president, information and operations. He headed for the bronze and marble bath off the master bedroom. The shower was perfunctory, but the shock of the hot spray allowed him to settle his racing mind, regain a degree of control, and rehearse his conversation with Tom. As president of Eaton Mark Securities, one of the largest investment banks in the world, Tom was a powerful man. Since his own promotion nine months ago, Keith had worked hard and skillfully to gain the confidence of his boss. After all, Tom would probably be chairman one day—and one of the eleven executive vice presidents would then be tapped for the slot of president. Keith had always hoped he'd be in the running. Perhaps it was still possible—if he could get through today.

A sleepy female voice greeted him as he stepped back into the darkened bedroom. "What's going on, honey?" The mumble was emanating from under a pillow on the king-sized bed.

"I'm sorry to wake you up. The head of the Y2K task force just called. There's been a big, big incident." Keith dressed rapidly, trying to coordinate both words and fingers as he fumbled with his shirt buttons. "You knew we've been doing this massive project to fix all the bad code in our investment computer systems, right?"

"Mmm." The pillow remained firmly in place.

Keith winced and plowed ahead. Carolyn knew perfectly well why she and the kids hadn't seen much of him lately—it was clearly still a sore spot. "Well, all our simulated tests of the fix looked great, and we thought we should finally conduct a real test—you know, a real-life operation rather than a simulation. So, at one o'clock this morning, the Y2K team was going to bring the fixed system into live operation and see if we had really fixed it." He sat down on the bed, suddenly out of breath, and put his head in his hands.

His wife rolled over and slowly sat up, pulling the sheet around herself and resting her hand on his hunched back. "Keith...what happened?"

He swallowed. "When they brought the system up, it took them a while to notice..." Keith raised his head, and Carolyn could hear the disbelief in his voice. "Somehow, we placed nineteen million dollars of our money into the account of every single investment client."

Carolyn closed her eyes. "Oh my. You have over half a million investment accounts, don't you?" She didn't need to hear his answer. "That's...a ten-trillion-dollar error. How did it happen? They can fix it, can't they?"

Despite himself, Keith smiled sardonically. "They'd better be able to, or you've just watched Eaton Mark vanish in a puff of electronic smoke."

Carolyn suddenly heard what he wasn't saying. She carefully measured her words. "Keith...who authorized that live test?"

"Guess." The two of them looked at each other for a moment. He had his back to the light pouring from the steamy bathroom, and his face was in shadow. He cleared his throat. "So...what do you think?"

"I think you'd better get down there right away."

Outside New York City, March 1998

Victor Luccio looked in his rearview mirror. The man in the backseat looked badly shaken by something. His face was white, and his glazed eyes were clearly not focusing as they sped toward the man's suburban destination. As the miles passed, the man seemed more agitated, not less. *Lord, what should I do here? I've never seen anyone like this before.*

Finally, Victor spoke up. "Sir, if you don't mind my asking—are you all right? Do you need me to take you to a doctor or something?" Victor had picked him up from a nuclear power plant. He didn't know anything about those facilities, but they always seemed rather ominous. Maybe the guy was sick from the plant.

The guy started at the sound of Victor's voice. "No. No, I don't think so. I'll be okay. Thanks for asking."

Victor waited a few minutes, then tried again. "You know, it might help to talk about it. I talk to a lot of people about a lot of things in this little taxi. They seem to find it a safe zone. Want to tell me what's wrong?"

"Well, I guess it'll be all over the news tomorrow, anyway." As if a dam had been breached, his words started to spill out. "We've been trying to completely update all the computer technology in the plant, to get it ready for the year 2000." Victor nodded as if he were following what the guy was saying. "And, I mean, we changed *everything*. We knew we couldn't risk losing power to the largest city in the country, so we just decided to take a slash-and-burn approach, you know? We thought we were so ahead of the game." The man's voice was dripping with self-condemnation. "We read every blueprint, investigated every nook and cranny, and replaced every single computer and computer chip in the place. We got all-new, compliant stuff. It was an enormous expense. Enormous! But all the tests looked perfect. All of them. So we decided to power the plant up and test everything for real. We took the rods out, of course, but we tested everything live. And you know what happened?"

Victor was starting to feel tense. "What?"

"We had a scram shutdown." The guy started shaking again, and in the rearview mirror Victor could see that his eyes had widened. "I've never been so scared in my life. Just for a second, I forgot that the nuclear power wasn't operational. But if it had been..."

The cab was quiet for a second, then Victor cleared his throat. "Um, what went wrong? Did a new piece not work right or something?"

"No." Victor's passenger was rubbing his temples. "We thought we'd gotten rid of and replaced every single chip and circuit and computer system in the plant, but when the scram happened, we found the problem. Just a few hours ago, we found it. We had missed a few chips embedded in a *sensor* in a smokestack! Who would have thought that *that* could have shut down an entire plant? I don't know how these nuclear plants all over the country are ever going to be able to track and solve all these Y2K problems. It's such a huge job..." His voice trailed off.

"If you don't mind my asking, sir, what exactly is a 'scram'?"

The passenger shifted forward to the edge of his seat, closer to Victor, really looking at the cab driver for the first time. "Let's just say that—if the nuclear rods had been in—it would mean your city was within minutes of having a really bad day. Ever hear of Chernobyl?"

Victor had. And suddenly, somehow, he knew there was more to this meeting than just providing comfort to a shaken passenger. Victor said quietly, "Well, we can thank the Lord that didn't happen here." He glanced in his rearview mirror again. "And if you don't mind, since we still have a long ride ahead of us, I'd like to understand more about this problem you mentioned."

Austin, Texas, June 30, 1998

Billy Phillips watched in disbelief as another large ERROR message appeared on his computer screen. "What on *earth?*"

As an analyst with the Texas State Budget Department, he had spent the last three months preparing for the new fiscal year that would start tomorrow. It took a whole team of people to prepare the annual state budget, which included the required two-year forecast as well. They had plugged the final 1998–1999 budget into the Texas information system just a few hours ago. Billy was now testing it, ensuring that the central state budget was interfacing effectively with the smaller budget departments of each Texas government agency. Or at least that was what he was trying to do. Some agency budgets just weren't responding properly. He was currently trying to access the budget for the Transportation Department—a budget that had looked just fine a few hours ago, before it had actually gone live. Now he was encountering an error message he had never seen before.

Billy frowned at the computer screen. *Lord, what on earth is going on?* He didn't necessarily expect an answer, but frequent prayers were a longtime habit. He grabbed a hard copy of the Transportation budget and stood up, intending to bring this problem to his boss's attention. At that moment, one of the Information Technology guys walked by his cube. "Hey, Warren," Billy called out. "Do you have a second?"

Warren turned, with the politely aloof look common among IT people when they have been interrupted from a more urgent task. "What's up?"

Billy explained, and Warren sat down and started punching buttons. He called up several odd-looking screens, muttering under his breath, and then suddenly stopped. Without turning his head, Warren asked, "Does this year's budget also include a two-year forecast?"

"Absolutely. It goes right through June 30, 2000. Why?"

Warren stood up, his aloof manner suddenly gone. He smiled wryly. "Well, it looks like we have a bug in the system, and we'd better take this to your boss right away."

"A bug? But what about our antivirus software?" Billy's home PC had been decimated by a computer virus the year before, but he thought the state was completely protected against such an outbreak.

"It isn't a virus. It's a computer programming glitch called the Millennium Bug. Basically, the computers at some of these agencies—like the Transportation Department—are having trouble dealing with dates in the year 2000 or beyond. Your two-year forecast has confused them, so some of them are shutting down." Warren looked sober. "Some of the agencies have fixed their systems to recognize the year 2000, but some haven't, and now it looks like a perfectly good budget may not run properly."

In one accord, Billy and Warren stepped out of the cube, heading toward the boss's office. As they threaded their way among a maze of government-issue cubicles, Warren continued, "Frankly, I'm not surprised to see this happen. You really need to go out and learn as much about this issue as you possibly can, you know. It's really important. Fixing this problem takes a *lot* of time and money. I could tell you stories that would knock your socks off. Early last year, for example, an outside consulting firm did a huge study and concluded it would cost some awful amount to fix some of the key state government computers—like $30 million, I think. If we'd started last year, we might have had a chance. But the state legislature refused to appropriate enough funds for the fix. They wimped out—they didn't want to incur the wrath of voters. So now, of course, we're one year closer to the deadline and still no fix. Now the consultants are saying the cost has increased to $75 million—even though it'll be almost impossible to complete on time."

Billy's head was swimming. He didn't understand everything Warren was saying, but like a good budget analyst he focused on the area he *did* understand. "Why has the cost gone up so much?"

"Well, for one reason, because the closer we get to the deadline the more impossible it becomes to just fix the old system you already have in place—instead, you just have to bite the bullet and pay for an entirely new one. It's like your personal PC—weren't you telling me last year that your PC got eaten by a virus?" Billy mutely nodded. "Well, suppose your PC got garbled by a virus on Monday; nothing works properly, and your computer repairman is telling you it will take him two months to fix it. Then suppose your entire life and business depends on having a working PC by Saturday, and you know yours won't be fixed by then. What do you do?"

"I guess I'd have to buy a whole new computer."

Warren beamed at him. "Exactly. It's the same thing for the entire state of Texas."

Billy felt numb. They had reached his boss's closed door, and he was suddenly loath to knock. "Is that the only reason costs are going up so much?" He leaned against the wall, waiting for Warren's answer.

"No, that's not all. The other reason costs are skyrocketing is that everyone in the world has this same problem, and there aren't enough technical people to go around. The cost of hiring them has gone through the roof, and state government jobs aren't exactly the highest-paying ones in the world. Governments are rapidly losing the programmers they have and they can't afford to hire replacements, much less fill new positions." Warren lowered his voice. "Don't tell anyone, but I'm outta here. There are three of us who are leaving in two weeks to go work for Data Services down the block. They just offered each of us two hundred thousand dollars a year and full repayment of our student loans." Warren's eyes gleamed. "It wasn't a tough choice."

At that moment one of Billy's coworkers rushed up to them, out of breath, with thick sheaves of papers clutched haphazardly in her hands. "The Social Services Department budget isn't working right! What's going on?" She looked blank as Warren briefly outlined the problem, then knocked loudly on the manager's door.

Ten minutes later, twenty-five people convened hastily in a conference room, listening to Warren's boss explain the problem. The group debated potential stopgap measures—such as pulling out the two-year forecast—but no one was happy. Everything was interlinked, and the now-unworkable budget had consumed nearly half a year's intense work. The tension in the room mounted sharply when everyone realized that many of the state's payroll functions were connected to the budget system, which meant that no state employee could be paid until they completely altered their payroll functions.

The IT director breezily closed the meeting by saying that he had full confidence that Warren and his team of "five outstanding IT professionals will surely conquer these temporary system problems over the next few months." Billy looked at Warren and said nothing.

Outside Houston, Texas, July 3, 1998

In the private conference room of the university president, the dean of students glumly reread the fax from the Texas State Department of Education:

> *Due to unavoidable complications in our computer systems we will be unable to immediately transfer monies for the 1998–1999 school year to state-funded schools and universities. This problem is only temporary and you will be advised when the situation is resolved, hopefully within a few weeks. Please contact our office to arrange release of emergency funds for the approved purposes noted below. Thank you for your understanding.*

The top university officials had been meeting for over two hours. Everyone knew that the university had to request emergency funds in order to stay afloat. They had, like many schools, borrowed heavily to prepare for the upcoming school year and were counting on the huge transfer of state funds to make ends meet. Unfortunately, some programs were going to have to be trimmed until they received the cash. Other programs, which now couldn't be started on time, might have to be suspended entirely for the year. The president regretfully informed the dean of students that all entering financial aid and work aid recipients should be notified that the status of those funds was "unclear at this time."

The dean's counterarguments were brief. The university, like many others around the country, was quite cash poor. Taking the cash that would have gone to financial aid and applying it to their debt and operating costs would at least keep the doors open. It was their only choice.

Austin, Texas, July 10, 1998

From his office, Jim Thicke watched his secretary disappear through the glass doors of their trading company into the high-ceilinged atrium outside. She had risen abruptly and seemed near tears. Concerned, he walked out to her desk. Nina was one of his favorite people. A short one-page letter lay face up on her neat desk, so Jim couldn't help seeing the relevant sentences: *We regret to inform you of a delay in processing financial aid for entering students. At this time, it is unclear if and when those funds will become available for the 1998–99 school year...*

"Oh, Nina, I'm so sorry," Jim said to the air. Nina and Pedro had been counting on that financial aid—Nina had a large merit scholarship—to complete their college degrees. They had two small children and had been looking for part-time jobs and cheap housing in Houston. Because they lived paycheck to paycheck and had little or no savings, Jim knew they couldn't afford to move to Houston without the financial aid cushion and the assurance that they could actually start school in the fall. After waiting eight long years to reenter college, Nina had been on cloud nine ever since receiving the scholarship notification. No wonder she was upset.

Well, at least trade is booming, Jim thought, *and I can give her that raise, if she's staying. They really need to scrounge together some savings. If they had savings, they might have been able to take the chance and move anyway.*

Jim's phone rang. It was Courtney, finalizing plans for the dinner party they were hosting that night. "Thanks for arranging this thing, sweetheart. Oh, just put it on the credit card. That'll be easiest. Love you, too." As he hung up, Jim realized that these last-minute expenditures might actually max out one of their cards, and that he also had forgotten to pay his student loan bill this morning. *Another late penalty.* Jim knew their credit card bills were probably high, and that they didn't have a large amount of savings either, but he wasn't particularly concerned. They always had plenty of cash to pay bills every month. He had an Ivy League MBA, great earning power, two incomes, no kids—and business was booming.

Just down the road, Deborah Carey walked shakily out to the parking lot of the walk-in clinic, clutching the hands of her squirming children. *I can't have diabetes! With no health insurance, there's no way I can pay for doctor visits!* Waves of despair crashed over her. Her AFDC checks and her two waitressing jobs were simply not enough to cover medical treatment, but she knew she risked horrible disability or even death without medical care. Reluctantly, she allowed herself to consider a way out: she could work a third shift, if her mother would agree to keep the kids late at night. She didn't like leaving the twins with her mom so much, since the older woman was so often strung out on something, but Deborah didn't see any other way. Maybe that would give her enough money to buy medicine and see the doctors. Maybe. She got the kids buckled in and sat in the driver's seat, resting her forehead on the steering wheel for a moment, trying to gather the strength to drive away. She was so, so tired. *Why is life so unfair?*

New York City, November 1998

Carolyn Hendricks reluctantly handed the manila file folder to her secretary, who scuttled down toward the managing partner's office before Carolyn could change her mind again. Carolyn slowly walked back to her office, sat down, and stared, unseeing, out her 61st-floor window. She had just handed over their first negative, "qualified" audit opinion of a Fortune 500 company. Food Pavilion was an enormous food distributor with billions in revenue and supermarkets and subsidiaries all over the world.

The mammoth company had been the client of the revered accounting-consulting firm of Monroe & Hubbard for more than ten years, and she had been the managing director for their account half that time. Food Pavilion's stated preference of working with her had given Carolyn good standing within M&H's largely male bastion of power. And she had greatly enjoyed the mutually beneficial relationship. But that was all about to change.

Her staff had been shocked when a routine audit had raised alarming questions about the client's readiness for Y2K, appalled when further investigation concluded that Food Pavilion would be at serious economic risk when 2000 hit, and grim when they realized that M&H would be legally liable if they failed to mention these concerns in their audit opinion and Food Pavilion later went bankrupt. After weeks of progressively tense meetings, the senior partners of M&H had agreed that her audit opinion couldn't be the usual boilerplate signoff that a client's books looked fine. Instead, their statement had to note that Food Pavilion "might be allocating insufficient resources to their Y2K remediation" and that "their income statements and projections might therefore not be reflective of their true financial position."

Audit statements were public, and Carolyn knew how seriously the market would view those innocuously worded but unprecedented phrases. They were the equivalent of a corporate plague—that a Fortune 500 company's own auditing firm didn't have faith in their books. She remembered her husband's near panic when that live system test had dropped $19 million into every brokerage account and hoped desperately that the market would not react to her client in the same way.

En Route to New York City, December 20, 1998

Julia Ashford stared pensively at the black void outside the airplane window. She was exhausted after two weeks of contentious meetings with her banking "counterparties" in Japan, Thailand, China, and other Asian Rim countries. She had spoken daily by phone with the other members of her bank's Y2K task force who were conducting similar meetings in other regions of the world. She took some small comfort in the fact that they all seemed as tired as she was.

Her gaze dropped to the second paragraph of the recommendation memo she was drafting on behalf of the group:

> *Not only are many of our counterparties still recovering from the Asian financial crisis, but technologically many are also completely unprepared for the Year 2000 rollover. In summary, we propose that for the next ten months the Bank extend only short-term funds and charge a risk premium to most counterparties in Asia, Latin America, and parts of Europe (a detailed list is attached), with the expectation of ceasing all transactions with these institutions after October 1999. However, these controls should be periodically reevaluated as the rollover approaches and the readiness of individual institutions becomes clearer.*

This executive summary would be attached to a huge stack of meeting notes outlining the minute details of each task force meeting with each financial institution the bank did business with around the world. These counterparties were not going to be happy when the bank implemented these suggestions. *Well, too bad,* Julia thought. *They are the ones swiftly driving their ships straight toward an iceberg.* The movie *Titanic* had been one of Julia's all-time favorites. She was just as exasperated with the stupidity of the present as with that of the past. *Everyone thinks they are unsinkable and don't need lifeboats.*

She put away her laptop and relaxed into the soft leather of her first-class seat. The darkened cabin, the weeks of jet lag, and the drone of the engines were irresistible, and she gratefully closed her eyes, glad for a few hours of sleep before the rat race started up again.

New York City—Eight Hours Later

As he waited for the elevator in his apartment building, Dr. Marvin Rogers stared, troubled, at the article in his hand. The lobby had just been done up beautifully for the holidays, but he wasn't looking at the decorations. One of his medical colleagues had somehow gotten his hands on an internal bulletin from a competing hospital. The bulletin discussed Y2K problems the hospital had found in many common types of medical equipment and outlined their exhaustive efforts to fix these problems as a part of their three-year "War on Y2K" initiative. *Three years?* Marvin thought incredulously, reading down the list of suspect medical devices. Infusion pumps...EKG machines...pacemakers...dialysis machines...MRIs... *Why haven't we seen this sort of thing at OUR hospital?*

He was abruptly jerked away from his thoughts by an exasperated voice behind him. "I said, ex*cuse* me!" A woman impatiently brushed past him, banging her suitcase and laptop case against his leg, and stepped into the elevator. He hadn't even noticed that the doors had opened. Before he could stir himself to action, she jabbed a sharp finger at her floor button and the elevator doors closed in his face.

And a merry Christmas to you, too. Marvin didn't know who that woman was, but she lived on the 18th floor, was always brusque and in a hurry, and didn't seem to notice that her selfishness usually came at the expense of someone else. He remembered when she had obliviously stolen a taxi right out from under the nose of Mrs. Beechman. The widow who lived on his floor—the 21st—couldn't move fast enough, and that impatient young woman had come out of nowhere to grab the cab and speed away without a backward glance, leaving a shocked Mrs. Beechman on the sidewalk.

Marvin had given the widow a ride in his Lexus, which she enjoyed immensely, the dear thing. Mrs. Beechman had later brought cookies over and they had talked for an hour about her cats, her grandchildren, and her long-ago trips with her late husband.

Another elevator arrived, and Marvin boarded. He smiled as he remembered Mrs. Beechman's visit. Everyone kept so much to themselves these days, shut up behind closed doors and blank faces. Only at the holidays did people relax and come out of their self-contained shells a bit. Church was different, of course, but cookies and coffee with Mrs. Beechman had been the first time in years he had felt connected to anyone in his actual building.

Wouldn't it be great if people would do that more often?

Champaign-Urbana, Illinois, January 1999

"Why won't we be receiving that shipment?" Becky Lee spoke loudly into the receiver, pressing her hand against her ear and straining to hear the reply. She was on the phone by the cash register, trying to block out the many chattering conversations in the grocery store. "Hold on. I can't hear you. Let me transfer to the office." She hoped he would wait. This particular supplier was notoriously impatient with his retailers, particularly with small regional grocery chains such as hers that didn't have the market power of the big national supermarkets. But she was troubled by what she thought she had heard, so she hurried into the office, dodging a group of well-dressed retirees who were slowly examining the wine and cheese options displayed on a glass-topped table.

She picked up the phone, and without preamble, repeated her question. "Why won't we be receiving that shipment? They *destroyed* it? What do you mean?"

The distributor was rather curt and unhelpful, but she continued to ask questions and gradually pieced together the troubling picture. A large food wholesaler, a subsidiary of Food Pavilion, had mistakenly destroyed thousands of tons of canned goods in its inventory. The list was immense, encompassing most of her shelf stock. The wholesaler had told all its distributors, which in turn had to notify the retail stores they supplied, that those particular foodstuffs would not be forthcoming as expected. The supplier calling Becky wasn't any more thrilled about this news than Becky was, although Becky knew that *he* was in a better position to withstand the loss of inventory. With two massive, modern supermarkets just a mile down the road, her customers had plenty of options if she couldn't keep the shelves stocked or her catering service supplied.

Becky replaced the receiver, her mind galloping through strategies for overcoming the problem. She'd been thinking about making contacts with other suppliers and wholesalers, and this seemed like the perfect excuse. Within minutes she was speaking with someone she knew casually through a food seller's association.

"Food Pavilion! *Hmph!*" The voice on the line snorted. "Everyone over here is howling. The mighty company brought low by two zeros. They've been so clueless, it's hard to believe this didn't happen before now."

Becky desperately wanted to know what was going on. "*What* exactly happened?"

"Their computer system mistakenly told them that a whole block of their brand-new canned goods should be destroyed because they had already expired! Isn't that a hoot?"

Becky set her jaw and patiently asked for a clearer explanation. Her contact was surprised she wasn't "on top of the Y2K problem," but he willingly brought her up to date. Her mouth dropped open as she scribbled furious notes. In the end, the levity left his voice. "Becky, I'm telling you, for the sake of your business you need to get up to speed on this *quickly*. Your whole chain of stores, your suppliers, your vendors, and even your customers could have Y2K vulnerabilities that could just leave you twisting in the wind come January 1. Start calling around and figuring out who's safe to deal with. Start diversifying suppliers. Get prepared *now*."

Weakly, Becky thanked him and hung up. She crossed her arms on the desk and rested her forehead on them, stunned. *Oh, Lord...help. What do we do here? I don't know anything about computers. God, protect the business you have helped me build.* She thought of all her employees and their families, all the customers and suppliers she dealt with every day—people she mentored and witnessed to, people she loved. *Lord, it sounds like this is serious. Help me understand what to do. Help me understand how you are working through this.* She found her prayers unexpectedly taking a different tack. *I praise you that you are mighty and just; you are the Master of all things. Help me see the opportunities you are laying before me.*

"You asleep?"

Becky jerked her head up, recognizing the man in the doorway with a start. "No, no. Just resting."

"It doesn't look good for a small-business loan candidate to be sleeping in the middle of a busy workday, you know." Don Kramer was testy. He'd driven in circles before he found the store, and he didn't want to be here in the first place. This client was small potatoes, but she had been with Midwest Bankcorp for years, through all the mergers, and had stayed loyal while others had split. His boss liked her and insisted that Don visit her rather than making her come into the bank. Don was annoyed at having to take the time away from his larger, more prestigious clients to deal with this little Korean-owned grocery chain. He had been her loan officer for the last two years, but he wasn't particularly happy about it.

Becky's smile didn't waver as she stood up and shook his hand. *Oh, Jesus. Give me strength. Give me the beauty of a quiet and gentle spirit...so that I don't strangle him.* "Thanks for coming down, Don. Have a seat on the couch." The narrow office opened into a small but beautifully appointed room where major customers and other business contacts could be entertained. "Would you like a drink? Hot chocolate?" During the somewhat brutal winter, the store had a huge ceramic jug of hot chocolate standing ready for all customers.

Don took an oversized mug from her without thanks and got down to business, opening up her papers on the low antique sideboard that served as a coffee table. Becky had requested an expansion loan to add two more stores to her four existing ones. She was scouting likely sites and negotiating rent on one location and a property sale on another. She wasn't sure when she would need the loan; it might not be until much later in the year, when she hoped the sellers of the property might agree to reduce their price. They discussed preliminary loan terms, although Don officiously reminded her that they couldn't formally settle on interest rates until she was actually ready to sign the loan.

Becky was somewhat surprised that Don's arrogant manner wasn't wearing on her as much as usual. She suddenly didn't care that he so obviously thought her a waste of his time. Instead, she found herself thinking how unhappy and insecure he must be to feel such a need to put others down.

They concluded their business within an hour and Don drove quickly away to more important clients. Almost without realizing it, Becky found herself praying for him. *Lord, show me how to be a light in his darkness.* In her quiet way, she decided to put Don Kramer on her prayer list. She would watch and see what would come of it. *All in your time, Lord.* She turned back to her office, back to her rapidly jotted notes on this Y2K problem. She had a lot of studying and planning to do.

Two Days Later

"Okay. And if something changes, I'll be in touch. Good-bye." Becky put down the receiver and stretched, feeling the tension flow away like the tide. That was her last phone call to the stores she had been thinking of acquiring. They had been disappointed, but potential buyers came and went all the time. Few of them seemed to understand her explanation of Y2K or why she had suddenly decided against any short-term acquisitions, but every small business owner could comprehend her desire to save up some more operating cash before expanding.

After getting laughed at on the first phone call, Becky had stopped mentioning that she was going to use those savings to increase her inventory of certain basic and luxury foodstuffs. It would have sounded kind of crazy to her too, she admitted, if she hadn't spent the last forty-eight hours steeped in a crash course on the Y2K problem. All the newspaper and magazine articles warning of imminent business and economic failures had been interesting, but it was one incongruously positive sentence that had really caught her eye and completely changed her thinking. A major research firm believed 35 percent of large businesses would actually turn Y2K into such a competitive advantage that they would *thrive,* just as all their competition was failing. Becky had awakened in the night, determined that she would be among that 35 percent. First thing the next morning, she had drawn up a plan to reduce her debt, increase her liquidity, and store up essential goods in order to potentially meet demand that her competitors couldn't. Who knew what opportunities might come her way in the year 2000?

As she sat in her bustling store, she felt complete peace about her new direction. She looked at her "to do" list for the day. Ah, yes. She looked up the number for Grace Chapel. She had one last, very important phone call to make.

New York City, Saturday, January 1999—8:30 A.M.

Marvin Rogers gulped down his coffee as he drove swiftly up the FDR toward the Bronx. He didn't want to be too late. He knew that the guys at Good Shepherd Church had been planning this seminar thing—this "Y2K Community Awareness Event"—for the Bronx community since well before Christmas. After checking around at the hospital he had become increasingly convinced that the church was doing the right thing in informing the average resident of the potential issues. They had found a donated space that would hold 9,000 people—and were even worried that *it* would be way too small. Well, as they continuously said, it was only the first step. The real work of preparation would start immediately afterward, with plenty of chances for everyone to become involved if they wanted to. Marvin checked his watch and sped up a little.

Champaign-Urbana, Illinois, February 1999—9:15 A.M.

Tensely escorting an important customer through the lobby, Tadé Okebari nodded to Patrick, the office building's big red-haired janitor, but didn't stop to exchange morning pleasantries. Tadé had just been surprised by a representative of his biggest customer. This mammoth retailing chain, with hundreds of warehouse-like outlets around the country, purchased silk flowers and other craft items from his family-run company—accounting for nearly two-thirds of their business. When they phoned, Tadé jumped. He hadn't been expecting a visit from the business office, and his mind raced as he politely followed his client into their facility.

A few miles down the road, Pastor Gustavson slipped into a church sanctuary fifteen minutes late, silently closing the door behind him. The room was nearly full, and Johnny Barry, the pastor of Grace Chapel, was just finishing a welcome. The lights dimmed and a video started to roll as Gustavson found an aisle seat next to an elderly man wearing a crucifix and a cleric's collar.

He came from a very different church than Grace Chapel and didn't know many of the other pastors here, but what he knew of Johnny he respected. When he had received the invitation to this "Eastern Illinois Year 2000 Meeting for Christian Leaders," he had been skeptical at first. He knew of at least eight families in his congregation who were planning a sort of well-stocked hideaway on a farm about fifty miles away—they had even bought guns to protect themselves and goods to barter with in the event that the monetary system collapsed. Naturally, Gustavson had associated any discussion of the year 2000 with this sort of survivalist attitude and had wanted no part of it.

But so many of his more reasonable parishioners had been pestering him about the year 2000 that he finally decided to take the time to attend this pastors meeting. It was just a few hours, after all, and he quietly hoped he would learn something to settle his mind on the matter—one way or another. He thought back to the letter he had received: *An opportunity to discuss our role as Christian leaders in preparing for the Year 2000 problem.* He was still uncertain why pastors—rather than computer people—needed to care about such a technical issue, but he was willing to listen.

New York City, Saturday, March 1999—10:00 A.M.

As Victor Luccio settled into his seat at the front of the room, he grinned, watching the chattering volunteers compare notes about the things they had done since their last meeting. Several people had—again—encountered seemingly insurmountable obstacles, only to watch in amazement as miraculous events blew the roadblocks aside. This was the first time many of them had *had* to truly trust God to accomplish something they could never do on their own, and it had been a real eye-opener. Organizing an entire community as diverse and large as the Bronx was humanly impossible, so it was exciting to watch as the Lord guided and directed their ways. Watching for God's daily active, practical leadership was something few had truly done before, so there had been a few miscues, wrong steps, and overzealous activities—but generally the group had laid everything before the Lord in prayer and had found that, well, things just *happened.*

Because the Bronx Y2K Church Task Force was earning a reputation as the place to watch that sort of activity unfold, the group of volunteers grew and grew. After their Bronx Community Awareness Event in January, the first group of volunteers numbered about twenty-five...then forty...then seventy. Now, Victor estimated, nearly one hundred people met in the church every other Saturday to report on their findings and progress and to determine their next steps.

He called the group to order. After prayer and preliminary discussion, the reports started. A volunteer on the Mercy Ministries committee led off. "Well, as you know, we're most concerned right now about—" he ticked them off on his fingers—"one, whether the refrigeration appliances at the Good Shepherd center will work, and two, whether the food distribution network for their bulk foods will break down. The service people are not giving us a straight answer, but since we need to put together a contingency plan anyway, here's what we figure we can do..."

The young man outlined the committee's initial plan for an "option" contract with a small firm of refrigerated (and Y2K-compliant) trucks to bring in perishables daily after January 1. Then, after a theatrical pause, he dropped the bomb: this was another divine appointment, as the volunteer had quickly discovered that the coowner of just such a firm went to his church. Everyone laughed and applauded at the revelation, and Victor just shook his head. *Lord, forgive my irreverence—but you are so COOL!*

Champaign-Urbana, Illinois, April 1999

"Okay. OKAY! I'll get there right away—keep your pants on!" Travis Pitt slammed his phone back into his workman's belt and turned back to the mass of wires and circuits on the wall. He was working under independent contract with three different phone and cable companies and for several months now he hadn't been able to keep up with the exploding demand. The sixteen-hour days were making him irritable, despite the exceptional pay, and he had a four-week backlog of jobs—as did every other repairman in the world, it seemed. Unbelievable! And it was only going to get worse.

Ever since the *Today Show* had aired that feature on the Y2K vulnerabilities in telecommunications systems, every nitwit in the county wanted their phone company to come check them out—even if the phone company insisted that their system was fine. Not that he blamed them, Travis thought sardonically. He had already found seven phone systems that would have completely failed at year's end despite the fact that their vendors had signed off on them. Mostly older systems, like the one he was currently working on, had noncompliant chips from the early '90s embedded in the hardware—rather than EPROMs that could be easily popped out and replaced. Or some of them had operating software that needed to be reconstructed. He replaced a couple of connections and closed up the exposed panels in the drywall, then headed out into the client's main office, dusting off sawdust onto the dark blue carpet as he went.

"Well, what's the news?" Johnny Barry's eyes registered the trail of sawdust behind the repairman but his smile remained in place.

Travis scribbled on his clipboard as he talked. "Well, like a lot of other churches in the area, you have an older-model PBX phone system, and this one will need some parts replaced and some adjustments in order to work properly after the rollover." He ticked off the list of software adjustments the church would need to ask for. "But your biggest problem is the chips—you've got a bunch of them implanted in the phone system itself, so the whole thing will have to be transported to the factory to be fixed. They'll need to take out the old ones, manufacture and customize the replacements, then rebuild the phone system and reinstall it." He paused, grinning internally, waiting for the inevitable question. It was always the same.

"How long is that going to take?"

Travis put on his best sober face. "Well, sir, it's hard to say at this point. Last year it would have taken only a couple of weeks. Nowadays, when everyone in the country is doing the same thing—well, you'll be lucky to have it back in two, three months. And the fix is going to be expensive. Before you ask—" he correctly read the next question on Johnny's face—"the vendor is no longer able to provide rental equipment while your system is in the shop. They're completely out. So your church staff will be stuck with sharing just one garden-variety household phone for a while. Unless you want to buy a whole *new,* compliant phone system, of course."

He watched Johnny's face, taking mental bets on the next statement. These customers were all so predictable. They ignore the issue for years, despite all the attention, and then come whining to him at the last minute, expecting a miracle. *Well, no miracles today, boys and girls. Serves them right.* Travis carefully hid his smugness but prepared for the usual argument about the phone vendor's responsibility, good business practices, and—very likely—the veiled threat of a lawsuit.

This time, however, he was surprised.

"Okay." Johnny grabbed a blank index card from his desk and began writing on it. "We were expecting something like that. The whole congregation raised nearly ten thousand dollars for a replacement system, and a few other Y2K things, last month." Johnny continued writing, seemingly unaware of the repairman's surprised reaction.

"Well, um, sir, if you don't mind my saying so, I think that's the best course of action. Just fixing your old one would be almost half of that, after all. There are a lot of people getting very angry nowadays, but it's not going to speed things up for them." They talked about new phone system options for a few minutes, then Johnny walked him to the entrance. As they shook hands, Travis's curiosity finally overcame his customary superior manner. "Reverend, so many of the small businesses I've been to around here have been so clueless about this. Why are you so...so...unflustered by having to shell out for a whole new expensive phone system?"

Johnny handed over the index card and gripped the young man's shoulder. "Just following some good advice. Thanks for coming by."

Good advice? Travis watched as Johnny disappeared back inside the church building, then stared, bemused, at the small note in his hand:

> *A prudent man foresees the difficulties ahead and prepares for them;*
> *the simpleton goes blindly on and suffers the consequences.*
> Proverbs 22:3

He blinked in surprise. *Unbelievable. I actually agree with something in the Bible.*

New York City, The Bronx, September 1999

William Temple slowly lowered himself into his old blue chair and began sorting through his mail. The TV was on in the background, but he wasn't really listening. He just liked having it on for the company. The small stack of mail wasn't particularly engrossing, but retrieving and reviewing it was one of the highlights of his day. He always searched hopefully for his Social Security checks and for the occasional letters from his children and grandchildren. Just last week, his granddaughter Cindy had sent a videotape of his newest great-grandchild, William Patrick, just two weeks old. He had played the tape at least a dozen times, watching his tiny namesake yawn, sleep, cry, and stare through the screen with unfocused eyes.

He chuckled to himself, remembering that little pinched face. The baby's wizened, wrinkled countenance even *looked* like him. He'd have to remember to tell Cindy that the next time she called. All the children and grandchildren knew to call him, rather than the other way around—the phone had gotten so expensive these days.

A convulsive shiver passed through him and he pulled the afghan tighter around his thin shoulders. This fall was already unseasonably cold, and he couldn't control the central heating in his Bronx apartment. The landlord was so stingy! Mr. Jackson adamantly refused to turn on the heat for the building before the end of October. Nellie had sometimes been able to sweet-talk him into cranking it up earlier, but the landlord's penny-pinching ways had triumphed in the three years she'd been gone. William had thought about changing apartments, but he didn't really have the energy—or the money—to bother with a move. He and Nell had lived here for over twenty years; there were too many memories tied up in this little apartment, this neighborhood. He found himself unconsciously stroking the afghan she'd knitted. He missed her so much.

As he put the mail down on the tray by his chair, he brushed the little plastic pill box, his constant companion. He knew his heart was getting worse. One of these days he'd probably have to move into assisted living anyway. William mentally shrugged, relaxed into the comfortable softness of the old recliner, and turned up the volume with the TV remote control.

New York City, December 1, 1999

Teresa Luccio listened quietly to the tirade on the other end of the line. Her client was high-strung at the best of times, and this most certainly was *not* the best of times. She dimly noted that her colleague, Janice, was receiving the same treatment from a walk-in customer waving an airline ticket in her face. Business had been increasingly difficult for the High-Flight Travel Agency over the last few weeks, and it only looked like it was going to get worse. Her current phone call was from a senior partner at their largest corporate client, a big law firm on 52nd Street. He was calling from La Guardia Airport and had just lost any chance of making an extremely important meeting in Texas because of the extensive flight delays and cancellations that had begun to tie up every airport in the country.

She scanned quickly through screen after screen of flight information but was unable to find any available flights within the next twenty-four hours. "Mr. Kingston, I'm afraid everything I see is bad news. JFK, Newark...even if you went down to Philadelphia. They are all as backlogged as La Guardia. I'm so sorry, but there seems to be literally nothing we can do about it from here." Those words had not been in her vocabulary until recently, but she was finding herself saying them more and more often. "You could keep waiting for a standby seat to become available, but I know you're very busy and you may decide it's not worth it. I know it's no consolation, but there are thousands of other people missing their meetings all over the country right now... Yes, we'll get your ticket back from your secretary and you'll receive a full refund from the airline." *Which means another lost commission for us,* Teresa thought.

As she hung up the phone, Teresa struggled to stifle the anxiety that seemed to be swamping everyone these days. Because of continuing glitches in implementing and testing their Y2K conversions, the Federal Aviation Administration and the airlines were running on an increasingly reduced schedule, rather than compromise safety. Hundreds of flights were being either rescheduled or canceled altogether, leaving business and pleasure travelers stranded. Thanksgiving weekend had been a major headache. Twice, airports had been forced to revert to completely manual systems—thereby operating at only 15 percent of regular capacity. On top of that, airlines were beginning to lose both reservations and baggage with astonishing regularity. Over the last few days, the gleaming high-ceilinged airport lobbies of Chicago, Atlanta, and Denver had begun to look like the teeming and disorganized airports of the Third World. Because of these "mechanical" problems, the airlines had been forced to refund thousands of tickets—taking back thousands in travel agent commissions in the process.

Teresa tried to maintain a cheerful countenance, but privately she was very aware of the grim expressions on the faces of the agency's owners. She knew she was the least senior of the five travel agents there. It was only a matter of time.

Champaign-Urbana, Illinois, December 12, 1999

"Are you a shepherd—or a hireling?"

Although more than 400 faces looked up at him from the congregation, Johnny Barry saw only about two dozen—the hard ones, those who seemed unwavering from their chosen course. On those faces, fear and insecurity were etched so deeply that there almost seemed to be a shield about them bouncing off his pointed words—his arrows of truth and hope. Johnny had to force himself to look away, praying that the Holy Spirit would pierce their armor.

"If we are honest with ourselves, we don't know how this thing is going to turn out. Obviously, it is natural to fear the unknown, but scripturally we are told not to fear. It may be a natural response to want to run, to protect ourselves, but is that the biblical response?" Johnny had decided to address the issue directly. With only a few weeks left, he had to. There was a small but vocal group who were moving to a remote, well-stocked farm—their "Y2K Fortress"—in just a few days. This was their last Sunday in church. Johnny couldn't argue when they said that "God had told them to" remove themselves. *How do you counter that?* he thought. All he could do was point out another, harder, way.

"This could be the church's finest hour since the new converts of the first-century church sacrificed themselves for the world that 'God so loved.' This could be a divinely granted opportunity for the people of God. Will we give it up in order to save ourselves?" Looking out across the congregation, he saw other faces—those who wore thinly veiled expressions of boredom, exasperation, or even bemusement. Those who hadn't yet been affected, who had grown weary of the feverish national obsession with the topic. It was ironic, he thought with grim amusement, that the survivalists and the complacents were sitting side by side in his pews.

Lord, is anyone listening? The answer to his brief cry was immediate as other faces stood out as if spotlighted. Whether they agreed with everything he said, whether they had fully prepared themselves, these were the saints of God who would be in the vanguard—those who loved the Lord so dearly that they would be willing to take up the challenge when it hit. With renewed purpose, the pastor continued.

"During normal times, we tell our unsaved brothers and sisters that God loves them and sent his only Son to die for them. Now, as I said, we don't know how this is all going to turn out, but many people believe it will be bad enough that they should protect themselves. As you know, there are whole churches out there right now that have bought mountain ranches and caverns, built bunkers in remote locations, who are moving away from large cities. If this event is just a hiccup, then what the world is going to conclude is this: 'The church, in spite of all they said, really is only interested in saving itself—and not us.'

"Suppose something awful does happen? I'm not saying we shouldn't be careful—but do we wish to leave this world snatching and clawing to hang on to every last piece of it that we can grasp, or do we want to go out as an extension of our Lord, who was willing to—and *did*—lay down his life for the very ones who nailed him to that cross? After all, before he left his church, he did say, 'Feed my sheep.' We are now supposed to be the undershepherds for the great Shepherd. Are you going to be a shepherd? Or are you going to be a hireling—just hired hands of our Lord who are only looking after the 'sheep' of this world because we get paid to do so, and once the wolf comes, we take off—rather than being the shepherd who will wade directly into danger, willing to lay down his life for the sheep? You are going to have to make a choice—and there are only two choices."

As he peered into the eyes of his congregation, Johnny's heart jumped, and he nearly lost his train of thought. Before this morning's sermon he had prayed that the Holy Spirit would bring commitment and unity to the shepherds among his flock. Now, his discouragement drained away as he saw determination, resolve, compassion, and acceptance creep into one, then another, then another of the faces before him. He sighed a silent prayer of thanks. He had his shepherds.

CHAPTER FOUR

WHERE ARE WE NOW?

It has become conventional wisdom in the Y2K arena that there are two kinds of people in the world: those who don't know much about the Year 2000 problem and aren't particularly worried, and those who know a lot about it and are terrified. Dr. Bill Merrell, vice president for the Southern Baptist Convention's Executive Committee, recently noted the irony:

> It is normally the other way around. Usually, people who know more about a problem are less perturbed because they understand the real situation and are comforted by the knowledge. With Y2K, however, the more they know, the more they have reason for deep concern.[1]

To get a feel for the real situation (if such is possible), we must look at what the most credible experts are saying, the current state of the "fix" worldwide, actual Y2K-related disruptions that are already occurring and are expected to continue as the rollover approaches, and the reasonable expectations for what might occur when A.D. 2000 does arrive. Please remember that, while there is a great deal of credible evidence on the potential impacts of Y2K, all analysis of the problem is uncertain because of its very uncertain nature.

SNAPSHOT OF CREDIBLE COMMENTARY

Ernest Patrikis, the second-in-command at the Federal Reserve Bank of New York, summed up a common concern about attention to Y2K in his July 1998 testimony before the U.S. Senate Special Committee on the Year 2000 Technology Problem.

> My discussions with other [business and government Y2K leaders] have convinced me that successful efforts to address the Y2K problem will be dependent on the credibility of those calling for action. Those of us...who are seriously engaged and concerned need to be able to persuade others of the need to take appropriate actions promptly. It would be unfortunate if general perceptions of the Y2K problem are driven primarily by unofficial commentators whose rhetoric is seen to exceed the facts on which it is based, and therefore easily dismissed.[2]

As Christians, we must take careful account of the credibility of those publicly commenting on Y2K and avoid the temptation to lean toward the more sensationalist statements. We are supposed to be "the head and not the tail" (Deuteronomy 28:13) in our societies, and we must be able to—as Mr. Patrikis puts it—"persuade others" of the importance of this issue and of the need to take prompt action. In order to be able to both lead and help others, we must maintain our credibility by being of "sound mind" and "sober judgment" on all things (2 Timothy 1:7, Titus 2:6). We should not and cannot present an easily dismissed face to the world by relying on—or even giving ear to—sensationalist rhetoric. The factual evidence and comments from well-respected officials are sobering enough. For example:

- "Given the sheer number of organizations that are potentially at risk, it is inevitable that Y2K-related disruptions will occur. Today it would be impossible to predict the precise nature of these disruptions. However, we do know that financial markets have in the past survived many other serious disruptions." *—Ernest Patrikis, Senate testimony, July 6, 1998*
- "Worldwide problems are now inevitable from the glitch. It threatens electrical power, water utilities, airline and railroad traffic, telecommunications and international finance—all controlled by computers... Don't panic, but don't spend a lot of time sleeping, either." *—Senator Robert Bennett, quoted in* Deseret News, *June 3, 1998*
- "I believe we're going to win; that is, I think that civilization as we know it is not going to come to an end. It's a possibility [that], if Y2K were this weekend instead of seventy-six weekends from now, it would. But we have seventy-six weeks in which to try to get this under control...we are, in a sense, at war against this problem." *—Senator Robert Bennett before the National Press Club, July 16, 1998*
- "The likely failure of developing countries to head off widespread computer failure by fixing the Year 2000 computer bug could trigger bank panics, disrupt trade and cause civil unrest [in those countries]...fear will start to hit next year [1999]. People will start to take their money out of the bank, leading to further and further paralysis as we get closer." *—Joyce Amenta, United Nations Director of Information Technology, quoted in* Business Today, *July 1, 1998*
- "We do not know or cannot really realistically make an evaluation of what the economic impact is as a consequence of the [Y2K] breakdowns that may occur. We do not know the size. We do not know the contagion interaction within the system. And we do not know how rapidly we can resolve the problem." *—Alan Greenspan, chairman, Board of Governors, Federal Reserve System, testifying before the Senate Banking Committee, February 25, 1998*

CURRENT GLOBAL IMPACT ESTIMATES

As you can see from the comments above, the question is not *if* Y2K will have an impact on global business, government, and society, but *how deep* that impact will be. While that question is impossible to fully answer (especially since it depends heavily on the progress of the fix between now and the rollover), a realistic assessment of the evidence supports the conclusion that the impact may be more serious than we would like or can easily handle. Beyond that, there is a wide array of expert opinion as to degree.

High Costs

One of the most compelling proofs that the A.D. 2000 problem poses a very real threat is the vast sum of money businesses and governments are spending to combat it. Capers Jones, the highly esteemed chairman of Software Productivity Research, says, "Because this problem is embedded in millions of aging software applications, the costs of fixing the 'Year 2000 problem' appear to constitute the most expensive single problem in human history."[3]

In today's shareholder-driven economy, neither private nor public sector organizations can afford to spend millions of dollars on a single problem without an overwhelmingly good reason. A quick glance at the numbers shows, however, that they are doing just that as they urgently try to fix their organizations' Y2K vulnerabilities. Fortune 500 companies that have been forthcoming on this issue are disclosing very large Y2K costs. For example, according to their public statements, Citibank expects to spend more than $600 million, Delta Airlines $120 million, AT&T $520 million, General Motors $500 million, and Federal Express $75 million. The Securities Industry Association estimates that securities companies as a group will spend at least $5 billion. The U.S. government officially expects to spend nearly $5 billion, although numerous government officials believe that figure is low by at least 50 percent.

General Motors provides a good example for how quickly costs can escalate beyond just the cost of fixing one's *own* problems. Remember the statement "You are only as ready as those you do business with"? If even a few key companies that supply brake pads and engine parts to GM are disrupted by Y2K, GM will be unable to make and sell cars—and GM has more than 100,000 such suppliers. Similarly, GM is just as vulnerable to an internal disruption in its *own* distribution system, as evidenced by the fact that the July 1998 strike in one small part of GM's operations was able to shut down its national operations within a matter of days. Therefore, GM reports that it expects to spend *additional* millions to help its thousands of suppliers get ready for Year 2000 as well.

Significant (Perhaps Severe) Business Impacts

Virtually everyone looking at the problem agrees that there *will* be some impact from unresolved Y2K vulnerabilities, but there is disagreement on the degree.

Analysts and researchers have been trying to pin down both the worldwide total costs of fixing and responding to Y2K and the impact that unresolved problems could have. Because such an undertaking must be derived from both hard evidence and subjective judgments, these independent estimates vary quite a bit. However, the weight of credible opinion appears to lean toward Y2K having a "greater" degree of impact rather than a "lesser" impact, although some highly respected figures argue that the effects will be relatively moderate and easy to adjust to. No authoritative figure currently claims that Y2K will have no effect whatsoever. In fact, several highly respected individuals have publicly changed their beliefs on the possible severity of the problem. Robert Samuelson, a nationally respected economist and writer, even apologized to his readers for not attending to the issue more closely, saying that Y2K "may be one of the decade's big stories."[4]

This difference of opinion notwithstanding, several different and well-respected groups have independently demonstrated that the cost and impact of Y2K has the potential to be quite large. These researchers—widely recognized as leaders in Y2K analysis—include the Gartner Group, a respected technology consulting firm; Capers Jones, chairman of Software Productivity Research and the father of a field of science that studies computing-related productivity; and the Forrester Research Group, which conducts high-level business research for, among others, the MIT and Harvard business schools. After conducting sophisticated studies on the cost and impact of Y2K, these analysts have independently concluded the following:

- The cost of just fixing the problem may run from $300 to 600 *billion* worldwide (Gartner Group), although cost estimates have been rising and may increase further as 1999 progresses.
- The cost of litigation worldwide is expected to exceed $1 *trillion,* according to the Gartner Group and Lloyds of London.
- The total global cost of Y2K, including fixing the problem, lost business, and lost productivity, may be anywhere from $1.5 to 3.6 *trillion.* (Gartner estimates $1.5 to 3 trillion; Jones estimates $3.6 trillion.) As a comparison, that is an enormous portion of the entire annual Gross Domestic Product of the U.S., which was more than $8 trillion in 1997. Clearly, the global economy would be unable to easily absorb costs of this magnitude in a short period of time.
- Up to 15 percent of large U.S. businesses could be at risk of failure as a result of Y2K-related difficulties, with a potentially higher failure rate internationally. George Colony, president of the Forrester Research Group, in 1998 publicly estimated the following about the future of the Global 2000—the two thousand largest businesses in the world—as a result of Y2K:

- 35 percent would *thrive,* because they would fix their systems well in advance and use that as a serious competitive advantage;
- 50 percent would *survive,* although perhaps slightly battered by Y2K disruptions; and
- 15 percent would be at high risk to *fail,* due to failures in mission-critical systems. If correct, that will mean the failure of three hundred of the biggest household-name companies in the world.[5]

It is important to note that other analysts disagree that the problem will be so costly—either in terms of monetary or business losses. Among them is Capers Jones, the highly respected chairman of the Software Productivity Research Group, who currently estimates that 5 to 7 percent of midsized businesses will go bankrupt as a result of Y2K—sharply different from Forrester's 15 percent figure. Unfortunately, even if the more optimistic estimate is correct, that would still mean the failure of approximately one out of every fifteen or twenty midsized businesses, which in itself is a very sobering result. In the end, the more pessimistic figures are gaining more attention and credibility within industry and government. *SmartMoney* magazine, for example, reports that the National Association of Securities Dealers agrees with Gartner's $600 billion cost estimate.

Likelihood of a Recession

While the amounts of money businesses and governments are spending to prevent Y2K problems are pretty spectacular, the importance of these costs goes beyond the "wow" factor. In large part, much of this money is being spent in unproductive fixes. In other words, in many cases a company will spend tens of millions of dollars finding and fixing code, but the sum result is merely that they get to stay in business. The cost is like a pure loss; there may be no increase in the company's efficiency or productivity. Some forward-looking businesses, however, are using Y2K as a convenient excuse to completely upgrade their systems, thus reaping efficiency benefits as well.

This high incidence of unproductive fixes has to take a toll on the economy, and indeed many respected economists are predicting a high likelihood of a global economic recession. Ed Yardeni, chief economist for Deutsche Morgen Grenfell, has generated a great deal of publicity with his escalating predictions of economic recession. At the time of this writing, he is forecasting a 70 percent chance that the world will experience a recession worse than that of the 1973–74 oil crisis.

Not everyone agrees with these predictions, however. The Federal Reserve's "educated guess" in mid-1998 was that Y2K would shave just one-tenth of one percent off GDP growth in the coming year (i.e. that the economy, for example, would grow at a rate of 1.9 percent rather than 2 percent). Though not insignificant in economic terms, it is much less alarming than Ed Yardeni's prediction. It is worth noting, however, that Yardeni enjoys a freedom that the Fed doesn't have: the markets watch Fed statements so closely that a negative Fed forecast could become a self-fulfilling prophecy. The Fed's public forecasts, therefore, are always extremely conservative. It is worth noting that Ed Yardeni himself is a former Fed economist and that Fed governor Susan Phillips has said she expects slower growth and possibly higher inflation.

Likelihood of "Ripple Effects"

The possibility of Y2K "ripple effects"—which magnify a relatively small and isolated problem into a large and widespread one—is one of the hardest areas to analyze but one of the most troubling. As Y2K watchers become more informed, they generally realize that society's extensive interconnections have led to a degree of macrolevel vulnerability unprecedented in our history. You can get a sense for this by examining the crux of the issue: Two missing zeros have the ability to cause massive business failures worldwide.

In an environment where "When Wall Street sneezes, Asia catches a cold," and where information, financial transactions, and business communication seem to speed around the globe faster than light, even relatively simple problems can become enormous headaches. The previous example of GM's reliance on potentially noncompliant suppliers provides one picture of an enlarging ripple effect. The problem, obviously, is that many different types of ripple effects could occur. The most fundamental characteristic of the Millennium Bug is its uncertainty.

PROGRESS OF REPAIRS

While many businesses have made great strides toward combating their Y2K vulnerabilities, others are either just beginning to take action or are planning no Y2K remediation at all. Frequently, the larger companies are more aware and are further down the road, although that is not universal by any means. There remains a high degree of denial of pending problems among businesses, governments, churches and other nonprofit organizations, and individuals.

Status of "Cornerstone" Companies

Most programming experts agree that a medium- or large-sized business will require at least two to three years of full-time work to find, fix, and test their Y2K problems. It has become an inescapable fact that the testing process requires roughly 50 percent of the total time a company spends on Y2K. Some of the more forward-looking and perhaps more vulnerable businesses, such as banks, have been working on the problem since at least 1995, and are planning to use all of

1999 to test their fixes. Even so, many still have concerns about being done in time. Capers Jones's study analyzed the U.S. capability to address Y2K as a whole and determined that if the U.S. essentially dropped everything else computing-related and devoted its available resources nearly full time to the effort of fixing Y2K, we would have had to start no later than January 1, 1998, to finish on time. His conclusion, therefore, is that it is mathematically impossible to fix all Y2K problems by the time January 1, 2000, rolls around.

Even if they may not have the necessary two to three years to fully fix the problem, most large U.S. businesses are at least on the road to Y2K remediation. Unfortunately, even with the life of their businesses on the line, examples still arise of very large companies that have not yet begun the process. In mid-1998, major consulting firms around the country were shocked when one of the top national food distributors/supermarket chains began asking for bids to *start* their Y2K project. For this very reason, many of these consulting and auditing firms are beginning to refuse lucrative Y2K projects; they know that the majority of these late clients cannot possibly fix their vulnerabilities in time, and they don't want to be sued by angry shareholders when the client inevitably encounters problems.

Most Vulnerable Sector Unprepared

Unfortunately, the segments of our economy that are most vulnerable to Y2K also appear to be the least prepared. They are also the most likely audience for this book: nonprofit groups, churches, small businesses, community organizations, and individuals.

For example, in April 1998, the Gallup Organization conducted an extensive survey of American small business owners (*excluding* the self-employed). There are currently more than six million small business employers in the U.S. A Wells Fargo report based on this survey concluded the following:

> [While] more than four in five (82 percent) of all small businesses could be vulnerable [to Y2K problems], less than one-fourth of the nation's small business owners believe Year 2000 poses a serious problem to their operations, and less than half are implementing—or even considering—strategies to ward off the...problem.[6]

Other key findings include:

- Only 41 percent of small businesses have begun or plan to take Y2K action.
- "Vulnerable" small businesses estimate that nearly 25 percent of their sales or production would be lost during Y2K disruptions, on average. However, some had a much higher level of concern. Fifteen percent of the small businesses surveyed estimated that they would lose nearly *all* of their

business during Y2K disruptions (between 70–100 percent of production). The Wells Fargo report says, "In short, approximately 330,000 businesses could come to a halt during Y2K downtime and a slightly larger number could be seriously crippled."

- Nearly 20 percent of all small business owners—translating to more than *one million* businesses—reported that they had limited or no awareness of the Y2K problem.[7]

A Gartner Group study in April 1998 concluded that while large companies were 20 to 40 percent done with their Y2K fix, small businesses had completed only 0 to 10 percent of their repairs. Gartner believes that unless events dramatically intervene, these small businesses are almost certain to experience a mission-critical failure of their systems—that is, something that would endanger their ability to continue as a going concern.

Churches appear to be just as unaware as many small businesses—if not more so. Profit-seeking businesses at least have the powerful incentive to avoid bankruptcy. Unfortunately, churches and other nonprofits are at least as vulnerable to the sorts of cash flow and operational disruptions that could cripple some small businesses, and just when the need for their ministry is the highest.

Furthermore, it is sobering to realize that small businesses account for roughly 40 percent of GDP. If the large companies are the engines of our economy, the small business sector is the oil that makes it run. Even a minimal Y2K impact on small business could have a very large ripple effect throughout the economy. Richard Scurry, a former vice president at IBM and currently a financial executive in New York, says:

> What you tend to hear about Y2K is that it's costing the big companies an arm and a leg and that the economy may therefore be damaged from their "wasted activity." Obviously, there is also concern that some large businesses won't be ready. As I see it, the problem is that the *smaller* companies won't be ready. And if they aren't, and they encounter large problems, it will almost certainly cause a recession because they will either have to shut down until they are fixed or run well below their capacity...and these are the businesses that supply and purchase from the *larger* businesses.
>
> In 1973, when the foreign oil crisis started, I told my boss—a very senior executive of my company—that I was seriously concerned about a risk of inflation. But then our company economist came in and said that the oil shortages would not be a serious threat to the economy because only a small percentage of U.S. oil came from overseas, and oil was just a small percentage of GDP. He said, therefore, it basically didn't matter. I argued that on a direct basis foreign oil may be only a tiny fraction of GDP, but that since energy sales ripple through the entire economy, even a small foreign oil disruption almost *had* to cause a reces-

> sion here. And sure enough, it did. Y2K seems to be the same way. My concern with Y2K is that it will be a relatively small business problem, but that—when it winds its way through the economy—it will multiply.[8]

OTHER INDEPENDENT COMPUTER PROBLEMS

Believe it or not, Y2K isn't the only major computing-related challenge facing our world today. It actually is intermixed with so many other one-time and seemingly unrelated glitches that we might begin to wonder if this can all possibly be a "coincidence." For instance:

The New European Currency

The introduction of the euro, the new currency for the entire European Union, is slated for January 1, 1999, and poses enormous technical problems for many European companies (particularly banks) completely aside from Y2K. Peter de Jager, widely regarded as the leading Y2K expert worldwide, says:

> When you move to a single currency, like Europe is...all the computer programs that manage that currency must be modified.... It's a huge computing task. At the same time you're doing that, you also have this looming deadline of the year 2000, and that must also be done. To try [to] do both these tasks at the same time is like trying to dance a ballet while...lifting weights. It's not a wise move. Some people will achieve it, but many will fail because they are attempting too much.[9]

Because the euro deadline is one year earlier, companies that are behind in their conversions are focusing on the euro and have hardly started on Y2K. Government regulators worldwide are beginning to publicly wonder whether some institutions will even come close to the Y2K deadline.

A.D. 2000 Leap Year

Another computer glitch, completely unrelated to Y2K, also occurs in Year 2000—and it alone will have the ability to cause serious problems. Year 2000 is a leap year that does not conform to the most common mathematical rules for leap years; therefore, February 29, 2000, is not accounted for in some computer programs. While this situation is less pervasive than Y2K, it will likely cause some time-consuming problems in corporate billings, bank interest calculations, and similar endeavors, effectively compounding those problems already caused by Y2K.

The "99" Problem

The same sort of individualized programming techniques that led to Year 2000 problems may also cause problems in 1999. Programmers have long used 99 in two-digit year fields as a special command, such as *End of File* or *Delete All Records More Than 60 Days Old.* (You may have seen similar shortcuts in which a desktop printer recognizes the command to *Print From Page 1 to Page 9999* as *Print to End of Document,* since very few documents have more than 9,999 pages.) Any unfixed shortcuts such as this could very possibly cause all sorts of strange problems during 1999 itself. As Y2K watcher Jim Lord says, "The extent of this '99' problem is not known and is considered by the experts to be a real wild card in Y2K."

Solar Maximum

Looking at the volume and complexity of the unrelated computing problems that are cropping up independently and simultaneously raises the question of whether all this can possibly be coincidence—particularly given another approaching major and uncontrollable event. Year 2000 is the estimated timing for a major natural phenomenon that has had serious consequences in the past. The solar maximum, the maximum output of solar flares, has occurred only twenty-two times since records were first kept in the 1600s; scientists expect the next solar maximum to occur sometime around A.D. 2000. Solar flares—and particularly the solar maximum—have been tied to a high incidence of crop failures and technological disruptions around the world, although scientists cannot explain exactly why. The National Academy of Sciences warns that "Increasing effects of solar…disturbances on human activities are *expected* during the period of the [next] solar maximum" [emphasis added].[10] In the past, such "space weather" disturbances have affected not only our agricultural productivity, but also satellites, power systems, underground pipelines (e.g., for oil and gas), communications systems, and the Global Positioning System. These all sound eerily familiar to potential Y2K disturbances. It does make you wonder what on earth (or in heaven) is going on!

Some Christians may try to link the potential impacts of all these events with end-times speculation, but that is beyond the purpose of this book, and, in any case, unproductive for believers. It is not ours to "know the hour or the day." We must simply be faithful servants until our Lord Jesus Christ returns. Obviously, there are no real coincidences in our world. Thankfully, God is sovereign and knows exactly what is happening here, even if we do not.

HAZARDS OF FIXING PROBLEMS

As if all this weren't enough, the very act of fixing our Y2K problems is actually causing other problems, such as the introduction of new errors in the system and Y2K-like disruptions caused by the testing process.

A common problem in the computing industry is that the act of reprogramming code actually introduces new errors. After a system is revised or replaced, the new system is usually riddled with these bugs, which take time and diligence to find and fix. Y2K expert Jim Lord notes that, under normal circumstances, seven new errors are introduced for every 100 lines of code programmed. And most Y2K projects are *not* occurring under "normal circumstances." Under the intense Y2K deadline pressure, the error rate has risen to ten per 100 lines of code, or 10 percent. These errors can spark either unnoticeable or enormous glitches.

Partially because of these hidden errors, the process of Y2K testing of hastily fixed companies will itself cause disruptions, such as with real-process controllers that wouldn't otherwise have a problem until the rollover. Jim Lord expects that we will "see accidents at these facilities...as Y2K repairs are completed and then rushed into on-line testing."[11]

TRIAGE IS NECESSARY

As noted, the focus of expert opinion on Y2K disruptions has shifted from *if* to *when* and *how much*. Many of the individuals who are managing the process are beginning to shift their focus away from trying to fix every single system, since that is impossible for many organizations at this point. Instead, these managers are deciding to focus on fixing mission-critical systems—those that are necessary for the organization to survive and continue its mission—and are developing contingency plans for the rest. In the Y2K community, this has become known as "triage"—the long-standing medical technique of prioritizing treatment by focusing on the most critical but saveable patients, and waiting to address the non-life-threatening problems (or those that are beyond saving) until later down the line.

Senator Robert Bennett, chairman of the Senate's Y2K committee, said in a July 1998 National Press Club speech: "We cannot get this problem [fully] solved. So what we have to do is start making priority choices. To go back to the medical term, we have to do triage and say, 'We will allow these systems to die, because these [other] systems are absolutely critical for us to survive.'"[12]

These sort of "system triage" decisions are being made every day by those governments and businesses who recognize that since they cannot solve the whole problem, it is better to cut their losses and focus on the most important areas. Unfortunately, as time has passed and our slow progress has become increasingly apparent, some organizations have found that the choice is no longer between critical and secondary systems; they are now being forced to decide between one very important system and another. *PC Magazine* editor Jim Seymour wrote in June 1998 that those companies less far along are already "deciding which of their vital systems they're going to let [fail] on January 1, 2000, and which absolutely, inescapably must—and still can—be fixed by then."[13]

This can pose uncomfortable quandaries which must nevertheless be faced. As a Georgia state official queries: "Is our system of paying benefits to employees more important than collecting revenue?...If we can't collect revenue, that's a big problem."[14]

A FEW ENCOURAGING FACTS

Amid all of the melancholy predictions, there are a few bright and important rays of hope.

- New automated techniques are being invented and adopted to speed the fix. While none can ever be the single, longed-for silver bullet, they can assist the process enormously. Peter de Jager compares the task of fixing our global Y2K problems to the enormous and labor-intensive job of building the Panama Canal: the automated utilities act like sticks of dynamite rather than picks and shovels. They may not build the canal, but they are an invaluable aid to the work of digging.
- Even though it is impossible to fix all of our Y2K problems in time, some percentage of our remaining vulnerabilities are either in less critical systems or are the types of failures that will not actually threaten the functioning of a mission-critical item.
- Y2K will, as described above, actually provide a competitive advantage and opportunity for many prepared organizations. It is highly likely that prepared banks, manufacturing plants, and other businesses will start fortressing themselves as 1999 progresses by avoiding potentially noncompliant organizations and dealing only with those known to be Year-2000-ready. This should dramatically increase the fortunes of known Year-2000 "stars," not to mention the financial benefits they will derive if Y2K problems knock out their competitors.
- Much more concretely, the swelling need for Y2K repairs and workarounds (both before and after the rollover) will likely translate into direct benefits for many businesses—including several segments of our economy that have diminished noticeably in an era otherwise dominated by computers. While programmers and other entities providing fixes are an obvious beneficiary of Y2K madness, there are many others, including secretarial and administrative services, old-fashioned mechanics, repair and maintenance services, and those companies that are manufacturing Y2K-compliant replacement parts. Michael Fletcher, who authors a "Y2K on the Job" column on Westergaard's online resource, noted in his February 24, 1998, piece about car mechanics that "you may want to look for those old-time mechanics and tradespeople who can get a job done regardless of the amount of electronic wizardry hanging off their belts.

Their value is going to soar." (Check out Fletcher's column at www.y2ktimebomb.com.)

SURVEY: ARRAY OF EXPERT OPINION ON IMPACT SEVERITY

As previously noted, those who are most aware of the Y2K issue are the most concerned about its impact. However, even within that community there exists a fairly large difference of opinion on how severe that impact might be.

A highly informative survey was conducted by Bruce Webster, chairman of the Washington D.C. Year 2000 Group—widely recognized as one of the most (if not *the* most) active Y2K groups in the country. The Washington group is primarily comprised of individuals who are heavily involved in hands-on or high-level management of the Y2K problem in a wide variety of business or government organizations—in other words, those most likely to have a truly informed judgment on the issue. The March 1998 survey asked members to estimate the impact of Year 2000 problems within the United States, using an explicit and cumulative scale developed by Capers Jones. Jones's scale goes from 0 to 10, with every step defined.

Nearly half of the 700 members responded to the survey. The following summary results are drawn directly from an analysis of the survey published by Bruce Webster in April 1998:[15]

Scale	Impact of Y2K Problems within the U.S.	Percent in Agreement (Cumulative)	Percent Choosing Each Level
0	No real impact	100 percent	1 percent
1	Local impact for some enterprises	99 percent	3 percent
2	Significant impact for many enterprises	96 percent	12 percent
3	Significant market adjustment (20 percent+ drop); some bankruptcies	84 percent	18 percent
4	Economic slowdown; rise in unemployment; isolated social incidents (e.g. strikes, riots)	66 percent	10 percent
5	Mild recession; isolated supply/infrastructure problems (e.g. food shortages, public utility and transportation disruptions); runs on banks	56 percent	22 percent
6	Strong recession; local social disruptions; many bankruptcies	34 percent	9 percent

7	Political crises; regional supply/infrastructure problems and social disruptions	26 percent	15 percent
8	Depression; infrastructure crippled; market collapse; local martial law	10 percent	3 percent
9	Supply/infrastructure collapse; widespread social disruptions and martial law	7 percent	6 percent
10	Collapse of U.S. government; possible famine	1 percent	1 percent

These results are not only informative, they are quite sobering. Two-thirds (66 percent) of these experts believe Y2K will cause *at least* an economic slowdown accompanied by isolated incidences of social problems such as strikes, looting, and demonstrations. Frankly, it is of more concern that one-quarter of the respondents believe those sorts of problems will not be isolated but will be widespread across entire regions. Further, one-quarter believe Y2K will also cause widespread regional shortages in necessities such as food and fuel, and disruptions in utilities such as power and telephone service. It is hard to know how to judge the realism of the remaining responses, but fully 18 percent appear to believe that Y2K will cripple our national infrastructure and collapse our markets.

The reason this is sobering, of course, is that these are the individuals who should know. These are the corporate or government officers, consultants, and technical managers who are most deeply involved in the process of analyzing and addressing the scope of the Y2K phenomenon. Unlike much other expert analysis or commentary that could be dismissed as self-serving (such as one Y2K study done by a consulting shop that will profit if it "scares in" enough clients), this survey was confidential and anonymous, asking members to identify themselves only by categories such as corporate, military, educational, consultant, government, etc.

DISRUPTIONS HAVE ALREADY BEGUN

One of the most important things to realize about the Year 2000 problem is that disruptions are going to start becoming apparent well in advance of the actual rollover. The scope and severity of such advance disruptions (or lack thereof) will be a compelling indicator as to the final nature of the problem once the rollover actually occurs. Some experts believe we may see an increase in business glitches as early as January 1, 1999, when many business applications begin to look ahead one year. Further, different industries may have different "spike dates" for facing these advance disruptions. For example, in a health care industry survey conducted by Rx2000 Industry Solutions—a central Y2K resource for the medical community—62 percent of respondents' organizations had *already* encountered actual Y2K failures.[16] Therefore, because our time horizon is considerably shorter than the time to the actual rollover, all organizations are encouraged to take remedial precautions immediately.

The following are representative examples of problems already sparked by the Millennium Bug, disruptions caused by computer glitches of the same nature, or potential problems found during Y2K testing.

- As in the fictional scenario in the previous chapter, a large Wall Street investment bank made a ten-trillion-dollar error in June 1997. CNN reported that "a computer glitch at Smith Barney overnight briefly put $19 million into each of [its] customer accounts, the brokerage said Thursday morning.... The brokerage has 525,000 such accounts."[17] While the reasons were not officially announced, unofficial reports widely indicate that this occurred while programmers were conducting a live Y2K test, since all repairs had been successfully tested offline.
- In several major incidents, businesses have destroyed millions of dollars' worth of inventory when noncompliant computer systems mistakenly assumed that products with expiration dates of '00 or '01 were one hundred years old. In other cases, testing of Y2K systems showed that the inventory *would* have been destroyed if the system had been running in the year 2000. In reporting on U.S. government readiness for Y2K, the Associated Press stated that "several major Y2K tests have failed. In one case, the system that manages the military's vast inventory wrongly marked 90,000 items for deletion."[18]
- Other offline Y2K tests have shown what unprepared companies could be in for. *Business Week* reports that in the fall of 1997:

> Phillips Petroleum Company engineers ran Year 2000 tests on an oil-and-gas production platform in the North Sea. The result: in a simulation, an essential safety system for detecting harmful gases such as hydrogen sulfide got confused and shut down. In real life, that would have rendered the platform unusable.[19]

- In a more sobering example (fictionalized in the previous chapter), the past head of a large southern power company reported being seriously shaken when a seemingly Y2K-ready power plant experienced a "scram shutdown" when a live Y2K test was run with nuclear capability offline. They had conducted a head-to-toe system replacement, intending to use that plant as a Y2K prototype for others to follow. Upon investigation, they found that the problem was caused by something as seemingly trivial as a few noncompliant sensors in a smokestack that they had missed during their excruciatingly thorough replacement process.[20]

• The much-touted July 1998 opening of Hong Kong's new airport was marred by a small computer glitch with large and embarrassing consequences. Although it was not a Y2K problem, *Bloomberg News* made the natural comparison:

> If you can't imagine how the Year 2000 computer bug might bring world commerce to its knees, look what happened last week at Hong Kong's new airport when cargo-handling computers malfunctioned. Hundreds of scheduled flights were delayed, thousands of pieces of luggage were lost, millions of dollars in perishable goods were left to rot.... The magnitude of disruption...estimated as high as $2 billion during the first nine days, is a vivid illustration of what can go wrong with highly sophisticated systems, dependent on fail-safe computers.... The entire debacle was blamed on poorly written software [put into place too quickly].... Because baggage-handling computers malfunctioned, a delicately synchronized network that controlled virtually every system in the airport broke down.... During the first two days, passengers missed planes, flight information monitors throughout the stunning new terminal went blank and one of every two bags was temporarily lost.[21]

• A series of refinery incidents that occurred at midnight on New Year's Day 1996 has long been touted as a preview of potential Year 2000 problems. A system that hadn't been programmed to recognize 1996 as a leap year caused production cold-stops in at least three separate aluminum smelters in New Zealand and Australia, as each smelter passed into the New Year. This caused millions of dollars' worth of damage to the refineries and immediately gave New Zealand the dubious honor of being a Year 2000 early-warning post, as its proximity to the International Date Line will make it the first major industrialized country to enter the new millennium.

• While most of the government lags behind in Y2K preparation (as described below), the Social Security Administration is one of the few agencies that might make the deadline. The reason is that they discovered the potential gravity of the problem in 1989 when they experienced a major computer failure during long-term forecasting.

• The *Chicago Tribune*, in an interview with the technology director of an advisory firm, learned of a simple Y2K glitch in an inadequately prepared company the director has dealt with. "Half of this company's business comes from trading futures contracts on a particular commodity," he explained. "Some prices for that commodity in the year 2000 went into the system, but because the system has not been readied for Y2K, prices came out lower than they actually were and lower than anyone else's. Their phones rang off the hook. The [futures] were set at these prices and the company had to honor these contracts, costing the organization several hundreds of thousands of dollars."[22]

• Although the May 1998 failure of the Galaxy IV satellite and its backup system didn't appear to be at all Y2K related, it provided a great real-life example of the processes and services that may not work if Y2K *does* cause satellite disruptions. Most notoriously, nearly 90 percent of the 45 million U.S. paging customers lost service. Some other effects included the postponement of several television and radio broadcasts.

• Early in 1998 a retailer in Michigan lost hundreds of thousands of dollars in revenue when a customer used a credit card with a '00 expiration date and all cash registers in the store suddenly froze. They could not be reactivated until a company software specialist arrived the next day. This led to one of the first (but certainly not the last) Year 2000-related lawsuits for financial harm arising from lack of preparedness—in this case, against the cash register company.

SO HOW MIGHT THIS END UP?

The above examples of Y2K impact provide a peek into the types of events that *could* occur as the turn of the century approaches. But predicting *actual* outcomes is nearly impossible. As noted, the final outcome in your industry or area will vary considerably based on the effort expended between now and then to fix the problem and prepare for potential effects. While opinions about the eventual results are as varied as the people providing them, several good sources do exist for informed and credible judgments about the areas of greatest and least concern. Senator Robert Bennett and Representative Stephen Horn, chairmen of their respective Y2K-related committees in the U.S. Senate and House, both provide helpful summaries of these areas. Further, a landmark report by Capers Jones has statistically predicted the likelihood of various Y2K impacts on different areas of our lives.

Senator Robert Bennett: Areas of Greatest and Least Concern

While some self-described "Y2K alarmists" express extreme blanket concern over every industry and area, it is important to recognize that there *are* some areas that are further ahead than others in their preparations for the century date change. Some extremists rightfully point out that poorly prepared industries might have a negative effect on the well-prepared ones; for example, it doesn't matter how well your business fixes its computers if the power utility shuts down. Yet the fact remains that, in order to have any hope of affecting meaningful change in the time remaining, we must find and focus our attention on the areas of greatest concern.

At a National Press Club luncheon on July 15, 1998, Senator Bennett discussed the areas of his greatest concern and those with which he is more comfortable:

• *Power.* "I believe the power grid [as a whole] will work [but] we will have brownouts and regional blackouts...in some areas of the country."
• *Water.* "I think water will be available in most municipalities, but [in some] the water system will break down. And there could be serious, serious difficulty in those communities."
• *Telephones.* "The phone system, I think, will work. But I wouldn't guarantee that you could get a dial tone in Taiwan. So if you have a supplier in a foreign country that is not Y2K-compliant, you'd better start looking around for alternatives and drafting some contingency plans."
• *Banking and Finance.* "I believe the financial system will work [as a whole].... I think you will still be able to trade stocks on the New York Stock Exchange [but perhaps not on some foreign exchanges]. I think the banking system will work [but there will be] individual banks that will probably go bankrupt."
• *Health Care.* "I am very concerned about the health care system. There are health care entities that may very well go bankrupt because they cannot get [Medicare/Medicaid] reimbursement. That is, in my view, one of the number-one issues.... There are medical machines that will fail in ICU units."
• *Air Travel.* "I think the air traffic control system will work, but I expect we will probably be rationing flights. I don't think it will work at the same level that it currently is."
• *Municipal Governments/Welfare.* "I'm concerned about counties. What's going to happen to the social fabric in this country if a county in a large, populous area cannot deliver welfare checks? What kind of riots might occur?... That's an area where I have great concern."
• *National Defense.* "Do I think the Defense Department will fall apart? No. But I am glad we're not engaged in a major war when this hits, because the Defense Department will have serious challenges. I think the satellites will work, but I'm not sure about all of the weapons systems here on the ground."
• *Social Security.* "Of all the government agencies, I think the Social Security system is in the best shape and will be in a position to see to it that Social Security checks will go out."
• *Other Government Agencies.* "The government agencies that concern me the most [include the] IRS; serious, serious troubles at IRS. [Also] our experience [at the Federal Emergency Management Agency], has been, shall we say, less than reassuring.... We have not found FEMA to be either as understanding of the problem or as forthcoming as they need to be with information."[23]

Some pundits believe Y2K won't cause many difficulties because we can always return to a more manual method of doing business. Senator Bennett explained why that is probably not a viable option as a whole:

> Somebody asked [me], "Why are we worried about the fact that the switches that control the rail traffic in this country are all computerized? Let's [just] go back to somebody standing there and throwing the switch in advance of the train." There are no switches to throw. All of the manual switches have been replaced.... We cannot go back because the infrastructure that undergirded our entire society

twenty-five years ago has been dismantled. It is gone. The skills are gone, the people are gone, the equipment is gone. Like it or not, we have no choice in this situation but to plow forward and, one way or the other, make it work.[24]

Representative Stephen Horn: Government "Y2K Report Card"

Obviously, the readiness level of both federal and state agencies is an enormous concern to all of us. In the "war on Y2K," our government is fighting the battle under unequal conditions. Due to their constant struggle for financial resources, government agencies rely more heavily on older systems, which have more Y2K problems and are unable to match the private-sector salaries for talented programmers to conduct the Y2K fix. It is highly likely that certain critical government agencies—such as the Departments of Energy and Defense and the Internal Revenue Service—may not be completely ready for the rollover. As the Energy Department deals with the power and natural resources that keep our modern society running, the Defense Department ensures our safety as a nation, and the IRS ensures that all U.S. government functions will continue, we should be as concerned as they are about their lagging readiness for the century date change. The table below is Representative Horn's "report card"[25] of the Y2K readiness of major federal agencies based on what the agencies themselves report:

Official U.S. Government Y2K Report Card

Y2K Ratings for Progress at Major Agencies (Ratings by U.S. Congress)
Based on Agencies' Self-Reporting
(As of August 15, 1998)

Grade: A
Social Security Administration (SSA)
National Science Foundation (NSF)
Small Business Administration (SBA)

Grade: B
General Services Agency (GSA)
Department of Commerce
Environmental Protection Agency (EPA)
Veterans Administration
Federal Emergency Management Agency (FEMA)

Grade: C
NASA
Department of Agriculture
Housing and Urban Development (HUD)

Grade: D
Department of the Treasury
Department of Transportation (DOT)
Office of Personnel Management (OPM)
Department of Defense (DOD)
Department of Labor
Department of the Interior
Nuclear Regulatory Commission (NRC)

Grade: F
Health and Human Services (HHS)
Department of Energy (DOE)
Department of State
Department of Justice
Department of Education
Agency for International Development (AID)

Overall Grade: D

Note: Some agencies (such as FEMA) have dramatically changed their standing by changing what they report. Such changes may not reflect real improvement. The full report card is available at http://www.house.gov/reform/gmit/y2k/

Capers Jones: Statistical Probabilities of Y2K Impacts

Capers Jones, the father of a field of computer science called "software metrics," is highly qualified to forecast Y2K software impacts. The chart below[26] is a sampling of his conclusions:

From "Probabilities of Y2K Damages"
Report by Capers Jones
Chairman, Software Productivity Research
February 27, 1998

YEAR 2000 PROBLEM	PROBABILITY
Bad credit reports from Y2K errors	70%
Cancellation of year 2000 liability insurance	60%
Loss of local electric power (>1 day)	55%
Litigation against corporate officers	55%
Loss of regional electric power (>1 day)	40%
Loss of international telephone services	35%
Errors in 2000 tax reporting (1099 forms)	35%
Errors with Social Security payments	35%
Errors in first January paycheck	30%
Errors or delays in tax refunds	30%
Delays or cancellations of airline flights	25%
Loss of local telephone services	20%
Errors with motor vehicle records	20%
Medical or hospital billing errors	20%
Manufacturing shut-downs (>1 day)	20%
Process control shut-downs (>1 day)	20%
Reductions in stock values	20%
Errors in 2000 tax reporting (W2 forms)	15%
Errors in bank account balances	15%
Disruption of stock market trading	15%
Shut-down of pharmaceutical manufacturing	15%
Errors in hotel/motel reservations	12%
Delays or cancellations of shipping	10%
Errors in prescription dates	10%
Delays in UPS, FedEx deliveries	10%
Delays or cancellations of rail shipments	10%
Urban bankruptcy due to year 2000	7%
Water shortages/rationing	7%
Corporate bankruptcy due to year 2000	5%
Food shortages/rationing	3%
Escheatment of bank accounts	2%
Death or injuries due to year 2000	1%

These estimated probabilities are a helpful starting point but may not tell the whole story. Mr. Jones's report and research are highly focused on software damages, and some experts caution that embedded chip problems will significantly increase the likelihood of certain disruptions (such as food shortages).

Watch for New Information

While good "predictive" information isn't widely available yet on many specifics (such as the Y2K readiness level of your individual bank or telephone service provider), better information is expected to become more widely and publicly available as 1999 progresses. It is likely that "consumer guides" and other such rating mechanisms will be developed to help guide your personal and professional decisions about where to concentrate your preventive efforts.

CHAPTER FIVE

January 2000

Champaign-Urbana, Illinois, January 1, 2000—9:45 A.M.

Patrick O'Neill groggily rolled over in bed, shading his eyes from the winter sunlight streaming through the curtains. Something about the angle of the sun clicked in his brain, and he squinted through bleary eyes at his wristwatch. *Oh no!* He sat bolt upright in bed, startling Cindy awake. "It's almost ten o'clock!"

Cindy threw off her sheets and propelled herself out of bed, gasping at the coldness of the air. She stared briefly at the darkened face of their digital clock. "The alarm didn't go off. How on earth are the kids still asleep?"

Patrick was already down the hall and in the bathroom, futilely flicking the light switch. "Honey! The lights are off! That storm must have knocked out the electricity."

But the electricity was working when we got home last night, Cindy thought, *and the storm was over by then.* She hustled into the kids' rooms, rousing Erin and picking Will up out of his crib. He was still sleepy after such a strange schedule yesterday. A whole passel of kids had slept in the two big beds at the Lees' house last night, but—due to a bunch of overindulgent dads—they had gone down way too late. She couldn't help but be thankful that a whole contingent of moms would have just as much fun as she would, coping with two overhyped and cranky kids while their Promise Keepers were gone this New Year's Day.

Cindy heard Patrick mumble in the bathroom and grinned to herself as she changed Will's diaper. *That's right—no electricity, no hot or cold water.* Frankly, she didn't mind the few occasions when their electricity would go out because she loved to tease her husband about what she called his "obsession" with creature comforts. She was the one who had grown up in the big city, but she was proud of the fact that she was much more of a country girl than her home-grown, afraid-of-spiders husband. He had agreed to go camping with her once—only once—and had decreed afterward that next time she wanted to go hiking they could do it on a mountain that had hotels with hot water. She knew he was fastidious and would probably use buckets of ice-cold water from their backyard stream for a semblance of a sponge bath.

She called brightly down the hall, "Oh, Paddy—before you make like a polar bear, could you fill a couple of buckets for the toilet?" She couldn't resist reminding him that their toilets required electricity to flush as well, and was rewarded by a whiny wail from the direction of the bathroom.

She giggled as she got Erin and Will dressed. Erin was a four-year-old handful and kept wanting to play with her Barbie Christmas present instead of putting on her clothes. By the time Cindy finally got her dressed, Will was crying to be picked up. Exasperated, Cindy told Erin to "go pick out a video," completely forgetting that no such distractions were possible.

This, she thought in grim amusement, *is going to be a very interesting day.*

Austin, Texas, January 1, 2000—11:00 A.M.

> *We regret that we are unable to process transactions at this time. Please try again later, and thank you for using Midwest Bankcorp.*

Jim Thicke stared at the ATM screen in frustration. The machines were conspiring against him—and this was his bank! He'd gone to three machines from other banks already, since they were closer to home, but although they had spit out cash for other people they were not working for him. Finally, he'd had to give up and drive around to pick up the other guys he'd promised to bring to Promise Keepers. The guys had agreed to this brief detour so he could get some cash out of an actual Midwest ATM near the Promise Keepers rally. And now he couldn't get cash here, either.

He climbed back in the driver's seat of the Jeep, trying to hide his embarrassment. "Well, is anyone willing to spot me for lunch today? Still no telephones, so no credit cards—and it looks like my own bank won't give me cash either." The other guys joked that since he was the chauffeur of the day, the least they could do was pay him minimum wage.

In his rearview mirror, Jim noticed that Billy appeared thoughtful and wasn't joining in the good-natured ribbing. He suddenly remembered that Billy used Midwest Bankcorp too. "Billy, are *you* okay? Do you need cash?"

Billy jerked his head up. "Me? Oh—no. I did the envelope thing last summer and saved up two months' worth of cash for expenses. Best to be prepared, you know."

In spite of his current circumstances, Jim smiled to himself, thinking how simple Billy was. This wasn't their great-grandparents' era, when money was safest under a mattress at home. What did Billy think, that Midwest was going to fail and his money disappear, like those banks in the '30s? Since the advent of the FDIC, bank runs were a thing of the past.

He was just about to tease Billy about that when he heard Mel—one of the older guys from Community Church—responding to Billy's comment. "Yep, we did that, too. Not sure if we could trust our bank not to garble up our accounts after the rollover, so we followed Burkett's advice and pulled out some cash. I'd forgotten what it was like to have a few thousand dollars in cash at home. But, you know, that was pretty normal before the ATM era."

Jim held his tongue. He respected Mel and was surprised at his statement. This certainly wasn't something that had been addressed at church. He wanted to ask him about it, but not in front of the other guys.

When they finally arrived at the Capitol steps, the throng was abuzz with discussion and rumors of Year 2000 incidents all over the country—utilities disruptions, dead gasoline pumps, manufacturing meltdowns, and even a train crash. Supposedly, the collective wisdom said, the Promise Keepers speakers were going to address the issue directly. Austin's loss of land-based telephone service had reportedly been a big topic of conversation in the New York news, as it was the most prominent domestic market with serious telecommunications problems. One man had heard a CNN report that serious power shortages in some major city markets—such as Chicago—were being countered by drawing electricity from more rural areas nearby. Apparently the power companies in several states had decided it was better to ration electricity in the smaller markets than risk a power loss in the larger, more volatile, cities.

As he listened to the energetic exchange of facts and speculation, Jim began to feel a growing sense of foreboding. Like everyone else on the planet, he had heard about Y2K. It had just seemed so ludicrous that anyone would let anything so major go unfixed. He had even called a couple of business school buddies on Wall Street, who had laughed and assured him the problem was overblown and that aside from a few annoying inconveniences here and there, everything would be fine. He and Courtney had even talked about Y2K, but figured that if their VCR conked out or a PC had trouble at work, they would deal with it then.

But what he was now hearing went way, way beyond a few "inconveniences." *That guy said eight states in the midwest had to ration power! Eight states? How is that possible?* Jim thought about the malfunctioning ATM card in his wallet. Surely he could depend on the bank to fix it. Surely he could trust his credit cards to work soon. And suddenly a shiver that had nothing to do with the cold air passed down his spine.

Champaign-Urbana, Illinois, January 2, 2000—11:30 A.M.

Johnny Barry stepped to the pulpit and looked out over the congregation. The church was filled to overflowing, and an additional four hundred people were reportedly sitting on the floor in the small gym where they could hear and participate indirectly in the service. Next week, he thought dimly, they would set up sufficient seating. He stood for a moment, fighting an urge to weep that rose unexpectedly from the inexpressible emotions inside of him.

"I'm glad you are all here this morning. It's good to see you," he said simply, and bowed his head. "Let the words of my mouth and the meditations of all of our hearts be pleasing in thy sight, O mighty King and Father. Amen."

He looked up again, feeling the gentle presence of the Holy Spirit among this gathering of the faithful and the unsure—the fiery believers and the desperately lost. They all needed to hear the words that were on his heart for this time.

"Friends, you have all come here today with one cry in your heart—one plea. That plea is *Help, Lord. Help me. Comfort me, provide for me, love me.* The events of the last thirty-six hours have been historic and challenging in many ways, and in your hearts you are crying out for comfort, for sustenance, for security. Whether you know it or not, you are crying out to God. A God who loves you and who has promised never, ever to leave or forsake you." Johnny could see the faces of his congregation—the beloved sheep of his suddenly expanded flock, many of whom he hadn't even met yet. He barely registered what he was saying as he reminded these precious people that God is the only true security we have or will ever have. That though the world may crumble around us, he will remain steadfast and faithful in his love for us. That God desires nothing more than our hearts, fully entrusted to his wise and good care, in an intimate relationship with him.

Johnny stepped from behind the podium and walked a few paces onto the open platform. His voice reached into every corner of the room, resonating with conviction. "Friends, I believe that our calling isn't just to renew our trust in a good and faithful God who will provide for all our needs. We are living at a unique time in history, and we have a unique opportunity—a unique role to play in our Lord's plan for this world. Over the last few months, and the last week in particular, we have seen so much that we have taken for granted come crashing down around us. Our world is being mightily shaken. What will our response be?" He nodded toward the piano at the end of the platform, where two young women waited. "I have something I'd like you to hear. The words to a beautiful Rich Mullins song, *If I Stand,* are printed in your bulletin. I know many of you know and love this song, but I want you to really *listen* to it this morning."

The pianist played a few gentle notes as Becky Lee stepped to the microphone and began to sing:

> There's more that rises in the morning than the sun, and more that shines in the night than just the moon. There's more than just this fire here that keeps me warm, in a shelter that is larger than this room. There's a loyalty that's deeper than mere sentiment, a music higher than the songs that I can sing. The stuff of earth competes for the allegiance I owe only to the giver of all good things.

> So if I stand, let me stand on the promise, that You will pull me through. And if I can't, let me fall on the grace that first brought me to You. If I sing, let me sing for the joy that has born in me these songs. But if I weep, let it be as a man who is longing for his home. There's more that dances on the prairies than the wind, more that pulses in the ocean than the tide. There's a love that is fiercer than the love between friends, more gentle than a mother's when her baby's at her side....

Becky fought to keep the words from trembling as she sang, but she could feel the deep emotion inside her and hear the tears rising in her voice.

> And there's a loyalty that's deeper than mere sentiment, a music higher than the songs that I can sing. The stuff of earth competes for the allegiance I owe only to the giver of all good things.

The last few words were practically a whisper, choked out against the ocean welling up inside of her. She could see the tears in many of the eyes before her, as well as the undaunted hope and life in the faces of her many wonderful friends. Suddenly overwhelmed by both trepidation and expectation, she was almost at a loss as to how to continue, but heard a few voices join in from the choir...then from the people before her. The song from the congregation grew in volume, swelling through the church, ringing through the empty hallways outside:

> So if I stand, let me stand on the promise, that You will pull me through. And if I can't, let me fall on the grace that first brought me to You. If I sing, let me sing for the joy that has born in me these songs. But if I weep, let it be as a man who is longing for his home![1]

The chorus was repeated again and again, and as they sang Becky began to feel the presence of the Lord showering comfort and peace upon his people. She noticed that the pianist was crying but playing through her tears, leaning into the notes as if she needed their physical support. With a peculiarly uninvolved part of her mind, Becky remembered that she had a small son with a special medical need. How many more people needed to really trust God's provision, even more than she did? She put her hand on the pianist's shoulder and squeezed gently, passing along comfort. They had to trust. They had no choice.

Austin, Texas, January 2, 2000—11:35 A.M.

"He *will* supply all your needs in Christ Jesus! That is a promise, not a suggestion." The pastor of Community Church spoke earnestly to his large and diverse congregation. "The last thirty-six hours have tried and tested many of us, asking us to evaluate where our trust lies. Do we trust the Lord to supply all our needs—or do we look to our elected officials, our banks, our telephone companies? We do have many among us and in our community with serious needs today. We must start acting like the true body of Christ, reaching out with hands and feet ready to bless others."

The pastor had been quietly working on this sermon for months, ever since he had started to suspect that the Year 2000 problem might actually be, well, a real problem. He had decided *not* to discuss it beforehand, though, because it was very clear that no one could know how it would turn out. He hadn't wanted to contribute to the general paranoia that was becoming all too rampant as the date approached. But now that the day had actually arrived, he wanted to stir his flock to action. It never occurred to him that they might not be in a position now to take any.

As he spoke this exhortation, Deborah Carey sat quietly at the end of a pew. Hope and despair battled within her. She didn't know the Bible all that well, but she knew that Jesus called himself the Good Shepherd. And never had she needed a Shepherd more than now. She wasn't experienced at talking to God, but now she found herself praying with all her might. *God Almighty, I need help. Please, God. I don't know how I'm going to fix the van, to keep my job. God, you know I don't have the money to pay even the electric bill or the rent. I wouldn't be able to feed the twins without the church food kitchen. Oh, please, God.* Deborah didn't realize she had started to cry. She blew her nose softly, trying to staunch her tears with the back of her hand. The twins were playing quietly with crayons and an old dirty coloring book. They looked up at her curiously before going back to their drawing.

Down the pew, Mr. and Mrs. Whitmore glanced over with politely concealed distaste. They had seen this ragged woman and her two children in church sporadically over the last few months but didn't know quite how to deal with it. This church was a grand cornerstone of the community, filled with society couples such as themselves, and they were secretly embarrassed about what holiday visitors might think of this unkempt family in their midst. The woman must be very poor, and there never seemed to be a husband around. Probably a welfare mom, Mrs. Whitmore thought. She hoped the poor soul was getting help from the church's Mercy Ministry. Otherwise, why bother putting five dollars in the offering plate every week? She would go suggest to them that they approach this woman and get her some decent clothes.

After the service, Deborah ventured into the warmly decorated fellowship hall to get a few holiday cookies for the twins. She was painfully aware that she had begun to look increasingly out of place among the winter finery of the other congregants, but she knew how much little Gary and Gail would enjoy the cookies as a treat. The small sign almost stopped her: *Suggested Donation: $1*. Courtney Thicke, working behind the refreshments table, smiled at her. She worked at the church's food kitchen; she and Jim knew Deborah and adored the twins.

Courtney whispered behind her hand, "Don't worry, Deborah. Here, have a little bag for the kids." Courtney's eyes twinkled as she scooped a dozen cookies into a small gift bag and handed it across the table.

This small act of kindness almost undid Deborah's careful reserve. Courtney watched with compassion as tears welled up in the corners of the young mother's eyes. She stepped out from behind the table and held out a tissue, patting Deborah on the back as she steered her to the side of the room away from the embarrassment of prying eyes. "Things must be getting difficult?" she asked. She listened as Deborah explained about the van's breakdown, her fear of eviction, her fear for her job and her health.

"Oh, that is such a shame. We will definitely pray for you." Courtney thought for a minute. "Have you approached the church about any of this?" When Deborah shook her head, Courtney beamed. "Well, that's a good first step. I'm pretty sure they have a fund and other ways to help people in desperate straits." She watched hope spring into Deborah's eyes. "Let me bring you to the pastor in charge of our Mercy Ministries. He's the guy you need to speak with."

Courtney found the pastor and introduced him to Deborah, explaining how she knew her. She walked away as Deborah nervously began to explain her situation. Courtney smiled inside, feeling happy that she was able to accomplish something nice for someone today.

Ten minutes later, Courtney noticed Deborah walking through the foyer toward the parking lot with something in her hand. She called out to her. The young mother didn't turn around. Courtney quickly caught up with her, intending to ask how her conversation had gone. Deborah unemotionally held out a slim sheaf of papers clipped together. Courtney examined it. *Dairy Products–$10.00. Meat Department–$20.00. Toiletries–$8.00.* It took her a minute to comprehend what she was seeing. She flipped through the small stack. They were all the same. "But these are *coupons!* You mean they couldn't give you any actual money?" Deborah shook her head, not looking at her. "But what about your car? What about your rent—your doctor's bills?"

After a moment, Deborah responded quietly. "He said the deacon's fund was low because of the bad economy and could only meet life-threatening needs...like food. He said under the circumstances maybe I should change jobs closer to home so I wouldn't have to drive. Maybe I should move in with my mom so I wouldn't have to pay rent."

Courtney sighed, shaking her head. She knew perfectly well how stuck Deborah was; it was a miracle she hadn't lost the job she had, given the economic downturn. There were no easy answers here. She hugged Deborah with all her might, even though Deborah was too emotionally drained to respond. *Well,* Courtney thought, *there's at least one thing I can do.* She pulled out her wallet and handed over two twenty-dollar bills. "Deborah, please take this, at least. I wish I could give you more, but we're out of cash until Midwest Bank opens tomorrow—their ATMs aren't working right for some reason. But please take this. We'll help you as much as we can." Reluctantly, Deborah accepted the money and thanked her.

Courtney felt so defeated as she watched Deborah head toward the bus stop half a mile away. Forty dollars was just a drop in a very large bucket.

Champaign-Urbana, Illinois; January 2, 2000—3:00 P.M.

As a fresh storm raged outside, Becky, three of her employees, and the truck driver worked furiously to transfer the last perishables from the truck to her special energy-efficient refrigeration units. She couldn't hear the sound of the electrical generator over the snow, but she knew it was working perfectly. *Done!* she thought triumphantly as she helped close the truck door against the wind.

As the truck driver came in for one last look around, Becky impulsively reached up and gave the big burly man a swift hug. He was startled, but broke out in a broad grin. "Just glad I could help, ma'am," he said. "I'll do this run every morning if you want me to." Becky had made advance arrangements with several independent food wholesalers—and with this driver, just in case—and was she glad she had. Even after switching from the Food Pavilion conglomerate, her newer supplier had been slightly put out by the rollover and was telling customers that some items—including some perishables, breads, and imported foods—might not arrive properly for a while.

As she said good-bye to the trucker, she sighed in relief and said a quick prayer of thanksgiving. Her business would be okay. The shelves of the supermarkets nearby were already being picked clean, but she could keep her stores stocked with a decent supply of food and stay open for some semblance of normal business. Even if the power shortages continued for weeks, she now had generators in each of her stores that could run her special refrigeration units around the clock and power the rest of each store at least three hours a day. Even if power conked out entirely, she decided, she would keep her stores open daily from 2 to 5 P.M.

It was going to be all right.

New York City, The Bronx, January 2, 2000—9:00 P.M.

"Hand it over. Now!"

Teresa Luccio stood stock still, scared witless by the perfectly calm, menacing voice in the thick darkness surrounding her. A moment later, a few feet away, she heard a woman's muffled scream as another voice made the same demand. *They've been ready for this.* The inconsequential thought floated somewhere in her brain as she jerkily unwrapped her purse from her arm and passed it back to the waiting hands. She could feel the flat of the gang knife cold against her neck and quivered silently. *Oh, Jesus.*

It took her a moment to realize that they were gone. She leaned against her car, trembling violently now that the threat had passed, too shocked even to pray. Ten minutes ago, the power had dimmed, flickered, and suddenly gone out in the small shopping center where people were returning presents and catching up on all the news. A few emergency lights had come on, enabling shoppers to find their way out. Everyone had been fairly good-natured about it, but she had noticed a few nervous looks as they split up to search for their cars in the inky blackness of the underground parking garage. With good reason, it turned out. After checking to be sure the other woman was unhurt, she fumbled to unlock her car door.

Her head snapped up as a scream echoed across the garage. Several male voices shouted incomprehensibly, and the sounds of a struggle broke out on the level below her. Teresa quickly jumped into her car and turned on her headlights. Several others did the same thing, until the darkness was punctuated at all levels by pools of light. A few figures darted among the cars, running up and out of the garage structure.

Two hours later, safe in Victor's arms and behind locked doors, Teresa listened weakly to the local newscast. A very well organized gang had apparently been thoroughly prepared to take advantage of any power disruptions caused by the Millennium Bug. Within minutes of the blackout report they had responded by beeper (ironically), reporting to predetermined favorable places for "saturation"—their term for simultaneous mass muggings. Attacks by similar "Y2K bandits" were being reported in several other big cities as well. The Bronx blackout, which had been caused by a series of cascading circuit failures in some machinery, had been limited to a fairly small area and had lasted only twenty minutes. But it had been long enough for 131 muggings, including more than a dozen knifings and two fatal shootings.

At the last bit of information, Teresa closed her eyes. Victor held her tight, rocking her slightly, remembering the subject of the sermon this morning. *His faithfulness will be your shield and rampart. Oh, dear God. Oh, Lord. Thank you for your protection.*

Outside Chicago, Illinois, January 3, 2000—10:00 A.M.

"I'm sorry, ladies and gentlemen, but that's the situation at this time. We'll notify you the minute anything changes." The regional director swept out of the room as suddenly as he had come in, followed by two assistants. They had another roomful of people waiting for the bad news at their small securities affiliate down the road.

Like half the other people in the room, Don could only sit and listen, stunned, as his boss began to detail the temporary plan to put half the staff—including all the loan officers—on temporary leave. It had taken them all a while to realize that that innocuous phrase did little more than mask a mass layoff—as the "temporary" leave was of indefinite length, without pay. Don felt a surge of anger at the sympathy in his boss's voice. Wasn't this the man who had assured them all that Midwest Bankcorp would be "just fine" when Year 2000 rolled around? Yet here they all were: the trusting staff of a bank that was now so screwed up by Y2K that it had to shut its doors for an undetermined period of time, in order to—what were the words the regional director had used?—"get our books in order." The regulators had approved the plan on an emergency basis the day before, the director said, when it became clear that thousands upon thousands of accounts had serious errors in balances, loan payment history, interest, and investment calculations—pretty much everything a bank could track. It was decided that the bank would be at great risk of failure if it opened for business in such a condition.

A few other banks around the country were having this level of systems disruption, the director had said, but Midwest was by far the largest. Most of the others were small community-oriented institutions with few branches. Management believed the series of mergers three years before had precipitated some of the problems, since the melding of those different banks' computer systems had complicated the process of spotting all the potential Y2K problems. Unbeknownst to most of the regular bank staff, the regulators had been concerned about Midwest's readiness for some time and had forced them to cease certain operations—like some securities activities—even before the rollover.

Don's boss droned on, repeating and rehashing what the regional director had said. Bank management had reached the unavoidable conclusion that the computer system might take some time to fix completely, and that while the key elements were being "phased back in," the bank would have to revert to a slightly more manual mode of operations—through all seven states it served. Therefore, once the bank was sure it had all its most important customer and interbank accounts right, it would reopen for old-fashioned, branch-based business. This would be a mammoth task, especially since the ATMs, phone banking, and some internal automated systems were expected to be off-line for a while. Under some new Y2K regulations no one had thought would ever need to be applied, they even had been forced to suspend their securitization interfaces, such as credit cards and packaged mortgage loans, until it was clear that the bank's system could handle the settlement mechanism.

The whole staff seemed shocked and angry, Don observed. However, the administrative staff seemed relieved that they would continue on the payroll. Those placed on "temporary leave" were chiefly mid- and lower-level professionals; their high salaries throughout the year meant that they were better able to withstand a few weeks or a month without pay. It was the poorly paid secretaries who were the heroes now, who would be doing most of the administrative work to get the bank's books back in order and set up to function with less automation. The bank had received a government-brokered line of credit allowing it to pay its administrative staff through an external third party (since payroll systems were just as garbled as the rest). Because the staff—like the customers—couldn't access their accounts until the bank reopened, a competing bank had graciously offered to cash the paychecks of the remaining staff.

As Don listened to the discussion, something became clear: While the extent of system failures had been unwelcome to the bank's senior management, they hadn't been a complete surprise. It sounded like this contingency plan had been well prepared and well rehearsed. Of all the bad things that could happen to a person, Don most hated being duped, being made a fool of. As he sat steaming in that cold room, he felt very much the fool.

Austin, Texas, January 3, 2000—Noon

Jim Thicke stormed out of the restaurant. *Well, this is just great,* he thought. His ATM card still wasn't working, and the bank branch had been closed that morning. With only a few dollars in his wallet, he had intended to use his credit card for lunch. But the restaurant had posted a sign beside its cash register: *CASH ONLY THIS WEEK.*

Most other restaurants in the area seemed to have sprouted the same sign. The phone service was back up, finally, so these establishments must be playing it safe until the Y2K disruptions died down. Which was all very well and good, but for Pete's sake, here he was, a well-educated, well-paid yuppie who couldn't buy lunch. In irritation, he bought a pretzel on the street corner for a dollar. *This whole thing is just so...strange,* he thought. He decided to run by the office and see if anyone had heard when the bank might get their act together.

As he entered his workplace, the whole staff was staring at the television set mounted prominently on the wall outside the conference room. What he heard sent a chill of disbelief through him. On the TV screen a harried anchorwoman was jockeying reports from all over the country. Manufacturing plants were being forced to shut down for lack of supplies. Deaths were reported following 911 malfunctions. Trains were stopping service. Pharmaceutical companies were curtailing production, and food distributors and merchandisers had "lost" large amounts of their bar-coded inventory. Giant oil tankers and cargo ships were adrift at sea. Radio and television broadcasts were being disrupted following the outage of some satellite services. Of course, domestic power, water, and telephone service continued to be sporadically disrupted, and many of the nation's nuclear power plants remained off-line. Companies all over the country were resorting to temporary layoffs of staff in an effort to reduce expenses while revenue-generating activities were disrupted. Overseas, the increasingly severe lack of essential utilities was causing fear of social unrest in some countries, and there had been runs on several major banks in Hong Kong, Germany, Spain, and Brazil.

The television anchor was about to cut to a commercial when she suddenly stopped. "This just in. We are receiving reports...okay, here it is. U.S. regulators today agreed to the temporary closure of Midwest Bankcorp, the banking conglomerate formed by the merger of three smaller banking companies several years ago. Again, Midwest Bankcorp has temporarily closed its doors. No further information is available at this time, but we'll bring it to you just as soon as we get it. Again, if you are just joining us..."

The office broke up in a cacophany of raised voices and fearful questions. Everyone knew that their corporate account was with Midwest. They conducted international trading here—how were they going to get their letters of credit, their short-term floats, and their operating cash? Then another thought seemed to occur to everyone in the room simultaneously: how were they going to get their *paychecks?*

Jim stood dazed, watching as the senior partners of the trading firm headed for their telephones. *This is not happening,* he thought.

Down the road at Community Church, the staff lunchroom was in a similar uproar. Unanswered questions filled the air as the newscast droned on, unheard, in the background. The senior pastor quietly returned to his desk, put his head down on his arms, and prayed.

New York City, January 4, 2000—10:00 P.M.

Dr. Marvin Rogers checked on Mr. Temple one last time before he went off shift. The patient had had a rough few days of it, but he was a fighter, and Marvin was finally convinced that he would make it. The gentle beeps of the monitors were reassuring. Marvin silently prayed for protection over his sleeping patient, as he had over all the others in the ICU that night. Thank God the blackout and the other two drops in power hadn't really affected them, as their good generator capacity had been able to handle the outages.

He spotted the patient's family in the common area and went over to see how they were handling things. They all looked exhausted. Since several of Mr. Temple's children were older and had their own health problems to deal with, some of the grandchildren had assumed responsibility for the paperwork and logistics. On hearing of her grandfather's illness, granddaughter Cindy O'Neill had tossed some clothes into a suitcase, loaded her two small children into her car, and driven cross-country from Champaign-Urbana, Illinois. Clearly she was tired from the sudden trip—and exasperated by the paperwork. Hospital records *and* the insurance companies *and* Medicare *and* the prescription services all seemed to be in an uproar. Each was depending on the other for something, and no one could give her a straight answer. The rest of the family drifted away to get some coffee, but Cindy stayed behind, looking after a gurgling baby in an infant seat and a small daughter asleep on the chair beside her.

"Billing is going to be a nightmare, Doctor," she said bleakly. "They can't even pull his *previous* prescription out of those stupid machines, and we have no idea how we're going to pay for anything." She sat down and put her head in her hands. "My husband got put on leave two days ago, and we don't know how we're going to pay the mortgage. There's no way this family can cover a hospital bill if Medicare doesn't kick in. Granddad has Social Security and VA checks coming to him, which would at least help, but apparently the VA has posted some notice that they may not be able to send checks out for a few *months*." She made a strangled noise, something between exasperation and despair. "And that's on top of everything else. They say Erin may not be able to go back to kindergarten next week because of the power shortages, so there's no way for me to do any part-time work to bring in some cash. I just don't know what we're going to do."

Marvin noticed the small gold cross hanging from her neck, and squatted down by her chair. "Cindy, are you a Christian?" He spoke quietly but earnestly. She nodded. "This may sound trite," Marvin continued, "but you need to start praying for God's help, protection, and intervention. That is the only way any of us are going to get through this."

He gestured around the ICU, and for the first time Cindy noticed all the other small knots of worried-looking people standing around. "Half the other families in this hospital have the same problem as you. We are going to have to start depending on God for daily miracles. And I think he probably wants us to."

A machine started beeping urgently in the background, and he smiled and squeezed her shoulder in hasty farewell. As Cindy watched him stride down the hallway, she felt—for the first time since Paddy was laid off—a sense of peace. She had never really *had* to depend on God before. Suddenly, inexplicably, she was looking forward to it.

Austin, Texas, January 5, 2000—9:30 P.M.

"Are you kidding? That's the least we can do. We work the same shift anyway."

Deborah tried to stammer out her thanks, but Margie Young—a fellow waitress—flapped a hand. "Look, you're in a bad spot, and we're supposed to do unto others as we'd have them do unto us, right? You need a ride every day, and it's only fifteen minutes out of our way. This way we don't lose a coworker. We're just blessed that we found out about your predicament before you quit on us!"

Deborah grinned ear to ear and hugged Margie with all her might. Her friend just laughed and patted her on the back, exchanging pleased glances with her husband. Deborah knew that she still could lose the apartment, and she still didn't know how she was going to pay the medical or car repair bills, but at least she could keep her primary job. *Thank you, God!*

New York City, January 6, 2000—7:00 P.M.

Marvin Rogers stepped wearily out of the Good Shepherd church, saying good night to Victor and Teresa and some of the other volunteers, and sank gratefully into the comfort of his car. He sat there for a moment, almost too tired to turn on the ignition, his thoughts in turmoil. From his long hospital rounds he knew that energy came in waves, so he simply waited and pondered the events of the evening.

They had been working for the last five days to implement their contingency plan. It was more than clear that they had to. They all knew that their church housed a large number of people for whom the events of the week had proven disastrous. Probably a third of the congregation were hardworking and careful but still lived paycheck to paycheck. Many of them had been placed "on leave" and wouldn't even *get* a paycheck this month—perhaps even longer. Just two weeks of missed income could literally threaten many of them with eviction.

Several of the families depended on some form of supplemental government support—mostly AFDC or another form of welfare—which, according to news reports, may not come in this month either. Even among the majority of the congregation with stable jobs, a large number still had trouble making ends meet and had indicated in the task force's special phone survey that they were running out of food, money, and basic necessities such as diapers for their children.

Marvin thought back to his conversation with David and Nancy Eagles, who were on his telephone list. David, a magazine advertising salesman, had been having an increasingly hard time making ends meet as his commissions dwindled along with the economy. Now his magazine was being forced to stop production until its printing process was debugged, and most of the staff were being laid off. He had quietly told Marvin that he and Nancy were going to have to rely on the church pantry for diapers and baby formula, and would have to ask the church for monetary help to replace the expensive leg braces that their disabled son was outgrowing. They were going to have to discontinue their telephone service for a while and use the pay phone on the corner to make necessary calls. Marvin had been shocked, particularly when David added, "It's not so bad. At least five other apartments in our building don't have phones either."

Marvin had been silenced by the thought of how difficult so many people's lives were and how incredibly *blessed* he himself was. As soon as he had gotten off the phone, he had walked to the bank branch down the block, thinking of Nancy's impending delivery and their son's worsening cerebral palsy. An anonymous $300 money order was in the mail shortly thereafter.

And now he was sitting here in the parking lot of his church, wondering how on earth the church would ever meet the many, many deep needs they could see all around them. His eye fell on his Bible in the passenger seat, and he felt what he called the gentle tug of the Lord.

Acts 11.

Acts 11? That was where Peter defended his act of dining with "unclean" Gentiles, wasn't it? He turned on the dome light and began flipping through his NIV Bible. *Acts 11. Look further.* In his haste, he flipped to the end of the chapter. And there it was, in verses 27–30:

> During this time some prophets came down from Jerusalem to Antioch. One of them, named Agabus, stood up and through the Spirit predicted that a severe famine would spread over the entire Roman world. (This happened during the reign of Claudius.) The disciples, each according to his ability, decided to provide help for the brothers living in Judea. This they did, sending their gift to the elders by Barnabus and Saul.

Marvin sat staring at his Bible. *Those believers loved each other so deeply, they gave* before *the famine actually came. Well, okay, Lord, if that's how you have decided to get us through this.* He thought a moment, then slowly flipped back to Acts 4:32–35, a passage that had always made him quail.

> All the believers were one in heart and mind. No one claimed that any of his possessions was his own, but they shared everything they had. With great power the apostles continued to testify to the resurrection of the Lord Jesus, and much grace was upon them all. There were no needy persons among them. For from time to time those who owned lands or houses sold them, brought the money from the sales and put it at the apostles' feet, and it was distributed to anyone as he had need.

In all his life, Marvin thought, he had never had such an overwhelming sense of conviction. His life was not his own, his money was not his own. Although he was a doctor, he wasn't wealthy by any means. He had a simple one-bedroom apartment, a nice car, and probably $25,000 in various retirement accounts—but he also had $135,000 in student loans. His Manhattan rent and student loan payments totaled more than $3,000 a month, well more than half of his monthly disposable income. He didn't have a whole lot of cushion, but if God was calling him to sacrifice for his brothers and sisters—so be it.

The next second, doubts assailed him. *What about my student loans? What about my car payment...insurance bills...taxes...savings...security for my old age?* An image of a truly wealthy couple from church popped into his mind; they lived in a penthouse in Manhattan, overlooking Central Park. They were clearly multimillionaires. *That's the answer! There are plenty of people in a better position to meet these needs than me.* He turned the ignition key and drove out of the parking lot. A nagging disquiet rose in his mind, and he pushed it away. He turned on his car

CD player, fiddling with the volume. The disquiet rose again, and he pushed it away.

Finally, a gentle tug got through. *You said you would obey me, no matter what I asked.* Marvin distinctly remembered promising the Lord that he'd be a medical missionary in Latin America if that was what he wanted. Instead, God had brought him this prestigious hospital posting. Marvin remembered the faces of people he had treated on short-term medical missions trips to Guatemala—and their dirt huts, their disease-ridden water. Suddenly he heard David Eagles's voice: *"It's not so bad. At least five other apartments in our building don't have phones either..."*

Shame overwhelmed him, and he turned the car around, heading back to the church. Sure, he wasn't wealthy like that other couple, but he had riches to spare compared to David and Nancy. He had a checkbook in his pocket and at least $4,000 in savings in the bank. It wouldn't be enough, but it would be a start.

CHAPTER SIX

THE JOSEPH MODEL: A MINISTRY OPPORTUNITY

The word *wise* is used to describe just twelve significant people or groups in the Bible: Joseph, Moses, Bezalel, Joshua, David, Abigail, Solomon, Daniel, the Magi, Stephen, Paul, and Jesus. Most, including Joseph, are called wise because they exercised leadership according to God's precepts. As we look to Year 2000 and the potential crises that may arise, Joseph's story is a wonderful model of how Christians can wisely respond by leading, preparing, and serving our communities.

> Joseph told Pharaoh, "God was telling you what he is about to do. The seven fat cows...represent seven years of prosperity. The seven thin, ugly cows...represent seven years of famine.... The next seven years will be a period of great prosperity throughout the land of Egypt. But afterward there will be seven years of famine...so terrible that even the memory of the good years will be erased.... [Therefore] collect one-fifth of all the crops during the seven good years...[so] there will be enough to eat when the seven years of famine come. Otherwise disaster will surely strike the land, and all the people will die...."
>
> For the next seven years there were bumper crops everywhere. During those years, Joseph took a portion of all the crops grown in Egypt and stored them for the government in nearby cities. After seven years, the granaries were filled to overflowing. There was so much grain, like sand on the seashore, that the people could not keep track of the amount....
>
> At last the seven years of plenty came to an end. Then the seven years of famine began, just as Joseph had predicted. There were crop failures in all the surrounding countries, too, but in Egypt there was plenty of grain in the storehouses. Throughout the land of Egypt, the people began to starve....[so] Joseph opened up the storehouses and sold grain to the Egyptians. And people from surrounding lands also came to Egypt to buy grain from Joseph because the famine was severe throughout the world. (Genesis 41:25–27, 29–31, 34, 36, 47–49, 53–57)

When first considering this book's subject matter, many readers might ask themselves, "How is this a Christian issue? Why do we need a 'Christian response' to the Y2K problem?" Joseph's story provides the answer: *We are called to be ready to love and serve others in all circumstances.* Biblically, the people of God have a special responsibility to be "the head and not the tail" as God's ambassadors in the world.

Joseph, warned of the coming famine, prepared for it during years of extraordinary prosperity. He believed the warning, stored up what would be threatened, and organized others to prepare as well. When the terrible famine arrived, Joseph was not only able to save his community but also to bless the surrounding areas. He was able to save multitudes who were literally starving, eventually purchasing the land that they willingly traded to Pharaoh in exchange for food. Psalm 105 even notes that the Lord purposely sent Joseph into Egypt ahead of the famine, knowing he would wisely prepare, thus using this event in history to save the Israelite nation out of its stricken land, Canaan.

Once we recognize the potential hardship Y2K could cause in our personal and professional lives and overcome our initial rush of nervousness or fear, our natural desire is to get ourselves swiftly prepared for whatever outcome we think likely. That response is a good first step; biblically, we are supposed to cast out fear and be ready at all times for *whatever* God allows to come our way.

The challenge with Y2K is to go a step further and put into practice what we theoretically already believe—namely, "love your neighbor *as yourself*" (Mark 12:31). Although the outcome of the Year 2000 problem is far from certain, the potential does exist for Christians to be truly confronted by that verse for the first time. Many of us may have the opportunity to apply the Golden Rule to a degree that has never seemed necessary before.

Meeting this latter Y2K challenge may be unexpectedly difficult for us, testing our true commitment to the Lord and our willingness to sacrifice on behalf of others. We must focus our eyes on the author and perfecter of our faith to see the blessed opportunities he will be laying before us, to see this event in history not as a tribulation to be grimly endured but as an occasion to be a shining city on a hill that truly reflects his love and glory.

APPLYING THE JOSEPH MODEL

The hardship we may face in Year 2000 can be likened to the famine in Egypt. We have been warned of a potential problem on the horizon; the preceding chapters have outlined the need to take this problem seriously. During our current time of "prosperity" we should prepare for the possible "famine," both individually (for our own families) and corporately (for our church and our community), saving up necessities that may be threatened and fixing as many foreseeable Y2K problems as possible. For example, individuals and churches can store extra quantities of food and clean water, buy generators for emergency power, save up a few months' worth of operating funds, and head off or plan around the loss of some other modern conveniences. Churches and businesses can and should make every effort to be operationally ready for the rollover and be prepared with contingency plans for action. If and when disruptions arrive as a result of the

Millennium Bug—whether they entail problems with food, telephone service, finances, or medical technology—we should plan to generously serve and bless others in the name of Christ.

Larry Burkett's June 1998 newsletter of *Money Matters* notes that we should "ask God to use the impact of Y2K—whatever it turns out to be—as a catalyst to awaken millions of people and turn them to Jesus Christ. And pray that the Church will be ready to proclaim Christ to those who are ready to hear."[1] In a subsequent interview with me, Mr. Burkett added:

> What an opportunity! If the churches were prepared with food, water, and power, and this thing really happened, and they can say to the community, "Come on in, we'll help you," what a great opportunity God's people would have.... It would be very much like Joseph and his seven years of plenty and seven years of lean. After we prudently investigate to find out how serious this [Year 2000 problem] might be...we must then have a plan of action.

It is clear that we will be unable to help others unless we first prepare ourselves. Unfortunately, many within the Christian community are not yet focusing on the problem—and our time frame for preparation is rapidly dwindling. Remember that some significant disruptions *could* start occurring in 1999, and that the longer you wait, the harder it will be to fix your business vulnerabilities, ready your church, and store the basic necessities. In chapters 10 and 11 we will explore the practical specifics of preparation for families, churches, and businesses in greater detail.

If you began reading this book as a skeptic, by now you may be able to justify saving a little money or storing a few days' extra food. But you may still be unconvinced of the need for what seems like more thorough—more "drastic"—steps of preparation. As you read on, please consider that these actions, while they may be unfamiliar, may not be drastic at all. Millions of people around the world routinely "insure themselves" against events such as natural disasters with this type of preparation. And, as with Joseph, wise preparation will definitely put you in good stead as a loving witness to your community.

THE TORNADO ANALOGY

A natural disaster such as a tornado, blizzard, or earthquake may take only minutes to strike, but it leaves behind a trail of devastation that may still be seen and felt months or years later. In a split second, people may find their lives and livelihoods turned upside down; getting back to "normal" may take quite a while. Water, phone service, and power are lost; homes and businesses are damaged or destroyed; and residents suddenly face the daunting task of painstakingly piecing their records, finances, and property back together. In an age where millions live paycheck to paycheck, even a short interruption in income can have devastating consequences. Virtually all Y2K experts (even skeptics) agree that in a best-case scenario, Year 2000 *will* result in isolated disruptions similar to the effects of a natural disaster—only all at once, all around the world. The key difference is that we generally know when these disruptions will occur, if not exactly how and where, and we can better prepare for them.

Consider what typically happens after a tornado hits. The first people into the stricken area are usually from the local Salvation Army, the Red Cross, and the *churches*. Out of nothing more than love and compassion, Christians (and many others) will move in with food, water, blankets, and warm shoulders to cry on. Over the next few weeks, churches may eventually take over the day-to-day process of helping: They will invest themselves into the lives of the affected people, offering their expertise (distributing food, fixing houses, filling out insurance papers) and friendship during a time of incredible hardship. After giving so much time and energy, these caregivers earn the trust and gratitude of those they are helping.

Inevitably, someone asks, "Why are you doing this?" Christians can honestly answer that they are just pouring out the love that Christ has poured into them. For nonbelievers who may have previously equated Christians with undesirable politics, boring church services, or "intolerance," this brush with the true face of Christianity may permanently change their minds and hearts.

Similarly, consider the varying responses among those actually victimized by the tornado. At one address you have a family that is devastated and under extreme distress—picking through the wreckage of their lives and possessions, worried about looters, and venting their anger and helplessness onto relief workers. Next door you have another family; their house and all their possessions are completely destroyed, and they too are in tears over the loss of treasured memories. But they walk around to see whom they can help; they volunteer to participate in relief efforts; they give away their last blanket to someone in shock or go buy sandwiches for their neighbors and relief workers. These two next-door neighbors may never really have known each other before. Will the first family notice how differently—how "oddly"—the second family is behaving? You bet. When they ask why, they may hear for the first time that this house, these things, are just temporary—that their neighbors have an eternal home, an eternal security, that no disaster will ever be able to shake.

See the parallels to the Year 2000 threat? Ideally, we who have "built our houses" on the rock rather than on sand will not be shaken when the waves rise and the storms crash around us. However, the truth of our salvation will not do much to physically help or save others unless we are actually *prepared* to help. When a natural disaster hits, churches are often the human and physical infrastructure around which disaster relief is built. Unfortunately, in the case of Y2K, our churches are so unprepared that *they* are among the institutions at risk of being destroyed or thrown into panic by the approaching storm.

It is therefore critical that we as a Christian community respond and prepare wisely to meet the challenge of Y2K; not just for ourselves but for others. Jim Lord, the secular Y2K speaker and author, notes that "churches are incredibly important to community preparedness. They are *the* key, the one element able to mobilize people in large numbers. We need to use our existing community infrastructure to get ready for Y2K, and the churches are it."

WALKING THE TALK

In times of crisis, we know we can trust God in his mercy and power to miraculously care for his children. But we must also acknowledge that his Word continually exhorts us to an active faith that is lived out through concrete "works." For example, we are saved by his grace alone, through faith in Jesus Christ, but James 2 cautions us that faith without works is dead. Note the full statement:

> Dear brothers and sisters, what's the use of saying you have faith if you don't prove it by your actions? That kind of faith can't save anyone. Suppose you see a brother or sister who needs food or clothing, and you say, "Well, good-bye and God bless you; stay warm and eat well"—but then you don't give that person any food or clothing. What good does that do? So you see, it isn't enough just to have faith. Faith that doesn't show itself by good deeds is no faith at all—it is dead and useless. (James 2:14–17)

We must confront the inescapable fact that, in times of turmoil, a friendly demeanor, unflappable spirit, and heartfelt security will not please or glorify God if we are not in a position to minister to the real physical needs of others. We must therefore prepare to be a blessing to others—to be ready with what James refers to as extra "food and clothing." In other words, as witnesses of Christ's love, we must be ready and willing to take any action necessary to meet people's needs.

Preparing ourselves and serving our neighborhoods and communities can take several different forms. First, as noted, we can store those basic necessities that we and our neighbors could conceivably need—food, water, medicine, etc. Second, we can create awareness. Churches in a particular geographical area could band together to sponsor Y2K informational seminars for residents (see the afterword for how God has already arranged such events). Third, we can interface with other community and relief groups, such as the Red Cross, to prepare specific contingency plans in the event that serious disruptions occur. Fourth (and most important), we can pray for God's mercy and protection and that his glory will be shown through our lives, attitudes, and actions. Whatever happens in A.D. 2000 and its aftermath, his desire and our mission is that "all the world might know" that Jesus Christ is Lord.

While our discussion is currently in a Y2K context, it is important to recognize that—if we believe our own theology—we should be thus prepared *at all times.* God allows many serious events to impact our lives; Year 2000 is nothing more than one example. Paul exhorts us to "be prepared in season and out of season" (2 Timothy 4:2, NIV). Some religious groups take that exhortation much more seriously than evangelical Christians do. For example, while Mormon doctrine contradicts orthodox Christianity in many respects (for example, by stating that God is actually a perfected human being), Mormons read the same Bible we do in addition to their own *Book of Mormon.* They not only *see* the need to be ready for anything, they actually go one step further to actually *be* ready for anything. For example, the head of a Mormon household is required (under normal circumstances) to have enough on hand to feed his family for one year. It is a common observation in the Christian community that, when it comes to being prepared to care for one another in times of need, members of the Church of Jesus Christ of Latter-Day Saints (Mormons) seem to "walk the talk" better than most evangelical Christians do. Their actions sometimes speak louder than our words.

Since spiritual and physical preparation often go hand in hand, a lack of physical readiness on our part may actually reveal a dearth of spiritual readiness as well. In that case, under extreme stress we are likely to revert to more worldly responses despite our best intentions. Consider Christian financial counselor Larry Burkett's response when I posed this question:

> SCF: You've said that [with Y2K] we might see some wonderful opportunities to serve and be a witness. What happens if we don't prepare?
>
> LB: We'll be part of the problem. We'll be just as fearful and frightened and frustrated as everybody else. And probably we'll be the ones out there crying, begging, pleading and robbing, just like anybody else. That will be the problem.

In point of fact, we *are* more likely to be graceful and unflappable under stress—to be the individuals who are calm in the aftermath of the tornado—the more spiritually *and* physically prepared we are.

WHAT HAPPENS IF IT GETS BAD?

As the rollover approaches, particularly if serious disruptions do begin to emerge, it is likely that we will see an increase in "survivalist" attitudes. Realistically, we must confront the possibility that Y2K could cause anything from minor personal inconveniences to major global turmoil; again, *no one knows.* We will, however, know the answer soon enough.

So what *do* we do if events on the Y2K spectrum look as if they are leaning toward a more traumatic scenario? Some experts are focusing on the potential turmoil in urban centers, where small disruptions can cause disproportionately larger problems due to the potential for social unrest and the general lack of infrastructure flexibility. These experts, including some voices in the Christian community, are encouraging people to move out of heavily populated cities and relocate to areas where they can grow their own food, dig a well, and protect themselves and their families during a time of turmoil. One pastor, when asked what would then happen to the poor in the inner cities, responded resignedly that since we lack resources and time, "We might have to write off the inner cities." His counsel was that, since Christians are unfortunately just as financially and practically unprepared as everyone else, we should primarily try to help and protect our families and our church and realize that we cannot help many others.

Unfortunately, it is true that larger cities may be inherently riskier during times of technological disruption (imagine New York City during a blackout, for example), and that many people may in fact decide to remove themselves from that risk as the year 2000 approaches. An honest look at the evidence shows that this fear of economic and societal unrest is not entirely unfounded—but neither is it forecast as a certainty. Wanting to protect and care for our families is obviously a natural and good reaction. We must, however, take care that we don't stop "loving our neighbors" just when they may need us most. As with all things, Christians should carefully and prayerfully consider whether we are called to protect ourselves or to help those less fortunate. Perhaps the classic question, "What would Jesus do?" serves as a reminder of all the reasons we should consider placing sacrifice ahead of self-preservation.

Many Cannot Move or Prepare

On a purely practical level, it is clear that everyone does not have the ability to protect themselves by moving to a more remote location in times of societal crisis. As evangelist Pat Robertson told me, "That's the conundrum we've all faced with these survivalist alarms over the years. What do you tell the people in New York City to do? The [survivalists] say, 'Go out to northwest Arkansas and get a farm and milk a cow, and live off a garden.' That's a nice concept but you can't do that to twenty million people in a city."

In addition, many people live on such a financial razor's edge that they simply do not have the ability to "store up," as Joseph did, to prepare for the potential disruption. Larry Burkett notes that "in reality, for the majority of people, it's too late. They don't have enough time to save. They're spending all they make." These facts are among the primary reasons why churches should take the lead in preparing their communities. Paloma O'Riley, founder of the Cassandra Project, a nonprofit organization dedicated to preparing individuals and communities for Year 2000, notes that "individual preparedness is for people who *can*. Community preparedness is for people who *can't*."[2] If it does come to pass that Y2K causes unpleasant disruptions and social turmoil, millions of believers and nonbelievers alike will not have the option of escape or of dipping into a surplus.

We Are an Army

I asked Larry Burkett and his colleague Dean Webb, a Christian Financial Concepts vice president, what our response should be if Y2K were to "get bad." Should Christians try to leave their communities if they are able to? And if we are unprepared, should we try to help ourselves and a few neighbors but resign ourselves to the fact that we can't have a much broader impact?

LB: That's foolish. Why does God raise up an army if, in fact, the army quits when the battle starts? That doesn't make any sense to me. God put us here to lead people to the Lord. If this is the opportunity that God has provided, take maximum use of that opportunity. If it means that you can only eat a fourth of a meal per day rather than a full meal per day, and you can feed three other people, eat a fourth of a meal and feed three unsaved people. Why does God put us here in the first place? Like Paul said, "If this life is all that we ever see, we are to be most pitied among all men." Do we believe that or don't we believe that? If we believe that, then our job is to take these people who are going to hell and lead them into salvation. If this really is a crisis, is it worth going through that crisis to do that? Absolutely; no doubt about it.

SCF: Tell me if you agree…that sacrificial generosity, sacrificial love, has always led people to the Lord.

LB: Oh yes, that's why the martyrs of the past gave their lives. You see, that other attitude [of self-preservation] would have never caused anybody to give their life because of Christ.

DW: If, in good times, you can barely tell the difference between a Christian from a non-Christian by looking at their checkbooks, what's it going to be like in bad times? At some point, you have to make a difference.

SCF: What would you say to the other two arguments that are commonly raised? The first argument is that, because Christians are just as heavily leveraged with credit card debt and just as heavily nonprepared, with a lack of savings—despite your best efforts, Larry!—that we therefore cannot expect to make a wide-scale impact. The second argument is that many poor people in the inner city are "just looking for a handout anyway," so some people argue that if you give them the handout, it serves no beneficial purpose. How would you respond to that?

LB: Well, if you're talking about the government handout and welfare, it would be less beneficial. Now, government welfare in and of itself was not a bad idea; the problem was it was totally impersonal. It had no motive behind it except to help somebody who could help themselves. That's not what we're talking about. We're talking about helping people who *cannot* help themselves. That's the number-one key. Number two, we're talking about one on one. Let's say I have the only food here and I have the right to keep it for myself. But I invite you two here and share it; it's pretty hard to deny that I care about you people. That's the difference. You can't equate welfare with this. I can understand some of the concern about the violence that would occur, because what we've done is raise a generation who believe "if I don't have it, I have the right to take it away from somebody else." Is that going to stop me from ministering as a result of that? I don't think so. What I would like to do is go and be able to share with them, and say, "You don't have to take mine away from me—I'm willing to share with you because there is a difference in my life. And, once I share with you, I have the opportunity to tell you *why* there's a difference in my life."

From a human perspective, I can understand people's concerns. If you have your wife and children in your car and a mob is coming at you, and you have a weapon in your car, would you use that weapon to protect your family? Anybody in their right mind probably would. Would I consciously go out carrying a bag of food and a machine gun with me and then shoot down people who wanted some of my food? I would not. It's a totally different attitude. What would I do? Well, I'd [open] my bag of food and say, "I'll give you as much as I can. I'll share it *all* with you if necessary." That's the difference in Christianity; it is the difference between what we *say* we are and what we really are. Do we just *say* we trust God or do we really trust God?

Why did God put us here? Who would have believed that the martyrs of the first century, based on what was happening to them, could have had such a dramatic impact on their society? But look at what happened as a result of their unselfish attitudes: They changed the world in which we live, forever. We're here today because they didn't raise an army to defeat the Romans. That was not their perspective. You only have to read history of that era to figure out what Christianity is all about. One of the stories that always comes back to my mind was of the Roman legions. Often they would force Christians to march into very cold country in the middle of the winter, stark naked, and then they would leave them there to freeze. The Romans had some unique ways to execute people and that was one of them. I read a story about a Roman legion that was taking up a very large group of Christians, men, women and children.... They were marching in the cold, knowing they were going to freeze to death, and it took them several days to reach wherever they were going. By that time, those people had such an impact on the Roman legion that hundreds of Roman soldiers themselves stripped naked and sat with the Christians to freeze to death. That was the impact Christianity was having on that society. Did they foolishly give their lives? I don't think so. Somebody in that era might have thought so, but today, I don't think so. What's Christianity worth? I guess we need to decide. It doesn't mean we're supposed to be stupid people, but we need to decide what we stand for and whether staying alive is our most important function. If it is, protect yourself and buy a machine gun or a cannon or whatever you can buy. But if it isn't, if that's not the most important thing in our lives, then let's decide: Why did God put us here? And if there *is* a crisis in the year 2000, did God not know it was going to happen? Did he make a mistake? I don't think so. Then why did he put me here? I'm here for the purpose of leading others to the Lord. If that's not true, we're in the wrong business.

The true story of the Roman legion related by Larry Burkett is inspiring and sobering when we consider it in light of the potential impacts of the year 2000. It is just possible that this impending event may require a faith commitment far beyond what most of us have thus far been called upon to make. But that level of devotion would, after all, be no greater than what millions of Christians throughout history have been willing to uphold. Are we prepared for what might be required of us? Are we willing to truly sacrifice ourselves out of love for others? If people do go hungry, are we willing, as Larry Burkett challenged, to eat a fourth of what we regularly eat in order to feed three hungry people?

I recently asked Dr. James Dobson, president of Focus on the Family, how he felt Christians should respond to the potential Y2K crisis. Dr. Dobson wrote me:

> I would urge Christians not to panic or despair, regardless of the circumstances. God often uses hard times to accomplish His purposes. If chaotic times come, our responsibility will be to remain faithful to Him and to spread the gospel of Jesus Christ in the circumstances with which we are presented.

BRAVING THE PLAGUE

Most of us alive today have never had to face a situation grave enough to require much personal sacrifice. We don't know for sure if Year 2000 may spark such a situation, but we do know that—contrary to our natural instinct—we really shouldn't *care* if it does. 1 Peter 2:11 (NIV) says we are "aliens and strangers in the world." Since this world is not our true home, we should be willing to lose all earthly things in order to reflect the light of the world to come. As martyred missionary Jim Elliot once said, "Wise is the man who gives what he cannot keep, to buy what he can never lose."

We can learn an important lesson from believers throughout history who *have* been faced with this choice.

In 1660s England, after the Cromwell Faction was ousted and Charles II was recrowned king, the monarchy and the Anglican establishment set about systematically persecuting the Puritans who dared claim that Christ—not the king—was the head of the church. True believers were ejected from the pulpit, from positions of power, from universities—or were summarily shot if they refused to vow that Charles II was the head of the church. The Puritans were forced underground into a house-church movement and were barred from official office and society.

That lasted until 1665, when the bubonic plague rolled through London and devastated all in its path. As the people literally died in the streets, the aristocracy fled the city. Those who could—the educated and the powerful, including all the doctors—escaped, leaving the uneducated and poor to the ravages of the plague.

The Puritans stayed. Many had previously held positions of power, were highly educated, and could have easily protected themselves from the turmoil in the city. Instead, they not only *stayed* in the city to minister to the sick and dying, but they actually *came into* the city from the surrounding countryside. To meet the desperate human need and ease the suffering of their neighbors, they willingly surrounded themselves with death and disease. Many paid the ultimate price in the process. These believers poured themselves out on behalf of a society that had severely ridiculed and repressed them, sacrificing themselves on the altar of love for Jesus Christ and for their fellow man.

After the plague had run its course, killing 20 percent of the population, public attitude toward the Puritans changed dramatically. The people of England had experienced the fruit of their godliness firsthand, and many made the personal choice to follow Jesus Christ as their King. The Puritans received so much popular support that the aristocracy and the Anglican priesthood eventually stopped persecuting them; they were allowed to publicly flourish again. A number of spin-off denominations were finally allowed to be established, such as Presbyterians, Quakers, and Congregationalists. This rebirth laid the foundation for the first Great Awakening just a few decades later, out of which arose the British abolition of slavery, free medical care for the poor, prison reform, and the founding of orphanages for thousands of homeless children.

What looked like a disaster was actually a divine challenge and an opportunity for the people of God. The fruit of their love and sacrifice are clear. Are we willing to meet such a challenge today?

"THE NOBILITY OF SACRIFICE"

Many Christian leaders (in fact, most of the individuals interviewed for this book) believe that the church in America has become anemic. We hardly resemble the fiery church that blazed forth the glory of God in the first and second centuries, transforming everything it touched. What makes the difference?

Rodney Stark, a sociologist at Princeton University, studied the reasons behind the explosion of Christianity in the first and second centuries. He was puzzled at how a marginalized, persecuted, often uneducated group of people were able to not only survive but thrive, changing the face of the world forever. In his book *The Rise of Christianity,* he concludes that a key reason was their willingness to sacrifice themselves out of love for each other and for their world.[3] This sacrifice released an explosion of light and heat that the world had never known, transforming those around them forever.

The sacrifice of which he speaks is embodied in circumstances very similar to those confronting the Puritans of the seventeenth century. Two great plagues swept the Roman Empire, starting in the years A.D. 165 and 251 and killing *one-third* of the population each time. Rodney Stark's article in *Christian History* notes:

> The willingness of Christians to care for others was put on dramatic public display.... Pagans tried to avoid all contact with the afflicted, often casting the still living into the gutters. Christians, on the other hand, nursed the sick, even

> though [they] died doing so.... Christians also were visible and valuable during the frequent natural and social disasters afflicting the Greco-Roman world: earthquakes, famines, floods, riots, civil wars, and invasions. Even in healthier times, the pagan emperor Julian noted that followers of the Way "support not only their poor, but ours as well."[4]

In his book, Stark relays the words of Dionysius at the height of the second great epidemic, when 5,000 people per day were perishing in Rome alone.

> Most of our brother Christians showed unbounded love and loyalty, never sparing themselves and thinking only of one another. Heedless of danger, they took charge of the sick...ministering to them in Christ, and with them departed this life serenely happy; [or] in nursing and curing others...died in their stead.[5]

Stark notes that this visible sacrifice absolutely overwhelmed the reigning classical philosophy that regarded mercy as a "pathological emotion...[since] mercy involves providing *unearned* help or relief." Instead, Christians demonstrated the power of human mercy as required and modeled by a merciful God; they lived the doctrine that "Christian love and charity must...extend to 'all those who in every place call on the name of our Lord Jesus Christ' (1 Corinthians 1:2). Indeed, love and charity must even extend beyond the Christian community,"[6] given Jesus' revolutionary command to love even one's enemies.

Given the condition of our modern society, it is interesting to note Stark's judgment that societal paganism was strongly entrenched in Roman culture until the epidemics started, but rapidly fell away thereafter. He believes paganism "acquired its fatal illness during these epidemics, falling victim to its relative inability to confront these crises socially or spiritually—an inability suddenly revealed by the example of its upstart challenger."[7]

TRUE COMMITMENT

Jesus Christ says, "If any of you wants to be my follower, you must put aside your selfish ambition, shoulder your cross, and follow me. If you try to keep your life for yourself, you will lose it. But if you give up your life for me, you will find true life. And how do you benefit if you gain the whole world but lose your own soul in the process?" (Matthew 16:24–26). Jesus is clearly not calling us simply to a faith of loving feelings and heartfelt prayer, but to a vigorous, active, total commitment to *him,* and to anything he asks us to do. Even if we recognize, and theoretically agree, with that total dedication, we somehow are too often reluctant to actually make the adjustments and sacrifices required of us.

In the personal workbook study *Experiencing God,* Dr. Henry Blackaby emphasizes that such holding back is not an option for the Christian:

> [God] has a right to interrupt your life. He is Lord. When you accepted Him as

> Lord, you gave Him the right to help Himself to your life anytime He wants.... Many of us want God to speak to us and give us an assignment. However, we are not interested in making any major adjustments in our lives. Biblically, that is impossible. Every time God spoke to people in the Scripture about something He wanted to do through them, major adjustments were necessary. They had to adjust their lives to God. Once the adjustments were made [in obedience], God accomplished His purposes through those He called.... What you DO reveals what you believe about God, regardless of what you say.[8]

We may very earnestly want to be of use to God. We may weep during Sunday worship and *feel* desperately in love with the Lord, totally committed to a life centered in Christ. In order to *be* truly committed, however, we must overcome our tendency toward complacency and ease. We must take action and join God where he is working in the world. If the Lord sets an assignment of any magnitude before us, will we accept and act on it willingly?

Elizabeth Dole refers to this challenge in her essay titled "Crisis and Faith" in the book *Finding God at Harvard.* She recounts the Old Testament story of Esther, the Jewish girl who became queen of all Persia just when the Jews needed a mediator with the king to save them from extermination. At first reluctant to take action when her guardian Mordecai beseeched her to, Esther eventually risked her station, and her life, by making a full commitment—and God used this commitment to save the entire Jewish people. Elizabeth Dole comments:

> I can sympathize with Esther's dilemma. She had all the comforts, a cushy life, and when you get all those things around you, it can build up a resistance to anything which might threaten the comfort and security they seem to provide. I know all too well how she felt. Maybe you do, too.... I had built up my own little self-sufficient world...until it dawned on me that I share the predicament; that [Esther's] call to commitment is like the call [to take up His cross] which Jesus Christ presents to me.... Those are hard words to swallow when you are busy doing your own thing, but it is the most compelling logic I have ever heard. For if Christ is who He says He is—our Savior, the central figure in all of history who gives meaning to a world of conflicting priorities—then I had to realize Christ could not be compartmentalized....
>
> [Because] Jesus Christ was my Lord and my Savior...I knew it was time to cease living life backwards, time to strive to put Christ first, preeminent, with no competition, at the very center of my life. It was time to submit my resignation as master of my own little universe. And God accepted my resignation.... God began to teach me that it is not what *I* do that matters but what a sovereign Lord chooses to do through me.... In submission to Him, life is not just a few years to spend on self-indulgence and career advancement. It is a higher calling—God's calling. This alone gives true meaning to life. Mordecai's warning to [a reluctant] Esther is sobering. God forbid that someday I look back and realize I was too distracted by things of this world, too busy, too driven, and therefore my work was given to another....

> "Esther, who knows but that God in His providence has brought you to a royal position for such a time as this?" What Mordecai's words say to me is that each one of us has a unique assignment in this world, given to us by a sovereign God, to love and to serve those within our own sphere of influence. We have been blessed to be a blessing; we have received that we might give. The challenges Esther needed to hear were the challenges I needed to hear, and continually need to hear: the call to total commitment. [In the end, Esther] cast herself—indeed her very life—upon God in dependence on Him. "If I perish, I perish."[9]

We Christians must honestly confront one of the reasons why we do not want to believe the potential ramifications of Year 2000: *If true, we will be required to take action.* And given the potential scope of Y2K problems, that action seems overwhelming for us. It is much easier to relax back into half commitment, reasoning that if millions of people truly risk suffering around the world, then someone will surely do *something*—most likely the government, since dealing with broad-scale disaster is usually the government's job.

Obviously, our government has an important role to play, but unfortunately our federal, state, and local governments are likely to be somewhat unprepared themselves. For example, the U.S. government agency that is *supposed* to respond to the disasters that disrupt our society received a grade of F on the government's own Y2K Readiness Report Card in the spring of 1998, and at the present rate of preparation will not be fully Year 2000 compliant until many years after the rollover.

More importantly, *why shouldn't* the church be the first line of defense in arenas where the people of God can truly make a difference? There are obviously many important societal functions—such as national defense, public safety, and public utilities—where the church has less of a role than government (although individual Christians can have a large impact). But there are many other functions that could more easily and effectively be accomplished through the church—if only Christians would totally commit to joining God where he is working through this event in history.

OUR OPPORTUNITY TO "BUY THEIR LAND"

While this full commitment to "honor God by serving others" may come at a price, what we gain is far more precious than what we give up. It seems likely that we might find within the Millennium Bug a pearl of great price—a shining opportunity that is worth all our sacrifice.

The biblical story of Joseph tells us more than just to bless those around us; it tells us what happens when we do. Year by year, as the famine worsened and the surrounding peoples became increasingly desperate, they had less and less to trade in return for the food Joseph had stored. First their money ran out, then their livestock. Eventually, all they had left to trade were themselves and their land. "Buy us and our land in exchange for food; we will then become servants to Pharaoh," they said. "So Joseph bought all the land of Egypt for Pharaoh.... Thus, all the people of Egypt became servants to Pharaoh" (Genesis 47:19–21).

While at first we may be offended by this story and consider it the worst case of loan-sharking ever seen, we must look deeper. Instead, this account conveys a fundamental truth about what happens when desperate people are provided for: in exchange for having their needs met, they freely and willingly give themselves to the provider. In fact, God created us this way so that we would run to him when he meets our deepest needs in the way he longs to (Deuteronomy 30:1–10; Isaiah 43:1–13).

In ancient times, a family's land was like their name; it represented their heritage and their very lives. Selling their land meant that they were no longer their own; the purchaser had, in a way, bought their lives. During the time of turmoil that may potentially be on the horizon, people's gratitude and loyalty will be acquired by whoever helps them—whether that be the federal government, a religious cult, or Christians on behalf of almighty God. God can use such a time to stake a claim on the love of those whom we love in his name.

Consider the start of Victor Hugo's poignant novel *Les Miserables*. The hero, Jean Valjean, is embittered and self-serving after spending nineteen years in prison on a trumped-up charge. Experiencing freedom for the first time in almost two decades, he is aware with every scornful glance of the seeming impossibility of returning to an honest living. After he finds kindness and temporary shelter with a humble priest in a monastery, he steals some of the the priest's precious silver and flees into the night.

Local police catch and detain Valjean. He feebly protests that the priest gave him the silver as a gift, but as he is manhandled back to the monastery he knows he will be sent back to prison. Instead, to everyone's astonishment, the kindly priest corroborates Valjean's story...and begins to give him the remaining silver, telling the ex-convict in front of the police that "he left the best behind." In the Broadway musical, the police then leave Jean Valjean, shattered and humbled, alone with the priest. The priest sings with a previously hidden power and authority:

> And remember this my brother, see in this some Higher Plan. You must use this precious silver to become an honest man. By the witness of the martyrs, by the Passion and the Blood, God has raised you out of darkness. *I have bought your soul for God.*[10]

As the body of Christ we must reach out, lavishing his bountiful, plentiful, tangible love upon a hurting and needy world. When we do, we can indeed make a difference. Mark and Betsy Neuenschwander, directors of the A.D. 2000 Crisis

Relief Task Force (which trains Christians to witness in the midst of natural disasters worldwide), put it this way in their essay, "Watch the Window Open Wider":

> In the turbulence of a disaster, our Christian mandate is to give water *plus* Living Water; to give rice *plus* the Bread of Life; to provide shelter *plus* the Refuge of Psalm 91; to bring health *plus* the Great Physician; to help give physical life *plus* Eternal Life. Are we not agreed—the greatest of all disasters for anyone is an eternity spent in hell.[11]

Dale Mosley, founder of Greater Love Disaster Ministries, told me about the aftermath of a recent, terrible flood in Oregon. His volunteers were on the front lines of disaster relief, spending hours side by side with devastated families as they bailed water and salvaged what they could of their homes. He encouraged his volunteers to share *why* they were eager to help, and the reaction, he says, was remarkable. "It was like a connection straight to heaven. In nearly every case, the volunteer would barely mention the name of Jesus and the listener would begin to weep. That was how soft and open these hearts were during that difficult time."

OUR ULTIMATE MODEL

Our ultimate model, of course, is not Joseph, the early Christians, the Puritans, or modern Christians. Our ultimate model is our Lord Jesus Christ, "who, being in very nature God, did not consider equality with God something to be grasped, but made himself nothing, taking the very nature of a servant…[and] humbled himself and became obedient to death—even death on a cross!" (Philippians 2:6–8, NIV). We have the ultimate model for how to respond to any crisis, any turmoil, any opportunity the Lord puts in our path. Jesus so loved the world that he poured himself out on behalf of the world that hated him. He wants us to do the same.

It is clear that truly loving a hurting world in God's name might require both a level and *volume* of commitment that most of us have never summoned before. As we take careful stock of the potential size of the need and of the current level of Christian commitment in our nation, we might become discouraged. *How on earth,* we wonder, *can we accomplish all we might be called to?*

Henry Blackaby offers encouragement to all with that concern. He shared these thoughts with me:

> We don't see any anemic church bodies as problems as much as opportunities. Just like a doctor does not see a patient as a real problem, but as an opportunity to bring help. And Jesus said…the well don't need a physician, so he came for the sick. So he was criticized for always going with the sick folks and we've been criticized for going with the sick folks, too. But that doesn't discourage me. You see, if the doctor gets discouraged that all he ever sees are sick people, he can get the impression that there are no well people out there.…

> See, that's the reason God put you there. He didn't put you there for all the well people. I mean, anyone can coach the all-star team; it's the sandbox kids who really need you. You've got to go coach sandbox kids because it's easy to coach the superstars. But a lot of the spiritual leaders want to coach only the best, the finest and most spiritual people in their organization.... I say, "Anybody can do that. So why don't you just pick out some that are so discouraged they can hardly hold their head up, and say, 'Now, you're the kind of person I want to work with.'" Because you *know* that whatever happens, it is *God who is going to have to do it.*

We must not worry about how on earth we can ever meet such a large goal through our seemingly complacent and "settled" church bodies. Instead, let's do what we can to prepare, then watch with eager expectation to see how *God* (not us) is going to accomplish his ultimate purpose. Dr. Blackaby describes a swelling tide of Christian unity that many may not be aware of, but that could very well lay the foundation for God's work through his people:

> You can see that some people have a level of uninvolvement, but the other side of it is this: never have the people of God been marshaled so thoroughly and so completely, with one heart and one mind as they are right now. Mission America, or A.D. 2000, is the largest coordinated effort ever in Christian history to coordinate all denominations, all parachurches, all ministries—and it's hitting its top running speed as we turn into 1999. It's voluntary coordination, but there has never been this level of coordination. And it is on the local level.
>
> There is a huge coordination of all the youth groups in America, all the college groups, men's work, women's work, prayer movements, evangelism movements. And these are the top leaders who have agreed to work together, and that's never happened.... When I go to the inner city, churches are already talking and working together. The seminaries are working cross-denominationally and otherwise. I did a conference call recently with over 500 pastors and they were as excited as they can be about the day in which we live.

It seems clear that Year 2000 could be setting the stage for a mighty work of the Lord in our world, through those of his children who are willing to commit themselves totally to his will.

CHAPTER SEVEN

January–March, 2000

New York City, Monday, January 10, 2000—9:30 P.M.

Dr. Marvin Rogers had barely finished knocking on the anonymous door of apartment 18N when it swung open—and he came face to face with the woman who had stolen old Mrs. Beechman's taxicab. After recovering from his surprise, he smiled and introduced himself. The woman briefly shook his hand, saying only, "Julia. Can I help you?"

Marvin eased into his well-rehearsed spiel. A coalition of churches and synagogues in the five boroughs of New York City was seeking support for the community efforts to help those most impacted by the Year 2000 crisis. As an example, he said, his church was running a central effort in its area of the Bronx to provide meals and warm housing for those who had lost their jobs to the Millennium Bug.

Julia roughly interrupted him. "But most people haven't *lost* their jobs. That's such an exaggeration. Most people are just on temporary leave." She sounded impatient.

Marvin responded levelly, "It's true that the majority are 'on leave.' But for many of these people, even one missed paycheck is disastrous." The woman rolled her eyes, and Marvin tried to stay calm. "What we're doing is visiting everyone in the more affluent areas of Manhattan—where building management agrees, of course—to formally ask for a donation to this very large cause. Even a small donation, even five dollars, would help. Most of us—" his gesture indicated the grand building—"can afford to give five, ten, or twenty dollars without thinking about it, but it makes an enormous difference on the other end. Some people have given a thousand dollars, just like that. It affects all of us, after all. The affluent areas aren't so far away from the poorer areas, and I'm sure you can recognize that they are near a boiling point."

Everyone had heard about the incident a few days before. Water service had been inexplicably cut off from a section of the Upper East Side—primarily affecting a few blocks of ramshackle tenements that housed, among others, several hundred families whose public assistance had already been disrupted. A luxury doorman building just a half mile away had been overrun by a band of tenement teenagers who had been out to "get help and get even." No one had been seriously hurt, but the teens had smashed into nearly a dozen apartments, terrorizing residents and stealing valuables and food before the police had shown up.

Julia reacted to this reference with annoyance. "Look, I don't like scare tactics, and I don't give to random groups I know nothing about. For all I know you could take my money and buy drugs with it."

Silently, Marvin handed her a copy of a letter signed by the mayor, the governor, and several religious and charitable leaders. The letter endorsed the efforts of the "Five Boroughs Faith Community" to raise funds for the many who were hurting in their city. Julia read through it completely, and Marvin held his breath as she seemed to waver. He could see into the beautifully appointed apartment behind her. She was wearing a tailored designer suit. He guessed she could easily support a few families for a week and never even miss the money. But then the implacable expression returned to her face with finality and she handed the letter back. "Sorry—it's not my fault all these people weren't prepared." She stared at him coldly, eyebrows raised, as if expecting a protest.

After a pause, Marvin simply said, "Thank you for your consideration." He started to turn to leave, then stopped. "One day you will come to realize how blessed you have been with a good job and lots of resources that you could have used to help people. But by then, I'm afraid it'll be too late for you to do anything about it. Good evening, ma'am." He didn't look back as he walked away down the corridor. A few seconds later, he heard the soft click of her door latching. He felt a deep sorrow, and somehow he knew that it was the Creator's terrible pain over a lost and unrepentant soul.

Austin, Texas, Wednesday, January 12, 2000

"So either you vacate voluntarily by Monday, or I'll have Antonio come and move your things out onto the street—and you know what'll happen to them there." The belligerent face stared up at her, turning Deborah Carey's insides to cold knots. *This is it, then,* she thought. *No more extensions. I have just five days.*

She couldn't even speak, couldn't argue. The loss of her night job had been the final nail in the coffin. She had no way to pay the three months' back rent. The stooped little woman who owned the building nodded sharply, turned, and shuffled away toward her own apartment.

The twins were still running around the bare studio as Deborah stepped back inside. She willed herself to be strong. *Okay, it's not the end of the world. We won't be homeless. We'll just have to move in with Mom.* Her mother had been completely inebriated when Deborah had broached the subject. Mom had agreed they could move in on the condition that "you give me my privacy when *they* come over. Understand?" Her mom lived in a one-bedroom apartment and was often visited by a string of no-good male friends seeking drugs and who knew what else. Deborah sank into the last remaining chair—she had sold all the rest—and put her face in her hands. She had no idea what would happen when her mom "wanted her privacy" at three in the morning...which would happen, Deborah was sure. The twins dashed over with some toys she had gotten them for Christmas at the church's secondhand store. Their little faces looked so happy, so trusting. What would happen to them in their new home? Would they be safe?

She leaned down and scooped them into her arms, fiercely hugging them, suddenly fearful. The social services people had been talking about taking them away and finding a foster home if she couldn't provide for them. Surely, once they found out about her mom... *Don't even think it,* she scolded herself.

Her eye fell on a news article given her by a sympathetic nurse at the clinic she visited for her diabetes treatments and insulin supply—an article that had terrified her. A company supplying large quantities of insulin to the world had not gotten its production back on line. As a result, this vital drug was becoming critically scarce and its cost was soaring. Losing her home was bad enough; Deborah was terrified at the potential ravages of untreated diabetes. Her mind careened through the frightening possibilities until she forced herself to shut down her imagination. That was one thing she truly couldn't control. Her thoughts turned again, inexorably, toward the desire to keep her kids safe in her own home.

I have until Monday, she thought. *Maybe there is one last chance...*

Austin, Texas, Sunday, January 16, 2000

Courtney Thicke couldn't do anything but stand there, embarrassed and tearful, as Deborah turned and walked away, clearly trying to hide her overwhelming disappointment. Deborah Carey had been physically trembling when she approached Courtney and Jim after the service, obviously summoning all her nerve to finally ask them for the help Courtney had offered to give. And now they had been forced to turn her down.

The last two weeks had been the most frightening of their lives. Both of them came from fairly affluent professional families, were well educated and highly employable, and took financial stability for granted. While neither was close to their surviving family—Courtney's parents had both died of cancer, and Jim's family was not particularly friendly—they had never thought too much about whether they could depend on Jim's folks in a crisis. Now that the crisis had hit, they had learned that they couldn't. Jim's mother and father were financially stable, but for years they had stated firmly that their children had to stand on their "own two feet." They had paid every bill on the dot until Jim graduated from college, at which point they had warned him that he was now on his own. It had never really impacted Jim much, as he had always been well paid and able to buy most of what he wanted. But he had never saved very diligently. He and Courtney had always assumed that if they ever got into a real scrape, Jim's parents would soften their stance.

Still unable to access any of their funds, Jim had sheepishly called his father this week, explaining their predicament and asking for a "float." He had been shocked and embarrassed when his father reiterated his firm policy. He had enough problems of his own to worry about, his father said. Since the turn of the year the oil wells suddenly weren't pumping properly and his company was losing millions per day. He had brusquely rung off.

Before that phone call, Y2K had seemed unreal, impossible. Jim and Courtney had regarded it as a chance to see how resourceful they could be. They had gone through the odd cans of soup and packets of macaroni and cheese in their cupboards, eaten cold cereal (which they liked anyway) and even searched out two-year-old packets of Ramen noodles in boxes in the basement, still unopened from their last move. But then the Jeep had run out of gas, and now their Accord was near empty. Even if they braved the long lines at the service stations, they couldn't afford to fill their gas tanks. The service stations—like most retailers—had stopped accepting credit cards. Jim and Courtney were down to twelve dollars cash. If they couldn't buy gas, they'd have to take the bus to work—but even then they had cash for only a few days' fare.

A few days before, they had started to worry about how they were going to pay their monthly bills. Obviously, their checks were no good. Jim had blanched when he realized that they might not receive a paycheck in this month, since payroll for both his trading company and Courtney's church "pantry" job were run through Midwest. They had only enough in their (inaccessible) savings account for about half of their bills. They had decided to liquidate some of their investments and use the proceeds to open another account at another bank, but then they realized that their investment account was managed through Midwest Securities—also closed.

Midwest was still maddeningly unhelpful, saying in a recorded message that "account holders should contact their local bank regulator for details of emergency funds releases." Placards on their branch doors said the same thing. Feeling somewhat foolish, Jim had tried to call the Austin office of the national regulator only to find that their particular office was "closed indefinitely due to systems problems."

Jim had even called the regulatory headquarters in Washington, D.C. After a half dozen busy signals, he finally reached a government clerk who sounded as if she'd been dealing with irate citizens around the clock. "Regulators are working with the bank to reconstruct their records," she said, as if reading from a prepared script. "After this is done, your bank will be able to arrange the release of emergency funds." When Jim protested that he had literally been out of cash since the rollover and couldn't even buy food, the voice on the other end of the line replied crisply, "Then you should have paid more attention. Since last summer we've been recommending that people carry at least two to three weeks' worth of cash. We even sent out notices to that effect in your bank statements."

And now, here they were. It was unbelievable. It couldn't be happening—but it was. Now *they* were waiting in line to meet with the pastor who ran the deacons' fund at church, watching Deborah walk away down the corridor. And there was nothing—literally nothing—they could do about it.

They finally took their turn in the associate pastor's office, humbled and dejected. He noted their situation, scribbling a brief entry on a legal pad already filled with other names. He didn't say much, just handed them six coupons: dairy, meat, toiletries...and a slip of paper with the names of church members who had saved up food and water and were willing to share. Somehow, Jim wasn't surprised to see Billy Phillips's name on the list. The pastor explained briefly that the church was unable to do more because it also was experiencing its own cash crisis, as Courtney already knew. Cash offerings had dropped dramatically. They were trying to set up a temporary banking account at another bank to deposit the checks received from the last three weekly offerings. But that all took time, particularly since the other banks were all busy with their own systems problems. He was hopeful that some of the staff could be paid sometime in the next three or four weeks. Courtney closed her eyes and Jim looked fixedly at the floor. *This isn't happening.*

Austin, Texas, Monday, January 17, 2000—7:30 A.M.

Margie Young looked up from folding napkins as Deborah Carey came in from the bus stop, then stopped still. There was no mistaking the dark circles and the reddened eyes. Deborah walked stiffly; almost, Margie thought, like a condemned person approaching the gallows. Margie walked over tentatively, touching her friend on the shoulder, searching her eyes in concern. As if a dam suddenly burst at this small kindness, Deborah collapsed into her arms, sobbing her heart out. Margie didn't know what to say; she could only hold her, shooing away curious looks from the kitchen staff, stroking her hair. She didn't know what had happened, but she would find out. It was time to do something about it.

Champaign-Urbana, Illinois, January 17, 2000

"I'm sorry we can't accept credit cards, and we can't give away much food, but there is someone who can."

Becky Lee had become adept at delivering this information, as she said it roughly ten times a day. From a drawer in her desk she removed a small cloth sack with *WWJD* emblazoned on it in bright gold letters, and pulled out a token.

"If you take the Number 11 bus—" she pointed toward the nearby bus stop—"south about three miles, you'll see Grace Chapel. It's a big red-brick church on the corner. Ask the bus driver to point out the stop. They have a food pantry, and they can help you with some essentials. They'll give you a second token to get home. Okay?" She slid the WWJD bag back inside her desk drawer on top of a slim, innocuous-looking file folder. A folder, she thought with quiet delight, that contained the future of her business—the contract on the new store she was purchasing for just 20 percent of its previous asking price, and phone messages from two other stores that had approached her with the same request. Although Becky still couldn't access her account with Midwest Bankcorp, she was using her newer, "contingency" account at Illinois OneBank to conduct business. They had been wonderful—despite their own systems glitches—and had made it very easy to consider switching entirely whenever Midwest finally reopened.

With some effort, Becky pulled her thoughts back to the matter at hand. The young man standing before her was rather unkempt—the power shortages were making it difficult for residents to take daily showers, as many of the water pumps ran on electricity and people generally preferred to use the periods of power to work or cook—but he had an indefinably gracious air about him. He wasn't ashamed to accept her help and seemed willing to do what she suggested. She smiled up at him. "What's your name?"

He smiled back. "Tadé Okebari."

She stood up and held out her hand. "Becky Lee. Nice to meet you." She asked him about his situation. He told her about his family's small business, which was nearly bankrupt now that their largest customer had dropped them, and about his wife, Ruth, who was trying to get some answers from the manufacturers of a few of their essential machines that were no longer functioning properly. He smiled as he told her about their three grade-school-age kids who were running around at home enjoying their extended school holiday, causing Ruth to climb the walls in exasperation. Tadé related his story in almost amusing fashion, but Becky knew they must be running out of money and basic necessities or he wouldn't be accepting her pointer to Grace Chapel's food pantry.

She pulled up a chair for him. "Tadé, would you mind if I pray for you?"

He looked a little uncomfortable, but he sat down as she returned to her chair. Becky closed her eyes. "Lord God, we have so many needs these days—and we know you are the only one who can meet them. I pray that you would watch over Tadé and Ruth and their family, that you would provide for their needs in a miraculous way. Please help Ruth find the answers and the help she needs as she tries to get the business running again. God, you own all the money and all the resources in the world. I pray that you would restore their business and their family finances. God, help me to know how to help my new friend Tadé. In Jesus' name, amen."

She looked up and saw that Tadé was regarding her with an odd look on his face—a mixture of confusion, helplessness, and longing that was very much the opposite of his gracious surface demeanor. Becky had seen that look often in the past two weeks. And she knew what the Lord wanted her to do. In a matter-of-fact tone, she told Tadé that she felt God wanted her to extend store credit to him on an honor system. She told him that in addition to whatever support he received from Grace Chapel, he could count on this store to give him credit for essentials the food pantry couldn't supply. Then, taking a deep breath, she reached into her drawer again and pulled out a small bulletin Grace Chapel had developed. It explained both their "Y2K Pantry" and the Christian beliefs that led them to help their community.

"Tadé, this is why I want to help you. Because everything I have belongs to God anyway. He has given me new life through the amazing love and sacrifice of his Son, Jesus, and I want to do whatever he asks—and whatever would help you." She watched as Tadé glanced at the brochure, her heart pounding. She always fumbled over explanations of her faith and was glad to have something concrete to put in his hands. At the very end was printed a simple sentence: *"By this all men will know that you are my disciples, if you love one another"—Jesus Christ.*

Tadé still wore the odd expression on his face as he told Becky he was a non-practicing Muslim. He thanked her for giving him store credit and for the bulletin. He promised her he would read it on the bus to Grace Chapel. Becky saw him paging through it as he walked slowly toward the bus stop. Neither of them knew that this particular bus ride would be the most important fifteen minutes of Tadé's life.

Austin, Texas, January 17, 2000

Deborah Carey looked around in awe as Margie led her into the enormous warehouse. The shelves and pallets were stacked high with huge sacks, barrels, and cans of food. A group of women worked swiftly, efficiently, to measure and sort different types of bulk foods for storage or distribution. Margie guided Deborah toward one side of the building, where a line of people was already waiting to receive a portion of the plentiful foodstuffs. Margie loved to see people's expressions when they first saw the Cannery. It made all their hard work worthwhile. She knew how difficult Deborah's life had become and was so thankful that they could help.

"How—how is this possible?" Deborah finally found her voice as she stared fixedly at the smiling, clean-cut young men who were handing out grocery bags of food to the people in line. Little Gary and Gail were sitting up straight in their rickety double stroller, taking it all in with wide eyes, babbling and pointing this way and that. She looked down at her children and an overwhelming sense of relief swept through her. *This is for REAL,* she thought. After Margie and her husband had helped her move back in with her mother, Margie had brought Deborah and the kids to the Cannery for enough essentials to live through the next month or so. They were headed to Margie's church next: Margie had promised that one of the elders there would be able to help her financially.

Margie laughed. "It's sort of overwhelming, isn't it? Believe it or not, this is normal for us. This Cannery isn't stocked because of Y2K, actually. It's like this all the time...although we've maybe put more aside than usual during the last year or two. I work here one day a month. We take turns stocking it and keeping it functioning smoothly. Every now and then we actually fast—that is, we don't eat for a day—and give the money we would have spent on food to the church for just this use. It's cool to be able to help people who really need it." She hugged Deborah around the shoulders.

The twins were starting to bob up and down in their stroller, wanting to get out and run around. Deborah picked up Gary and Margie took Gail. As the two women stood in line chattering about all sorts of trivial things, Deborah smiled at the realization that, for the first time in weeks, she was having a normal, adult conversation that didn't focus on her dire straits. As the head of the line grew closer, Deborah noticed that the workers were handing out literature with each bag of groceries.

Forty minutes later, in the offices of Margie's huge church, a tall, friendly, white-haired man drew up an action plan to get Deborah some financial help. First, he said, they would immediately get her a room—if she liked—with one of the church families to get her away from the crowded, less-than-desirable situation with her mother. The family he was thinking of had four small children and another on the way, but their big house had a guest apartment Deborah could live in for free as long as she didn't mind pitching in on household chores and such. Deborah could only nod her head, stunned, as the elder continued.

Next, they would see whether a mechanic in the church could take a look at her van. He happened to know that one of the Y2K problems conking out automobiles was actually simple to fix, and he was sure he could find someone to do the job for free. They had a few guys, he said with a wink, who would be glad to do such a favor for a pretty lady.

Deborah, far from being flustered, actually felt a slow grin rising from ear to ear. She was suddenly beginning to feel safe again—a sense of security she hadn't felt in years. The elder discussed some of her other financial problems—especially the unpaid medical bills—and wrote out a check to help cover part of it. He explained that this was a free gift from the church and that, while there was no obligation, he hoped she would be willing to do some work around the church and in some of their community projects from time to time. Their ultimate purpose, he said, was to help people in difficult situations get back on their own two feet, with self-respect and dignity. They did it, he added, out of their love for God.

Deborah was more than willing to help out around the church; she was delighted. She jumped up and hugged the elder, hugged Margie, hugged her kids—

feeling all the while as if she would float away from the weight that had just been lifted from her shoulders. She would have a safe place to live, working transportation, money for food and medicine, and the certainty of keeping her children.

The kindness and generosity of this church was amazing, Deborah thought as Margie drove them out of the church parking lot, past the beautiful sign that read *Church of Jesus Christ of Latter-Day Saints.*

New York City, February 4, 2000—8:50 A.M.

The receptionist didn't even look up from her desk when Julia Ashford stepped from the luxury elevator and brushed by. She had learned long ago not to greet Ms. High-and-Mighty. She never received a response, and not for want of trying.

Surreptitiously, she watched Julia walk briskly down the hall to her corner office. It looked as if she had mud—or something—on her briefcase and on the backs of her legs. If Julia were anyone else, the receptionist would have pointed it out in private, sparing her the embarrassment of going into meetings looking like that. For Julia—the receptionist grinned in spite of herself, as she answered another phone call—forget it. She deserved it.

Up in the Bronx, Marvin Rogers watched as the second shift of breakfasters streamed into the Good Shepherd Center. The ever-present boom box continued to pulse energetically in the background. Some folks were new and didn't know the ropes, but volunteers signed them up, took a survey of their needs, and sent them to the breakfast line. Most days, the Five Boroughs Faith Community took stock of the important needs that came in and marshaled resources and people to meet them where they could. Most importantly, Marvin knew, a team of intercessors in several churches prayed over every one of the hundreds of people who came through the Good Shepherd Center, watching in delight as, one by one, God met their needs. And one by one, they saw lives slowly, radically changed. The faces of despair were turning to hope. The masks of pain and self-centeredness were melting, becoming softer, more open.

Everyone could see the change—and they rejoiced. The churches were filled to overflowing. New services were being added every week. Signs of spiritual revival were starting to show. Last night over one thousand people had remained at church after the service and raised the roof as they sang praise and worship music for nearly two more hours. Marvin had watched and cried, overflowing with so much thanksgiving he couldn't express his joy any other way. Even this morning, the memory of the heavenly worship of those ragged, unpolished, *beautiful* people brought tears to his eyes. *What a return on our investment, Lord! You truly do multiply those resources that are given back to you. What a privilege to serve you!*

Reluctantly, he looked at his watch. He had to make his shift at the hospital. For the past five years he had thought of medicine as his real work and the church as his "hobby"...but suddenly that all seemed so backward. What was happening here was much more *real* than anything he had taken part in before. And in that instant, a deep, immeasurable reverence came over him, a fleeting glimpse of the awesome power and purpose of almighty God. *O Lord, my God.*

Champaign-Urbana, Illinois, February 12, 2000—4:30 P.M.

Travis Pitt sank back into his soft leather recliner, flicking to a sports channel on his brand-new supersize television. The power was becoming more predictable—and more stable—and was now usually on from around 4 P.M. to at least 9 P.M. every day. Now that he was fully moved into his new place, he was finally able to relax.

Some place, he thought, grinning to himself. How did that stupid commercial go? *If my friends could see me now!* He felt bad for all the mugs who had been completely taken by the Y2K problems sweeping the nation, but aside from the power and transportation problems he hadn't been affected that much. And boy, he'd take those temporary annoyances any day! With all the phone problems around the city, Travis had made more money in the last four months than he had ever dreamed of. After saving nearly all of it in cash, he had purchased this three-bedroom, two-bath luxury home outright.

The doorbell rang. *That's Don, I bet.* Reluctantly, he pried himself from the softness of his chair. He had felt compelled to offer Don a place to stay after his old college roommate found himself out of his bank job. Unable to pay rent for either January or February, Don's landlord had made it clear he could pay up—in cash, at once—or leave. Travis had been happy to help, but now, as he opened the door, he thought how awkward it was to see Don in this state. In addition to his luggage, Don was carrying a nicely packaged box of foodstuffs. Travis recognized the grocer as one of Don's former clients—a client Don had previously made no bones about disdaining.

To Travis's surprise, as he helped carry in boxes, he found that a secret part of his brain actually snickered at this turn of events. He had always felt, somehow, inferior to his old buddy. In college, Don had earned nearly straight A's while Travis was lucky if he didn't have to repeat classes. Don's major was finance; Travis had chosen physical education. Nearing graduation, Don was flown to cushy job interviews all over the country; Travis had been fortunate to find a phone repair firm to apprentice him. Don had been the high-paid, designer-suited banker; Travis had spent his days in overalls, working for a string of office clients who looked down on him.

That is, until the last twelve months. Now, Travis was the go-to guy, the savior, the one who could command an hourly wage more suited to corporate lawyers than corporate mechanics.

And business showed no signs of slacking. So many companies and government agencies were still so screwed up by Y2K that he would have this level of work for a long, long time. He smiled as he thought about the number of times he'd been paid in cash by desperate corporate clients. He wasn't going to declare half of it. *And frankly,* he thought, *there's no reason to. The IRS will never know.* Like half the country, Travis was delighted that the IRS had been thoroughly demolished by the crisis and hadn't truly been open for business since day one.

Half a country away, in Washington, D.C., the president's cabinet was gathering for a special Saturday session—not an uncommon occurrence these days. The U.S. government was about to face its most pressing fiscal crisis in decades, as it was clear that the IRS would be unable to smoothly process revenues from corporate and individual taxpayers.

Cabinet members knew that many American citizens were rejoicing over this particular turn of events. But they also knew that this was deadly serious. Several foreign nations were working round the clock to take advantage of the weakened, disorganized condition of the world's more modern countries. The Defense Department was in its most vulnerable state in decades. At least four other essential government agencies had been thrown into chaos from which they had not satisfactorily recovered. Many essential public services would be disrupted—or completely unavailable—for far longer than the average citizen was aware. With tax revenues reduced to alarmingly low levels, there literally would be no way to keep many other government services running. Massive layoffs of thousands upon thousands of government employees were almost inevitable.

Quiet, grim conversations sprang up in small groupings around the table as the cabinet members waited for leaders from both parties on Capitol Hill to arrive. It was time to make some hard decisions.

One man at the table was very, very tired. Unbeknownst to the others, he had been in prayer all night, pleading with the Lord for help and guidance. The country, he knew, was in crisis—perhaps its deepest crisis since the Civil War. He had been appalled at his pastor's flippant joke from the pulpit on Sunday: "The Lord is definitely blessing us through Y2K—we don't have to pay taxes this year!"

Does he realize what he's saying? he had thought. *He's advocating economic and social breakdown.* He himself had actually been pushing for years to dismantle the excess government structures and turn more responsibility over to local municipalities and community organizations, but he—of all of them—wanted it to happen in an orderly and planned way. A wholesale collapse of the government would be disastrous. But that was precisely what would happen if a large portion of the citizenry refused to pay taxes. A surge of anger swept through him, and he physically trembled. *Don't they realize how important the government really is?*

He thought of the Scripture he had been reading that morning, the beginning of Romans 13:

> Obey the government, for God is the one who put it there. All governments have been placed in power by God.... The authorities are sent by God to help you.... You must obey the government for two reasons: to keep from being punished and to keep a clear conscience. Pay your taxes, too, for these same reasons. For government workers need to be paid so they can keep on doing the work God intended them to do. Give to everyone what you owe them: Pay your taxes and import duties, and give respect and honor to all to whom it is due.

Then, against the buzz of the conversations around the cabinet table, an idea came to him. What if he asked the major Christian leaders in the country for their support? If they could call on Christians nationwide to voluntarily step forward and pay their taxes, what an example that would set for the world! Everyone knew that many conservative Christians were among the most vocal critics of the federal government and wanted to see it reformed. Well, here was a perfect opportunity for that reform—such a chance for the Refiner's fire to purify, for the dross to be swept away—if only the country would provide the revenue to *allow* them to. If he could just convince Christian leaders to come on board, the Christian faith community, and the rest of the country would follow. He was sure of it.

Austin, Texas, March 26, 2000

Courtney Thicke finally hung up the phone and admitted defeat. *I'm not going to find her.* For the last three weeks—ever since she and Jim had finally gained access to their bank accounts—they had tried to locate Deborah Carey. She hadn't been to the food pantry, and she hadn't been in church. *Maybe she still doesn't have her van fixed and she decided not to bother with the bus,* Courtney thought. But a nagging feeling wouldn't go away. She had felt a tremendous burden in her heart for that woman, and she knew they hadn't been there for her when Deborah had needed them most.

Jim and Courtney still didn't feel they were in a position to help anyone; they were in arrears on so many bills that they could hardly keep track of them. Jim's trading company had been decimated by the crisis. The entire staff—what remained, anyway—were on a reduced pay schedule. The company had lost tons of irreplaceable cargo, their accounts receivable were still impossible to fully piece together, and the worldwide problems with the oil and gas industry were threatening to dismantle what semblance of global trade remained. They had survived the crisis by selling their Accord for half its book value. They didn't know how they were going to make their student loan payments. But still, they had felt compelled to seek out Deborah and offer assistance.

And now, for all they knew, she could be crippled by diabetes or injured in the violence that had sporadically plagued some sections of the city in the past few months. Courtney closed her eyes and prayed with all her might: *Lord Jesus, look after her.*

CHAPTER EIGHT

IN WHOM IS OUR TRUST?

The Year 2000 problem may be much more than just a public quandary to be attacked and resolved with our usual ingenuity. It may, in fact, be a message to us from a heavenly Father who sees his children looking to humanistic values rather than to him. Consider the following Scriptures carefully:

> Israel has vast treasures of silver and gold and many horses and chariots. The land is filled with idols. The people bow down and worship these things they have made. So now everyone will be humbled and brought low. The LORD cannot simply ignore their sins!... The day is coming when your pride will be brought low and the LORD alone will be exalted. In that day the LORD Almighty...will break down every high tower and wall. He will destroy the great trading ships and all the small boats in the harbor. The arrogance of all people will be brought low. Their pride will lie in the dust. The LORD alone will be exalted! Idols will be utterly abolished and destroyed. (Isaiah 2:7–9, 11–12, 15–18)

> Some trust in chariots and some in horses, but we trust in the name of the LORD our God. (Psalm 20:7, NIV)

> If my people who are called by my name will humble themselves and pray and seek my face and turn from their wicked ways, I will hear from heaven and will forgive their sins and heal their land. (2 Chronicles 7:14)

Have we, like the people of God Isaiah spoke to, stooped to worshiping these things we have made while relying less and less on the Maker of all things? We who love the Lord may rebel at the thought, but we must honestly consider whether we have complacently surrendered to the pervasive idolatry akin to that which brought God's discipline on ancient Israel.

The Bible instructs, "Dear children, keep yourselves from idols" (1 John 5:21, NIV). The New Living Translation puts it this way: "Dear children, keep away from anything that might take God's place in your hearts." Throughout the Bible, it is clear that the human heart is very prone to falling into idolatry—to worshiping and trusting so many things other than God.

The Year 2000 computer problem is not a surprise to God. He may be using it as a wake-up call to his children. As his people, we must see it for what it is: not just a thorny problem to solve, or a potential inconvenience, but a stumbling block to the wise. God may be taking advantage of this period in history to point out to us how dependent we have become on everything other than him—dependent on technology, economic security, even self-reliance. These are all good things, but perhaps they may have become idols in our land.

HOLY DISCIPLINE

> My child, don't ignore it when the LORD disciplines you, and don't be discouraged when he corrects you. For the LORD corrects those he loves, just as a father corrects a child in whom he delights. (Proverbs 3:11–12)

Tim Keller, senior pastor of Redeemer Presbyterian Church in the wealthy, vigorous heart of New York City, frequently reminds his congregation that we can best identify our idols by the pain we feel when they are taken away. The more you lean on something, the harder you fall when it is unexpectedly taken out from under you. All of the potential distress surrounding the Year 2000 problem underscores this principle in bold detail. When discussing Y2K, Pat Robertson notes that "if people are worshiping a false god, perhaps the best way to get people's attention is to bring the false god down."

Without even noticing or realizing it, we Christians lean on so many things other than God every day. If we are going to obediently understand what God is saying to us through this time in history, we must first examine our hearts and confess where we have built our lives around these idols, rather than solely on him. Many believers who sincerely try to love God with all their heart, soul, mind, and strength might be somewhat perplexed or defensive at the idea that they could also have a false god in their lives. But it shouldn't be such a surprise: the wayward tendencies of the human heart are clear throughout Scripture.

For example, when we consider that our bank could fail or potentially lose our money for a time, we get nervous. Why is that? Many of us have never stopped to think about it, but the more prosperous we become, the more we depend on our investments, our savings account, our easy access to slush funds. We can't comprehend what we would do if our ATM or credit cards no longer worked, or if our bank couldn't organize its books quickly enough to release cash for a few months' personal expenses.

Now, money, conveniences, and security aren't bad things. But our craven fear that they may be at risk (or our willingness to ignore the potential risk) points out that they aren't just "conveniences"; we actually *trust in* them. In fact, we worship them. Many of us, if we are honest in the quiet of our hearts, must admit that we depend on these things in a way that we don't truly depend—practically, logistically—on God. We are too good at being self-sufficient and in control for that. God becomes a standby. We dial his 911 hotline when things unexpectedly come up, but in general we coast along without feeling like we *need* him day to day. That feeling of self-made security, of course, is nothing but an illusion.

Take the "Y2K Christian Challenge" and ask yourself a key question. Imagine that it is January 1, 2000, and many of the negative predictions have come true. Your bank is temporarily closed (no access to your funds), you are fast running out of food and other necessities, your credit cards don't work, and you are almost out of cash. Which would you rather have on January 1, 2000: (a) the all-powerful Creator of the universe, who knows your needs and says, "Do not worry about what you will eat, drink or wear"; or (b) a magic credit card that would work no matter what?

Dr. Henry Blackaby comments on where our trust needs to be:

> When your heart shifts from God to technology, then you have sinned against God. But God never allows His people's heart to shift without discipline. So this 2000 glitch may be one of God's premier warnings to His people to say, "If you put your trust in this, it will fail." There is no technology of man that will not fail, but there is One that will never fail.

Blackaby also adds this crucial note:

> In the atmosphere of our generation, you'll have [a] large segment of Christian leadership blaming Y2K on the enemy...because everything negative is attributed to spiritual warfare. [But] if you see everything negative as spiritual warfare, then God doesn't have a chance at discipline.... I've always had a far greater fear of God than I ever did of the enemy, because I don't remember any time in Scripture where the enemy ever destroyed God's people; but I can tell you many places where God did. So the greatest fear I have is that God's people will misread the activity of God.

As Christians, are we really willing to put all our security in God? He may be allowing this event in history so we can find out. The Millennium Bug's message to us, however, may go even deeper than that.

ISAIAH'S WARNING

When considering the potential purpose or message of Y2K, perhaps the most sobering Scriptures are found in Isaiah 2 and 3. Isaiah spoke the Lord's warning to his people, who had become wealthy and prideful in their accomplishments and had begun to "worship these things they have made" and rely on their "vast treasures of silver and gold." Furthermore, Isaiah says, "They speak out against the LORD and refuse to obey him. They have offended his glorious presence among them.... They sin openly like the people of Sodom. They are not one bit ashamed" (Isaiah 3:8–9).

Sound familiar?

In response, the Lord says he "cannot simply ignore their sins." He has to "punish the proud," bringing their arrogance low by destroying all those things on which they worship and depend other than him. God says he will "break down every high tower and wall...the great trading ships and all the small boats in the harbor...Idols will be utterly abolished and destroyed" (Isaiah 2:15–16, 18). Further,

> When the LORD rises to shake the earth, his enemies will...abandon their gold and silver idols [and] will try to escape the terror of the LORD and the glory of his majesty...Stop putting your trust in mere humans. They are as frail as breath. How can they be of help to anyone? (Isaiah 2:19–22)

Now, keeping in mind the potential disruptions the Millennium Bug may cause, consider the remainder of Isaiah's forecast:

> The LORD...will cut off the supplies of food and water from Jerusalem and Judah. He will destroy all the nation's leaders.... Then he will appoint children to rule over them, and anarchy will prevail. People will take advantage of each other—man against man, neighbor fighting neighbor. Young people will revolt against authority, and nobodies will sneer at honorable people.
>
> In those days a man will say to his brother, "Since you have a cloak, you be our leader! Take charge of this heap of ruins!"
>
> "No!" he will reply, "I can't help. I don't have any extra food or clothes. Don't ask me to get involved!" (Isaiah 3:1–2, 3–7).

The end of that passage epitomizes the reason why the Christian church must be ready for Y2K. If A.D. 2000 brings turmoil, people will be looking for a leader—and will appoint whoever can step up to the challenge. People will come to the body of Christ and say, "You be our leader!" If we are to bring glory to God, we cannot reply, "I can't help. I don't have any extra...don't ask me to get involved." Instead, we *must* get involved. We must be ready, both physically and spiritually, to meet the challenge and be as the shepherds watching over the flock. As Jesus did, we must pray that God would help us "not lose even one of those" whom he has entrusted to our care (John 6:39; 17:11).

IDOLS ARE FALSE GODS

Although we have the sinful tendency to put our trust in the works of our own hands, we all know in our hearts that they are *false* gods—in other words, they are incapable of helping us in the way we desire. As the psalmist writes, "Their idols are merely things of silver and gold, shaped by human hands. They cannot talk, though they have mouths, or see, though they have eyes! They cannot hear with their ears or smell with their noses. And those who make them are just like them, as are all who trust in them" (Psalm 135:15–18). Idols, above all, provide an illusion with no substance, just as our feeling of man-made sufficiency and security is nothing more than a mirage on a parched desert.

While every individual struggles with different issues, God's millennium message appears to be focused on the areas where we as a people have placed our "functional trust" on a broad scale. These are the same traps that God's people—as a holy nation—have fallen into time and again through the ages. Considering the previously referenced passages from Isaiah, Psalms, and Proverbs, those pervasive idols appear to include:

- money and economic prosperity ("vast treasures of silver and gold")
- technology ("things…shaped by human hands")
- economic and national security ("every high tower and wall"; "horses and chariots")
- our own abilities ("mere humans")

What do we hope to receive from these things? Can money truly provide happiness or technology meet our deepest needs? Can a good economy or human ingenuity offer real security or accomplish important goals on their own? Of course not. Only the sovereign Lord, the Creator of the universe who loves his children, can provide these things, and he longs for us to *let him provide*. Picture the cry of Jesus as he grieves over Jerusalem: "O Jerusalem, Jerusalem.… How often I have wanted to gather your children together as a hen protects her chicks beneath her wings, but you wouldn't let me" (Matthew 23:37).

Remember Jesus' concern: When we trust in anything other than God, we are not just adding a false hope to our real hope; we are actually *displacing* God from the center of our lives. Please review his words carefully:

> "No one can serve two masters. For you will hate one and love the other, or be devoted to one and despise the other. You cannot serve both God and money. So I tell you, don't worry about everyday life—whether you have enough food, drink, and clothes. Doesn't life consist of more than food and clothing? Look at the birds. They don't need to plant or harvest or put food in barns because your heavenly Father feeds them. And you are far more valuable to him than they are. Can all your worries add a single moment to your life? Of course not. And why worry about your clothes? Look at the lilies and how they grow. They don't work or make their clothing, yet Solomon in all his glory was not dressed as beautifully as they are. And if God cares so wonderfully for flowers that are here today and gone tomorrow, won't he more surely care for you? You have so little faith! So don't worry about having enough food or drink or clothing. Why be like the pagans who are so deeply concerned about these things? Your heavenly Father already knows all your needs, and he will give you all you need from day to day

> if you live for him and make the Kingdom of God your primary concern. So don't worry about tomorrow, for tomorrow will bring its own worries. Today's trouble is enough for today." (Matthew 6:24–34)

By secretly trusting in the works of our hands, we not only thwart God's best for us, but we actually hurt our relationship with the one we profess to love the most. Joel Balin, a music producer and worship leader, told me of a conversation he had with a young man who was living with his girlfriend. The boyfriend couldn't understand why she wanted to get married until Joel pointed out that he expected everything from her—her full loyalty, her constant presence, her intimacy—but was not willing to fully give himself in return. Joel drives home the crucial point:

> When we don't trust the Lord fully, when we allow our commitment to stray, we become halfhearted. We want the blessings of God and want his presence and his intimacy, but are not willing to give ourselves fully in return. God says he will return to claim his church...but God is not coming back for a girlfriend. He is coming back for *his bride*.

OUR PLACE IN HISTORY

It is not only technology and self-sufficiency that we may have begun to worship. For a moment, put aside thoughts of the Y2K bug and take a wider view of where we are as a national (and global) community of believers.

As a nation, America has been powerfully blessed for centuries. It is historical fact that the United States was founded by men and women with deep personal relationships with the very God we Christians worship today. Our country was founded not on values or ethics or ideals, but on God himself. (Massachusetts, for example, was originally chartered as a theocracy with God as the official leader.) Few would argue, however, that we have lost that focus—both as a nation and as a Christian community. As our lives have sped up, our desire to do what is necessary to maintain intimacy with God has slowed down. Even if we truly love the Lord, we may not faithfully seek him "morning by morning." As a result, our relationship with the Lord our God may have become more distant, less tangible. Instead of worshiping him, we have gradually turned to the worship of more tangible things such as doctrines, family values, social justice, or personal morality. While these are all good things in themselves, they are not the Lord himself; therefore, they are mere idols—impotent substitutes for the presence of God.

My friend Kris Carter, a politically conservative technology lawyer in Washington, D.C., notes that "many of us Christians fall into the trap of being passionate about conservativism so that we don't have to be passionate about Christ." It's easier, somehow, to be passionate about a socially sanctioned discourse than it is to focus our passion on the person of Jesus Christ—who has rarely been a subject of polite social discussion. All the otherwise good and moral ideals may have become our idols as well, as they gradually replace the preeminence of Jesus in our intensity of focus.

Even worse, as our unsaved friends, neighbors, and coworkers have gone further and further astray, we Christians have followed—either in practice or through our silence. As David Wilkerson, pastor of Times Square Church in Manhattan, has recently emphasized, too many Christians throughout the United States have become complacent to America's soaring illegitimacy rate, incredibly high rates of abortion and teen violence, the prevalence of the occult, and society's "normalization" of homosexuality...when in fact we should be crying out to God for forgiveness and mercy, and looking for ways to help the hurting.

Such acts and attitudes are no less reprehensible in God's sight today than when, through his servant Moses, he declared them sin. Just because a "more enlightened" America deems God intolerant and sin relative does not make them so; neither does our arrogance excuse us from divine accountability. Sin is sin just as truth is truth, and God never empowered us to modify the definition of sin or truth to accommodate our wayward appetites.

The issue goes beyond our silence in the face of sin, for as Christians we know that we ourselves are just as sinful and in desperate need of God's grace. We also have faltered at the most basic and most important of all Christ's commands regarding our relationship with the world: to love our neighbor as ourselves.

We may soon get another chance. If the Year 2000 problem really does bring economic turmoil and social conflict, we will have a very important opportunity to show the kind of sacrificial love that Jesus said brings about repentance and conversion. In our discussion regarding Y2K, evangelist Pat Robertson reflected:

> I was reading just the other day in Zephaniah..."The day of the wrath of the Lord is coming." We see the gross immorality there is in the world and in our country, and the materialism that is all over the world, and that the nations are moving farther and farther from the laws of God.... But in the midst of that, you can sense hunger for spiritual things. I don't believe God is going to completely devastate the world while evangelism is exploding...but if people are worshiping a false god, perhaps the best way to get people's attention is to bring the false god down. If banks crash, cars don't work, and food supply is interrupted, it would lead to desperation on the parts of millions of people. It is possible that in that desperation they would look to God and it would fuel revival.

THE WARNING IS THE OPPORTUNITY

As Isaiah had done, Zephaniah spoke to a prosperous nation with no sorrow for its sins: "Rebellious, polluted Jerusalem...proudly refuses to listen even to the voice of the LORD...refuses all correction [and] does not trust in the LORD or draw near to its God" (Zephaniah 3:1–2). Israel's security and wealth had made it complacent. The

Lord warned his people, led by King Josiah, that his wrath was coming because they had forsaken him; even priests worshiped both God *and* Baal, Molech, and the sun, moon, and stars. But God held out an opportunity: he would use this judgment to purify his children, purge away all sin and evil, and then restore his people and give them hope.

> "I will reduce the wicked to heaps of rubble..." says the LORD. "I will...destroy every last trace of their Baal worship...[and] those who used to worship me but now no longer do.... Because you have sinned against the LORD, I will make you as helpless as a blind man searching for a path.... Your silver and gold will be of no use to you on that day of the LORD'S anger.... [Therefore] gather together and pray, you shameless nation. Gather while there is still time, before judgment begins and your opportunity is blown away like chaff. Act now...[and] beg the LORD to save you—all you who are humble, all you who uphold justice. Walk humbly and do what is right. Perhaps even yet the LORD will protect you from his anger on that day of destruction.... The few survivors of the tribe of Judah...will lie down to rest.... For the LORD their God will visit his people in kindness and restore their prosperity again." (Zephaniah 1:3–4, 6, 17–18; 2:1–3, 7).

King Josiah was one of the few biblical kings who "did what was pleasing in the LORD'S sight [albeit imperfectly] and followed the example of his ancestor David." He instituted radical reforms in a country saturated with Baal worship, turning the nation back toward God. Scholars involved in editing the *Life Application Bible* argue that the above prophecy may have played a large role in spurring King Josiah's reforms; the book of Zephaniah was probably written around 640–621 B.C., when the reforms began. God's warnings were taken seriously and a great revival rejuvenated his people.

Unfortunately, the people did not fully eliminate the pervasive idolatry in their land; they tried in vain to embrace their worldly gods at the same time they embraced the one true God. Only a few years after Josiah's death, as a result of their life of compromise, the Lord allowed his people to be taken into a captivity from which they didn't return for hundreds of years.

It is important to understand that the Lord in his mercy always gives us prior warning of his judgment so that we might confess and repent: "Surely the Sovereign LORD does nothing without revealing his plan to his servants the prophets" (Amos 3:7, NIV). Now, as we approach the year 2000, we have had many recent warnings. Many respected Christian pastors, speakers, and writers—as diverse as Charles Stanley, David Wilkerson, Michael Youssef, and Rick Joyner—have grown increasingly concerned that the Lord's judgment may be coming upon a modern world that has turned far from him. And frankly, as the evidence for the potential disruptions of the Millennium Bug are clear—and given the biblical parallels—it is not unreasonable to ponder whether the Year 2000 problem might be a modern means of God's judgment.

As Dr. Michael Youssef, pastor of Church of the Apostles in Atlanta and host of the *Leading the Way* radio ministry, wrote in his July 1998 newsletter:

> I must confess to you that during the past couple of years I have begun to sense that we may be the recipients of God's warning for judgment. The good economy and the blossoming stock market, I felt, are God's final loving warnings to us as a nation. However, instead of turning to Him in thanksgiving, our nation has placed its trust in the blessings rather than the one who gives the blessings.[1]

God longs for us to turn our hearts back to him. His loving mercy has triumphed over judgment for eternity, and may, for many years, have stayed him from moving against us. It may be that it is only through his great love for us that we are able to foresee the disaster that might occur.

HOW THEN DO WE TURN OUR HEARTS?

Turning from such a pervasive trust in false idols requires that we confess and repent. The same passage in Isaiah that delivers the terrible warning also provides the prescription.

> "Wash yourselves and be clean! Let me no longer see your evil deeds. Give up your wicked ways. Learn to do good. Seek justice. Help the oppressed. Defend the orphan. Fight for the rights of widows. Come now, let us argue this out," says the LORD. "No matter how deep the stain of your sins, I can remove it. I can make you as clean as freshly fallen snow. Even if you are stained as red as crimson, I can make you as white as wool. If you will only obey me and let me help you, then you will have plenty to eat. But if you keep turning away and refusing to listen, you will be destroyed by your enemies. I, the LORD, have spoken!" (Isaiah 1:16–20)

We know that, as individuals, those who have accepted Jesus Christ as Savior and Lord have been washed "as white as wool." His atonement for all our wrongs was perfect and complete when he went to the cross on our behalf, and we will enjoy eternity with him. Remember, however, that this passage was written to God's dearly beloved, chosen people. Although they were chosen—actually, *because* they were chosen—he still required their total obedience. He requires no less of his people today.

Some might argue that perhaps God's judgment (if it is coming) applies only to today's lost and rebellious unbelievers. But biblically, God holds us—his adopted children—to a higher standard. Because Jesus went to the cross for us, we have been redeemed at an unfathomable price. While nothing we can do will ever be enough to repay his unwarranted mercy toward us, that doesn't absolve us of the tremendous responsibility of obedience his redemption has conferred. "Much is required from those to whom much is given" (Luke 12:48). Let me encourage you to prayerfully consider Jesus' message in light of our place in history:

> [Jesus said,] "You must be ready all the time, for the Son of Man will come when least expected." Peter asked, "Lord, is this illustration just for us [the disciples] or for everyone?" And the Lord replied, "I'm talking to any faithful, sensible servant to whom the master gives the responsibility of managing his household and feeding his family. If the master returns and finds that the servant has done a good job, there will be a reward.... But if the servant thinks, 'My master won't be back for a while,' and begins oppressing the other servants, partying, and getting drunk—well, the master will return unannounced and unexpected.... The servant will be severely punished, for though he knew his duty, he refused to do it. But people who are not aware that they are doing wrong will be punished only lightly. Much is required from those to whom much is given, and much more is required from those to whom much more is given." (Luke 12:40–43, 45–48)

Until our Master returns, he has entrusted us with a special responsibility of reaching out and caring for his lost family. Although obedience is required of all people, much more, is required of us than of the lost. For he has given us much, much more; he has given us eternity. Have we met his standards?

I asked Dr. Henry Blackaby about the judgment of God on the believer versus God's judgment on the nonbeliever:

> SCF: If I could return to the issue of the Lord's potential judgment, how would you respond to the argument that the Lord may be coming to judge the increasingly depraved world, but not the believer?
>
> HB: Rarely have I seen that in Scripture. Most of the judgments of God in the Bible—and the most severe—are against God's people. Because as go God's people, so goes the world. Right now, I have consistently said the condition of America is a reflection of the condition of the people of God. It's not Hollywood; it's not Washington. Jesus said, "*You're* the salt." What happens when the salt loses its saltiness? There's nothing to preserve. So you don't fault that which is decaying, you fault the salt. And if things are getting darker, the darkness is acting like its nature. But it's getting darker because the light is not acting like *its* nature; the light is no longer dispensing light.
>
> So God goes straight for his people: his judgment always begins with the people of God. When the people of God return to him, the world sees the nature of God in his people. In the great Scripture passage on revival, 2 Chronicles 7:13–14, the verses are a reflection of God's covenant with his people, not with the world. He declares, "If you [meaning his people] walk in my ways, then I will bless you. But if you turn away, I will curse you."
>
> Unfortunately, there isn't a solitary sin in the world that's not also visible in our churches. So God says, "If you see that I'm withholding rain, if you can see that I'm sending disease among my people, and if you see plagues come—if *my people* who will call upon my name will humble *themselves* and seek my face and turn from *their* wicked ways, then I will hear from heaven and forgive their sin and heal their land" [emphases added].

> The healing of America rests on the repentance of God's people. If God's people will not repent, America does not have a chance of avoiding the judgment of God. But many of God's people don't know they need to repent—or at least they don't want to discuss it. Talk about repentance and you're likely to get a violent reaction: "We need to talk about the grace of God, not his wrath." But it is the mercy of God that his grace follows; God's people need his mercy right now to hold off the judgment we really deserve.

Out of his great love, God has called us and made us his own. Out of our imperfect but great love for him, we must confess, repent, and follow him anew. As "people who are called by his name," we must stand in the gap on behalf of the lost family God has entrusted to our care. Even as we pray for *their* salvation and repentance, we must urgently humble *ourselves* and seek his face.

A CALL TO RELATIONSHIP

As we walk this possibly unfamiliar path of repentance as a body of Christ, we must remember that God's purpose for repentance is not to degrade but to restore. Remember the previous passage from Zephaniah; after warning the people to repent before the judgment of the Lord, the prophet says, "Perhaps even yet the LORD will protect you from his anger...[and] will visit his people in kindness" (Zephaniah 2:3, 7). The call to repentance is ultimately so that God might again "visit his people." We need to return to the kind of holy relationship with him that he has been longing for.

Kelly Monroe, an evangelical chaplain at Harvard University and the editor of *Finding God at Harvard,* suggests that the judgment of God, and the potential difficulties of Year 2000, could actually be the ultimate blessing for a world that has strayed so far from relationship with him. She notes that time after time Jesus invited us to "come," "rest," "remain," "abide"—inviting his busy disciples to slow down and cease *doing for* him in order to *receive from* him. We have not voluntarily slowed down on our own; few of us are really good at "abiding" anymore.

Monroe recently spent time in a remote cabin, taking a week-long fast from electricity (exactly the sort of experience we might be given, involuntarily, in Year 2000). During that week, she noted how unusual it was to be forced to set all busyness aside. She told me:

> We might want to begin to see the Year 2000 problem as a blessing: the blessing of keeping the Sabbath. God could be teaching us to reorient our lives around the Sabbath—a time for ceasing and resting and embracing that which matters most: our intimate relationship with him. The first full day for Adam and Eve was the seventh day—the Sabbath. Their first full day was a time for really abiding in God and getting a sense for their calling. God could turn this curse [of Y2K] into a blessing by teaching us how to place our dependency entirely in him and nothing else.... If we would just slow down from our busy, noisy, profane

world and find in him that "fount of every blessing," we might truly see what it means that he is the true vine—our only source of life.

If we are honest about the scriptural charge to "observe the Sabbath and keep it holy," we will realize that it is not a mere suggestion—it is a mandate. Many Christians today do not even realize that keeping the Sabbath is one of the Ten Commandments (Exodus 20:8). Henry Blackaby notes an importance to the Sabbath that few of us are aware of:

> Almost every major statement of God's judgment in the Old Testament has at the top of the list the desecration of the Sabbath. When he brought the indictment against people, that was almost at the top of the list.... The Sabbath is very, very sacred to God. Have America and God's people claimed the Sabbath? Rarely. Churches will adjust their worship services so they can all go watch the football games.

In the New Testament, the book of Hebrews parallels Sabbath rest with salvation, then exhorts:

> There remains, then, a Sabbath-rest for the people of God; for anyone who enters God's rest also rests from his own work, just as God did from his. Let us, therefore, make every effort to enter that rest, *so that no one will fall by following [Israel's] example of disobedience.* (Hebrews 4:9–11, NIV, emphasis added)

It seems that not maintaining a weekly time of rest from our work, a time for focused refreshment and renewal in our relationship with God, is directly correlated with falling into disobedience. God desires for us to keep the Sabbath *so that* we might return to a time of renewing our relationship with him. By means of the Year 2000 problem, he may be providing us with just that chance.

CHAPTER NINE

March 2001

Austin, Texas

"Deborah?"

The call echoed through the east end of the mall, and Deborah Carey turned, vaguely recognizing the voice. Margie Young and two other girlfriends stopped to wait for her, chatting about the design of a store's window display.

Deborah smiled as Courtney Thicke rushed up, out of breath, and hugged her. Jim was close behind. "Deborah! It's so good to see you!"

In an instant, Courtney and Jim took in the obvious, wonderful changes. Deborah had a nice haircut; the twins' stroller was new; the clothes were simple but clean. Courtney couldn't contain her delight. "Wow! What's happened to you? You look wonderful! Once we finally got access to our bank account last year—" *Had it really been a whole year?* "—we tried and tried to find you, but you had left your apartment and nobody knew where you were." The unspoken question was left hanging in the air, and Courtney glanced over to the group of women Deborah appeared to be with.

A gleam of remembrance appeared in Deborah's eyes. "It was pretty awful there for a while. I actually was evicted from my apartment, and the kids and I had to move in with my druggie mother." She shook her head, grinning at Courtney and Jim's gasp of protest. "But it was really a blessing in disguise. My friend Margie from work—" she pointed her out—"came along at just the right time. She and her husband drove me to and from work, brought me to a place where I could get food, took me to their church for help. They even found me a safe place to live. I'm staying in a guest apartment with Kathleen over there. I do most of the housekeeping, and they give me a break on the rent. They have *five* children!" Deborah chuckled. "It's been an adventure."

Something raised a question in the back of Courtney's mind, and she contemplated the lovely, young, well-dressed group of women and the many children running around. "Deborah, what church do they go to?"

"The Church of Jesus Christ of Latter-Day Saints. Boy, isn't that a mouthful!" Deborah laughed again.

Courtney and Jim glanced at each other, then turned back to their friend. Courtney cleared her throat. "But, Deborah...as Mormons, you know they aren't anything like our church, right?" As she started to explain some of the differences between Mormon beliefs and those of orthodox Christianity, Deborah stopped her cold. Courtney was surprised by the fierce expression on her face.

"You're right, Courtney. They are *nothing* like our church—*your* church."

As Courtney tried to put a consoling arm around Deborah's shoulder, Deborah stepped back a pace and put her hand up as a barrier. "*Your* church didn't care whether I lived or died. And I could have died. The *twins* could have died. And Community Church would still have been handing me coupons." She was suddenly shaking with emotion, both at the long-suppressed memory and at Courtney's slight of her friends—the friends who had probably saved her life.

Courtney and Jim were stunned and speechless.

With a deep breath, Deborah calmed down a bit. "I appreciate your concern. But I'm fine now, really." Swiftly, she fished out a paper from her bag and scribbled a phone number. "That's where I'm living for the moment. I'll probably try to find my own place again soon. Since a lot of businesses still haven't fully reautomated, secretarial and administrative jobs have really made a comeback. Some members of the church helped train me, and I've been working now for a few months. I'm enjoying it." She looked over her shoulder to where her friends waited. "Well, I've gotta go. They're taking me shopping for a present for my one-year anniversary."

Courtney looked at the floor. She could guess what the occasion was. She pulled together a smile and took Deborah's hand. "Okay. Have fun and get something nice. We're truly so, so glad to see that you're all right." She looked Deborah in the eye and quietly slipped Jim's business card into her hand. "But if you ever need anything, you call us, okay?"

Deborah didn't really respond, just quickly hugged Courtney and Jim, gave a cheerful wave good-bye, and pushed the stroller back toward her friends. As the Thickes watched the transformed woman walk into the distance with her new friends, both felt hard lumps in their throats. They were relieved to see that Deborah's devastating poverty had been alleviated, but were shattered and contrite over their inability to help her.

In frustration, under her breath, Courtney muttered something about Mormon canneries. Jim stopped her with a swift hand on her arm. She was surprised at the depth of emotion in his voice. "No. Don't be mad at them. They did the right thing...they fed Jesus' lost sheep. We're the ones who didn't." Quietly they stood, arm in arm, watching as Deborah and her friends turned into a store and disappeared from sight.

Champaign-Urbana, Illinois

SNAP!

A cheer roared from a thousand throats as the ribbon was cut for the new church building. It wasn't completely finished—the Sunday school wing would be under construction for a few more months—but today would be the first day they would actually hold services in the new sanctuary. Laughing a protest, Johnny and Anne Barry dashed out of the way as the throng streamed inside, jostling to see the layout and design of the sanctuary and the rest of the building.

The church had anticipated this moment since last summer, when ground had first been broken. So many of the members had participated in the building's swift construction that it was a wonder they had been able to keep the final look of it a secret. Johnny had barely been able to keep the congregation's excitement contained as the countdown approached.

Their reaction was everything he had hoped for. Everyone talked excitedly as they admired the octagonal shape, the skylights, and especially the long wall of glass behind the altar which looked out on a grove of budding trees. Few, however, noticed the real triumph of this building, which was its solar paneling. The whole church building was energy-efficient and relatively self-contained. Not that anyone expected more problems, but if there was one thing they had learned from the last two years, it was the necessity of being good stewards, prepared for anything.

Grinning like parents at Christmas, he and Anne watched their congregants darting around, inspecting features and comparing notes. "There are so many of them!" Anne said in some bemusement. "How on earth can a church more than double in size in just one year?" The question was rhetorical. They both knew it had nothing to do with anything on earth.

Across the narthex, Johnny caught the eye of Becky Lee, who smiled and gave them a thumb's-up sign. She was walking toward the front of the sanctuary beside Cindy O'Neill, Cindy's elderly grandfather, William Temple, and a young man who—Johnny vaguely recalled—had come to church with Becky several times in the last six months. His name was Dan or Don or something like that. He'd have to find out for sure.

Then Johnny saw Patrick O'Neill and Tadé Okebari—who had overseen the construction—holding court before a throng of admirers. He snorted in amusement. *Well, I guess they do deserve the accolades,* Johnny thought. *This would never have happened without them.* He was in awe at Tadé, Ruth, and their kids. They had barely attended their first church service before getting so deeply immersed in the life of the church that Johnny couldn't remember what it was like without them. Tadé and Ruth might be new Christians, but they were already the pillars of Grace Chapel's intercessory team. And, boy, did they have a gift of prayer! Johnny and Anne were convinced it was the fervent intercession that had led the church to its current position of favor and blessing in the community, and its ability to reach out and draw hundreds of new brothers and sisters into the fold.

The explosive growth wasn't stopping. This sanctuary was designed to seat nearly 1,500 in a pinch, and it looked as if they might face that pinch sooner than expected. He had compared notes with his other pastor friends, and much the same thing was happening everywhere. Johnny shook his head in awe. *The world is finally seeing CHRIST rather than Christians.*

He looked over to one side, where four or five members of the press corps were respectfully interviewing a few congregants and snapping pictures. Despite himself, a chuckle escaped his lips as he pointed the scene out to Anne. He couldn't have imagined the media covering the opening of a random local church building two years ago—but now it just seemed natural. And Johnny had no doubts that the coverage would be favorable. A quick prayer of praise floated heavenward. He didn't know how God was going to top *this* day, but he sure looked forward to finding out.

New York City

Marvin Rogers watched the end of the breakfast rush with satisfaction. The buzz of conversation, the upbeat music, and the smell of good cooking permeated the Bronx Good Shepherd Center. The huge room was no longer filled, but a steady stream of men, women, and children still came through these doors every day. As Marvin wiped and cleared tables, he reflected on the changes that just one year had brought about.

The number of people seeking help was only one-tenth what it had been a year ago, while the center now had four times the number of helpful volunteers. Good Shepherd Church was holding three services every Sunday and additional services five nights a week—all filled to capacity. They had planted four "daughter" congregations in other areas of the Bronx, Manhattan, and Queens, and God already seemed to be raising up two other likely spin-offs. Money had suddenly started to flood in—and then back out into the community—as people began to spontaneously share from their incomes, their savings, their possessions.

Marvin shook his head, still amazed. They hadn't asked for it, hadn't really even expected it, but it had all just happened. Further, prayer meetings had sprung to life nearly every morning at 6:30. At the last one he attended a week ago, there had been almost forty people—a number unimaginable two years before.

He paused, thinking back. The explosion in prayer had been one of the most unexpected but wonderful aspects of the whole thing. It was as if the same power that had flung the stars into motion had been poured out upon them, so fully that they couldn't *help* but pray all the time—for everything! And what answers they had seen! *Just like in Matthew 10,* Marvin reflected. *"Go and announce to them that the Kingdom of Heaven is near. Heal the sick, raise the dead, cure those with leprosy, and cast out demons. Give as freely as you have received!"* Marvin closed his eyes, reveling in the awesome presence of God they had witnessed.

It had started quietly. The members of Good Shepherd, who had always believed in God's power to provide, protect, restore, and heal, had seen their faith grow by quantum leaps after the Year 2000 rollover. Jobs and utility services had been miraculously restored. Homes had been saved and sickness quickly averted. Generosity—of people's time, talent, and treasure—had sprung from abundant, joyful hearts. The church had praised God publicly, telling anyone who asked (and many who didn't) what they saw happening in their midst. In turn, those hearing the good news came to Good Shepherd to see for themselves what was happening.

The people of Good Shepherd didn't think their walk with the Lord could get any better. Then, almost one year ago, it did.

One evening, at the start of a congregational prayer service, Marvin and others had specifically asked God to direct their thoughts and prayers. "We want to pray according to your will, not ours," they had prayed humbly. "We want to honor you, Lord. Guide our thoughts, our desires, our requests." Within minutes, Marvin had felt particularly impressed to pray for David and Nancy's five-year-old son. The child's palsy had gotten so bad he could no longer walk, even with braces. Marvin had prayed fervently as others joined in, prayed with conviction and confidence born of intimate faith in God Almighty.

Suddenly a shriek jolted everyone's eyes open. The boy was walking! All trace of the crippling illness had vanished. Shouts of astonishment and unearthly joy erupted from the crowd as the young boy began racing around the front of the sanctuary, crying, "Mommy! Daddy! Look—I'm RUNNING!" A group of exuberant teen girls surrounded the boy and lathered him with hugs and kisses while he struggled to break away—he wanted to run! Men, women, and children rushed to envelop a trembling David and Nancy and celebrate with back-pounding embraces, smiles, and joyful tears. "Thank you, Lord!" they exclaimed. "Thank you!"

In a few moments a man wheeled himself forward in his wheelchair and asked for prayer. Then came a woman who had been deaf from birth. And on that day it had become clear that God wished to bless the obedience, faithfulness, and trust of this church in a very special way.

It was as if an explosion had torn away the bricks and mortar and cut a path straight to heaven. The earthly vessel was still there, and the saints were still just redeemed, clumsy sinners, but the presence of God had filled and indwelled them so fully that they couldn't help but receive and pour out his love on a watching, wondering world.

Marvin took a deep breath and turned back to his table-cleaning. He knew—they all knew—that this wasn't the final answer. They were still "aliens and strangers" in this world, and the world still did not necessarily understand or accept what it was seeing. But for the first time ever, he thought, he was finding what it was like to be a true disciple of Jesus Christ. And his heart overflowed.

At the next table, an exuberant little girl was making a mess as she stood on her bench and tried to dance to a catchy new song by the Christian group 4Him. Her chubby four-year-old cheeks, laughing eyes, and bristling cornrowed hair suddenly reminded Marvin of the church's divinely sparked vitality, which had reached out in the midst of chaos to touch all those around them. Impulsively, he scooped her up for an impromptu dance around the table—whirling, laughing, and dancing, dancing to the beat.

PART TWO

WHAT SHOULD I DO NOW?

CHAPTER TEN

PREPARING YOURSELF AND YOUR FAMILY

Hopefully the preceding chapters have demonstrated that all of us must immediately begin to prepare, both physically and spiritually, to meet the challenges and opportunities posed by Year 2000.

While physical precautions will vary by region, industry, and other factors, certain types of physical action are universal. Likewise, we can begin to take spiritual action: to earnestly pray for this event in history, to repent of any "unseen idolatry," and to renew our personal relationships with the Lord. While we must wait to see the results of the Year 2000 rollover, we can start right now to enjoy the fruits of an intensified focus on our personal walk with almighty God.

As we begin to explore together the physical and spiritual steps you might take, let me encourage you to pause a moment and focus on the apostle Paul's admonition to the Philippians. His words, I believe, could be harkened as the "theme Scripture" of every Christian and group of Christians during the next pivotal years.

> If you have any encouragement from being united with Christ, if any comfort from his love, if any fellowship with the Spirit, if any tenderness and compassion, then make my joy complete by being like-minded, having the same love, being one in spirit and purpose. Do nothing out of selfish ambition or vain conceit, but in humility consider others better than yourselves. Each of you should look not only to your own interests, but also to the interests of others. Your attitude should be the same as that of Christ Jesus: who, being in very nature God, did not consider equality with God something to be grasped, but made himself nothing, taking the very nature of a servant....
>
> Therefore...continue to work out your salvation with fear and trembling, for it is God who works in you to will and to act according to his good purpose. Do everything without complaining or arguing, so that you may become blameless and pure, children of God without fault in a crooked and depraved generation, in which you shine like stars in the universe as you hold out the word of life.... (Philippians 2:1–7, 12–16, NIV)

BLENDING TRUST AND PRUDENCE

As previously noted, the goal of this book is to encourage further personal investigation into how Y2K may specifically affect *you*. People in different geographic environments (e.g., urban versus rural), industries, age groups, and socioeconomic strata will need to tailor their approach to address their individual needs. As you read through the recommendations in the next four chapters, consider how they might be personalized to your individual situation. Some important checklists and more detailed resources for each of these areas are available in the appendix. As was noted in the prologue, there are also dozens of good books in mainstream bookstores that address the technical issues of specific topics (large business, small business, personal computers, family preparation, etc.) in great detail; these will help you specifically address the personal or business vulnerabilities you may identify.

God tells us that "the heart of the discerning acquires knowledge; the ears of the wise seek it out," and that "a man of knowledge increases strength" (Proverbs 18:15; 24:5, NIV). The more you know about how Y2K may apply to you, the stronger a tool you will be in God's hand to accomplish his purposes. As a Christian seeking to honor him, your entire framework for action must revolve around an abiding trust in God and his ability to help and guide you during this process.

As Christian financial counselor Ron Blue told me:

> I've approached every major problem, be it individual or business, from an understanding that God is not worried, nor is he surprised. He is not wringing his hands in heaven now, wondering how Y2K is going to work out or how his people are going to survive. That is not an issue. That is very important to me, because I don't want to get in the position of God and worry about something unrealistically. That doesn't say I'm not prudent: I will actively prepare. But I don't want to drive my life by worry or fear, because fear is contrary to exercising faith.

If you are still ambivalent about the importance of Y2K and are hesitant to take action, ask yourself this: What is your risk tolerance, and if this were any "normal" event, would you insure against it? Do you buy insurance on your house or business in case of fire? On your car in case of an accident? On your health in case of serious disease? You certainly never *expect* your house to burn down or to get in a wreck or to have serious health problems, but most people consider it only prudent to insure themselves against these possibilities.

For the most part, the statistical probabilities that Year 2000 damages will occur far exceed the chances of any of the other hazards you would routinely insure against. And in this case, we even have the luxury of knowing roughly when the problems are likely to occur. It would seem, therefore, massively imprudent to fail to "insure" yourself against these possible Y2K outcomes. Remember the Bible's words of wisdom: "A prudent man foresees the difficulties ahead and prepares for them; the simpleton goes blindly on and suffers the consequences" (Proverbs 13:16, TLB).

PREPARING YOUR HOME AND FAMILY

For most of us, this may be one of the most basic but challenging aspects of preparing for Y2K because it involves taking concrete, personal actions beyond what we consider the norm. While we can easily justify the need to prepare our business or organization against Year 2000 problems, it may somehow seem strange to take the necessary actions to ready our homes and families. However, remember that there are already millions of people around the world who take certain "family-readiness" actions for granted. Residents of the blizzard-stricken northwestern U.S. would consider someone foolish who didn't keep several weeks' worth of food on hand. Residents of certain rural areas routinely store potable water in case filtration systems are temporarily disrupted. And even in our biggest cities, people keep flashlights and candles nearby in case storms knock out power for a few hours.

For family and household readiness, here are the steps recommended by nearly all Y2K observers:

1. Assess physical household vulnerabilities;
2. Store necessities;
3. Prepare financially;
4. Maintain information records.

1. ASSESS PHYSICAL HOUSEHOLD VULNERABILITIES

Just as a business would evaluate its Y2K vulnerabilities from top to bottom, so should every individual household. Families should check their physical homes and possessions right away to allow time to correct any problems.

The most likely household vulnerabilities may include: (1) embedded microchips in personal possessions, especially those at-risk items that seem to have date functions; (2) individual computers and software; (3) "inputs" to the household (such as utilities). In some cases, you may also want to assess your physical surroundings.

Check all essential at-risk items.

List and check all essential and at-risk automated items to be sure they will work properly come January 1, 2000, then fix or replace the ones that won't. The most obvious way to tell a potentially at-risk item is if it has a date function of some kind (experts warn, however, that some items you would never consider date-sensitive may in fact encounter problems). Ed and Jennifer Yourdon's bestselling book, *Time Bomb 2000,* suggests how to identify potential embedded systems:

> If your household appliance, office machine or apartment-building elevator has an LCD display (e.g. a bright green or bright red display that tells you the temperature of your oven, or the phone number being dialed on your office phone, or the floor number of your elevator), then it probably has an embedded system. If the LCD display shows the calendar date, it's a dead giveaway that it's year-sensitive, and thus Year-2000-vulnerable. And even if it doesn't display the date, it may be Year-2000-vulnerable. The other thing to ask yourself is: *Does the device exhibit intelligent behavior?*... [which means it is] a device that responds in different ways to different environmental conditions—and in particular to different time-oriented schedules.[1]

The list of products you consider important should go beyond the fancy consumer products such as VCRs or fax machines. You should also make a list of all the items that keep your household running, such as your furnace, refrigerator, septic system, and so on. (See the Cassandra Project's Web site for suggestions.)

There are two ways of checking for Y2K compliance. One is to call the place of purchase or the manufacturer of your product and ask if your item will work when the new century arrives. You are likely to find this method quite frustrating. Unfortunately, because their products may have been made with chips from several different companies—some compliant and some not—many manufacturers themselves are unaware of whether their products will work. And some companies are simply unprepared to answer such questions at this point, although there are others that are forthrightly discussing compliance scenarios on their Web sites. The best advice: Be suspicious of glib assurances and be persistent. If an item is particularly important to you, all the positive assurances in the world won't matter if the item doesn't actually function when January 1, 2000, rolls around.

The second method is to self test—to go around your house and reset the dates on everything. That is, to set the dates to December 31, 11:59 P.M., and see what happens when they roll over. The only problem with this method is that the item might actually sustain damage if it isn't Year-2000 compliant. Bruce Webster, chairman of the Washington Year 2000 Group, told the following story on *The 700 Club* in July 1998:

> I have a friend...who has gone around her house testing anything that she can set a date on. She took her camcorder and she advanced the date to see what would happen. Well, it hit midnight, December 31, 1999, and it opened up and ejected the tape. She said, "Oh, that's amusing," and she tried to put it back in. Well, the camcorder had frozen in the eject position. Nothing she could do—changing the date or whatever—would fix it again. She finally had to send it back to the factory for repairs, after which her husband said, "Please don't do that again."

As Webster's story illustrates, it is important to allow enough time for glitches to be discovered and dealt with. You can just imagine the repair waiting times that will be likely as 1999 progresses, when everyone in the country sends their noncompliant microwaves or telephones to the factories to be fixed! Certain items with embedded chips are at risk only if they are actually in operation or plugged in during the rollover, so to be doubly safe you may want to simply unplug or turn everything off during that time.

In general, the most important possession of any household (other than the house) is the car. It is unclear at this time whether an automobile will truly be at risk, but given your car's importance it seems only prudent to check it out as well. I have seen several pieces of evidence indicating that, in rare cases, some very simple Y2K problems could prevent cars from starting.

Unfortunately it is outside the scope of this book to address specific product risks. However, it seems extremely likely that, as Y2K fever spreads in 1999, lists of vulnerable products will become available in all sorts of consumer guides. Keep your eyes open, but start your checking and replacing now. As Paloma O'Riley noted in a July 1998 *700 Club* interview, "As demand increases, the ability to meet that demand diminishes, unless business has time to gear up to meet it. So the earlier we start, the more [advance] time they have, and the better able they are to meet demand."

Check your personal computer and software.

Some personal computers (although not Macintoshes) are expected to have hardware problems, and many software applications (including Macintosh) will have glitches as well. Some of these will be so minor that you may not even notice them, while others could be quite problematic. Again, you should check everything of importance to you. Greenwich Mean Time, a leading Y2K research firm, has found that while 11 percent of brand-new PCs have hardware Y2K problems, hardware constitutes only a small fraction of the overall concern. In fact, what runs on the computer (applications, data, etc.) constitutes 98 percent of the identified Y2K personal computer problems. Most software manufacturers are starting to address their specific known problems and, in some cases, provide downloadable fixes for newer releases on their Web sites. It is likely that retail stores also will become more aware of specific problem areas as the rollover approaches. Unfortunately, software manufacturers in general will have little sympathy for someone running noncompliant, older software; they probably just expect you to shell out for upgrades.

To check your computer hardware, you will have to reset the machine's internal clock. It is *extremely* important that you first back up your machine's system software, applications, and documents, then follow the directions carefully for resetting the clock. (A suggested protocol is outlined in the appendix.) You may want to have a professional help you; some Y2K problems could cripple your very expensive PC during testing.

Assess your "inputs."

Remember, when it comes to Y2K, you are only as ready as those you do business with. Statistically, it currently appears that your *most likely* vulnerabilities will arise from the unpreparedness of those who service your household in some way—your utilities, government services, local supermarkets, and so on. We'll address this important issue in greater detail in a moment.

Assess your physical surroundings.

It is not impossible that Y2K could cause a measure of social unrest. Obviously, this is quite possible if the Lord actually intends to use this event to humble our nation. Depending on where you live, and in light of the more negative Y2K scenarios, you may want to consider steps to enhance the physical safety of your loved ones. As Christians, of course, we share in the security of our Lord and should not live in fear or anxiety. However, God's Word does tell us that a prudent person is one who foresees danger and takes obvious precautions (Proverbs 13:16). In other words: trust in God but use the brain he's given you.

As you have read in this book, I believe that most believers should stay put during the potential Y2K crisis in order to minister to their neighbors and bless their communities. I realize, however, that this is a highly subjective area and that you may have specific circumstances that warrant another course of action. As Year 2000 draws closer, I encourage you to prayerfully consider your potential responses under varying scenarios. There may in fact be situations from which you should try to protect yourself and others, and there may be ways that those in safer areas can provide shelter and protection.

Certainly, no one would blame a young parent for wanting to escape harm to protect his or her children. As Y2K columnist Victor Porlier pointed out to me:

> In advance of the destruction of Jerusalem in A.D. 70, some Christians left the city to minister and evangelize in other areas. Others stayed and ministered to one another as well as the unconverted. God does not have a one-size-fits-all calling on his children. We must find our guidance about where to be on January 1, 2000, from a deep familiarity with Scripture, from an intimate and continuing prayer life, and from seeking wisdom in a multitude of counselors.

As we prayerfully consider the role God has for each of us in the coming months, we should ask him for both guidance and courage. And we must remember Peter's counsel that we not necessarily shy away from physical risk:

> If you suffer for doing right and are patient...[during it,] God is pleased with you. This suffering is all part of what God has called you to. Christ, who suffered

for you, is your example. Follow in his steps. He never sinned, and he never deceived anyone. He did not retaliate when he was insulted. When he suffered, he did not threaten to get even. He left his case in the hands of God, who always judges fairly. (1 Peter 2:20–23)

2. STORE NECESSITIES

Mitigate risk of disruption in essential goods and services by storing necessities, developing contingency plans, and preparing financially and informationally. At the least, prepare for disruptions of a few weeks to a few months, for your family *and* several others.

A household's most important vulnerabilities will be: (1) the possibility of unavailable food, water, and medicine, and the possible disruption in power, telephone, and other necessary services; (2) financial hardships arising from Y2K disruptions—such as late or incorrect paychecks, bank account glitches, and temporary or permanent loss of employment; and (3) the risk of information losses or mixups arising from garbled computerized records.

Determine what your necessities are—in other words, those things you truly would have a hard time living without. Sit down with a pad of paper, your checkbook, and your last few credit card statements; review every expenditure for the last three months and list everything you have spent money on, including items purchased with cash. Then carefully and prayerfully go back through that list and place a check mark beside every item or service you cannot live without or every expenditure you must continue. A few guidelines:

- The number of "truly necessary" items will be surprisingly few, as there are actually very few things you can't live without, such as food, water, and shelter. If you have specialized needs, such as a medical condition or young children, you will probably list your medicine, medical supplies, or diapers. Finally, you might want to add other important items such as gasoline for the car or fuel for cooking.
- Next, you will probably want to add such critical services as telephone, power, and other utilities.
- Examples of expenditures you must continue will include such items as tithe, mortgage or rent, loan or credit card payments, and other specialized payments such as for your elderly mother in a nursing home.

Now that you have your list of physical needs, determine how much you will need to store to feel confident that your family will be provided for during disruptions of a few weeks to a few months. Then double or triple that amount so you can plan on aiding others as well. In a recent conversation about storing basic provisions for Y2K, Tim Keller, senior pastor of Redeemer Presbyterian Church in New York City, shared this advice:

> Don't get ready just for your family; get ready for two or three other families. I believe people *do* want to say that they'll be ready for their own families, in case there really are these shortages. Well, it would be selfish to only be ready for yourself: get ready for some people who aren't. Whatever degree of concern you come to after you've read the facts, and whatever preparations you are persuaded you need to make for yourself, you need to also make for two or three other families. If you are a Christian...prepare double or triple.

Keller hits on a crucial point: Every family will have to prayerfully determine the appropriate depth of their own preparation. Because only God knows what the end result will be, only he knows if shortages or disruptions will last a week or a year. Every family will have to determine what is possible for them to do. You should be aware that some leading experts on Y2K preparation, such as Paloma O'Riley of the Cassandra Project, recommend preparing for six months of disruptions. While that may seem extreme, it is true that if you gamble on only a few weeks and the reality is a few months, the consequences of your choice are pretty severe. It is far better, as nearly every Y2K expert says, to "hope [pray] for the best, but prepare for the worst."

Also, Jim Lord points out, "These preparations have very little downside. Having critical goods stored is a good practice even if Y2K did not exist. If Y2K ends up being nothing but a hiccup, eat the food. Drink the water. Spend the cash you have set aside."

Larry Burkett provides some practical insight on both the type and length of food storage:

> If you're going to store food, don't necessarily buy freeze-dried, dehydrated food—because if this thing doesn't happen, you're probably not going to eat it. I know too many people who bought that stuff back in the seventies, and they still have a garage full of freeze-dried food that nobody will ever eat. So what's the alternative? Well, store dried beans, store canned goods—things that will last a long time. Don't stock up as if this thing's going to last a full year. If it's going to be a year, there will not be a building standing in any metro area in the world, and certainly not in America. It's not going to last a year, but it could last a month, or two or three. So store enough food and water to get through that period. Now, most city people are not going to be able to put in wells. And if you do, and Y2K doesn't happen, what you've got is an embarrassing $5000 well out back. But it doesn't cost you very much to lay in 150 or 200 gallons of water. Granted, that's not enough under normal circumstances, but in a crisis it's enough to get by. And you can do that for yourself and two or three other families. What I'm saying is: Approach it rationally.

Victor Porlier, however, argues that the uncertainty of Y2K should lead us to a more comprehensive approach:

> Every family should store up as much as they possibly can, because your preparations may not carry you as far as you think. I live in an apartment building in a major city. If I put aside enough food for a year and we did have major food supply disruptions, I guarantee you that my huge stockpile would be gone within thirty days, because I certainly know enough people in my building who would need food. Some people can't afford to put aside more than a week of food, while some can afford more than a year's supply. I would argue that the latter groups should try to set aside a whole personal food pantry.

Whichever approach you choose to take, you can see the importance of beginning preparation immediately. First of all, storing a few months' worth of food and other supplies for three or four families will be a large task—and a heavy financial challenge for most of us. We will be much better able to meet this challenge if we start immediately and spread out the task over a longer period of time. Secondly, distributors of bulk and storage-friendly foods (such as dehydrated or "survival" foods) are already reporting shortages and backlogs of orders.

3. PREPARE FINANCIALLY

The Year 2000 problem poses the very real possibility of financial disruptions for businesses and livelihoods—and therefore for families. We need to be prepared in the case that some people may not have complete access to their bank accounts for some period of time, that our credit and ATM cards might not work properly, and even that our means of earning an income may not be particularly stable. Therefore it is essential that we begin now to assess our financial vulnerabilities and prepare to withstand potentially major disruptions in our personal income and cash flow.

Your first step should be to investigate the stability of your income. Check out online or library resources available on your industry's level of Y2K readiness. Ask your company what is being done to ensure readiness—both for the company's survival and for its ability to process and deliver your paychecks on schedule. If you work for a midsized or large company, your employer should be able to provide you with its detailed plan for addressing Y2K problems. If he cannot, that's a telltale sign that the company may not be adequately prepared. You may need to be persistent in asking questions, at digging beneath glib assurances.

Remember that some companies behind in addressing Y2K may be forced to put people on "temporary leave" until they figure out their problems—leave with or without pay. Prayerfully determine your degree of assurance regarding the stability of your income; if you are deeply concerned over its possible interruption, you may wish to consider a job change. One major downside to a job change is that you will have a lower level of seniority in a new job—which could work against you if your new employer also must instigate "leaves" or corporate downsizing.

Please pray and seek trustworthy counsel, as every situation is different and this book cannot make a recommendation for your specific situation.

Your second step in financial readiness is to prepare for possible disruptions in income and cash flow. As we have seen, there is a very real possibility that you could experience delays in pay or loss of employment, or be unable to access your bank account for some time. While Christians are supposed to be financially stable and prepared at all times, many of us are just as unprepared for a financial crisis as our unbelieving neighbors. The approach of Year 2000 should spur us to get our financial houses in order—and quickly. As Christian financial counselor Ron Blue describes it: "The ideal financial situation is to be out of debt, have good liquidity, be well diversified, and don't panic. That is the same type of advice we've been giving all along."

Let's personalize these four "financial cornerstones" as we prepare financially for Year 2000.

1. Be Debt-Free

Financial advisors such as Larry Burkett have always counseled believers to reduce and eliminate their debt. The burden of mortgage payments, car loans, student loans, and credit card and installment debt not only keeps you from saving and investing adequately for the future—it also can stifle your Christian flexibility by limiting your ability to quickly respond to God's leading in your life. With a load of debt, individuals are forced to maintain a certain level of income to service that debt. The guideline used to be, "If the Lord called you to be a missionary in Botswana, could you just pick up and go?" Most people, sadly, would have to say no—because of their material encumbrances and financial obligations. Today, as we face Y2K, the question could be, "If the Lord called you to care for four other families during the Y2K crisis, could you?"

Many of us have never developed a true budget with an aggressive plan for reducing or eliminating debt. If there ever was a time to do so, it is now. There are several excellent books and software programs that can help you systematically become (and stay) debt-free. You may wish to contact Larry Burkett's nonprofit ministry, Christian Financial Concepts, for some no-strings-attached assistance in this crucial area, or seek out a financial planner such as Ronald Blue & Company for a fiscal checkup.

Three or four months before the rollover, you might find it prudent to arrange to prepay certain key expenses to avoid problems the rollover might cause. For example, if at all possible, you might want to prepay key utilities, loans, and other critical bills through February or March of A.D. 2000. However, make sure you keep proof of those prepayments in case your creditors' computer system becomes corrupted by the Millennium Bug.

2. *Maintain Good Liquidity*

There are at least three very good reasons for increasing your household savings and ramping up your liquidity in the coming months. First, as noted, the cost of preparing for Y2K will be significant. Storing up necessary goods and preparing for disruptions in essential services—for yourself and two or three other families—will require a large amount of extra savings. You also may incur unexpected household costs if you find you have to fix or replace noncompliant items. Some families are even finding that the cost of *investigating* these potential problems is unexpectedly high, entailing hours of long distance phone calls to manufacturers, on-site visits by service personnel, and service visits to repair shops. Second, in the event of Y2K computer glitches in the banking sector, you may find your bank accounts inaccessible for a period of days or even weeks. Thus it is prudent to accumulate and set aside some cash reserves in a secure, accessible place other than your bank. And third, as Year 2000 approaches and plays out, you may find unexpected financial opportunities that you will need sufficient liquidity to take advantage of.

Our first good reason for savings and liquidity, that *the cost of your Y2K preparation may be high,* can be illustrated by the following example. Imagine that you were thinking of buying a $15,000 car in 1999, which you intended to purchase with $10,000 in savings and a loan of $5,000. But as you learn about Y2K, you decide to estimate (very simplistically) what Y2K costs you might incur between now and the rollover.

You hold a special family meeting to discuss how you as a family want to respond to Y2K. You, your spouse, and two children decide to plan for one month of disruptions in food and other shortages—for your own family, the elderly couple next door, and one poor family of five in your church. You estimate that your family of four normally spends $200 per week on food and critical goods. With economies of scale for bulk food purchases, you estimate that you might need roughly $1,800 to feed and otherwise provide for eleven people for one month. Next, you add in the unique costs of preparing for Y2K disruptions in power and fuel by purchasing some large drums for water storage, a camping stove, a few coal-burning lamps, and a few other items. You can easily imagine spending $2,500 to prepare for just one month of outages. As you think through the issues, you decide to set aside an extra $500 or so to be able to help others financially (you are concerned, for example, that your elderly neighbors won't get their Social Security checks and you want to be able to help pay their heating bill). That totals $3,000 for one very unusual month—and doesn't include setting money aside to prepay key bills such as your mortgage, telephone service, utilities, or loans.

Now that you have worked through some numbers, you and your family may see the need to save more aggressively to meet your Y2K goals. Your options may include: (1) continue driving the old car and delay purchase of the new car until the Year 2000 rollover plays out; (2) adjust your spending patterns to save quite a bit more money; and (3) set aside your existing $10,000 in savings as a Y2K "slush fund."

The second good reason for ample liquidity is *the likely need for cash on hand beginning January 1, 2000.* Most Y2K advisors, including Larry Burkett and Ron Blue, advise setting aside extra cash in case your bank experiences computer corruption and cannot grant immediate access to your account. (There is also a possibility that certain necessities will be unusually expensive due to shortages.) Find a secure place in your residence to store these funds. For obvious reasons, you will want to maintain strict confidentiality about any cash reserves kept in your home, perhaps even agreeing not to tell your children of this contingency.

How much should you set aside? Notwithstanding the simple scenario above, it is difficult to know exactly how much cash (and savings) you will need. I asked Larry Burkett about this.

> SCF: What should individuals be considering as far as their personal finances? For example, looking again at the Joseph story, they saw the famine coming and saved 20 percent of their income. Are there some prudent financial measures every family should be taking—and then if Y2K doesn't happen, no big deal?
>
> LB: In reality, for the majority of families, it's too late. They don't have enough time to save 20 percent. They're spending all they make. There are others, though, who can save that much. Regardless, what I would say to everybody is do what you can. If you can't do anything but put $500 aside, put that $500 in cash someplace where you know you'll be able to get to it. Some people can put aside $5,000, and some can put aside $10,000, $20,000, or more.
>
> SCF: Should they?
>
> LB: Yes, I would think so. I probably wouldn't keep $20,000 with me (that's too dangerous), but if I had the ability to do so, I would store $10,000 because it might not be just me who needs it. It could be my kids and their kids who need it, or my neighbor and their kids, because people are going to have to buy some things. Now, I suspect that some things are going to be extremely expensive at that time. For instance, if the supply of food is cut off, the food that's available is going to be extremely costly.... So you have to have cash. Therefore, to be prudent, you have to store some cash as well as water and food.

Given this discussion of keeping some cash available, we should take a moment to address a couple of key questions raised by some Y2K pessimists: Will your dollar bills still be valuable during such economic turmoil? And will your bank deposits remain insured by the FDIC? Some pessimists believe that, because the U.S. dollar is no longer backed by the gold standard (i.e., it is backed by nothing more tangible than the "full faith and credit of the U.S. government"), U.S. dollars will be nothing more than worthless green paper when the Year 2000 crisis hits. As noted below, it is quite prudent to diversify your investments and consider holding some hard assets such as gold and silver, but at this time there is absolutely no convincing reason to believe that a paper twenty-dollar bill will no longer be worth twenty dollars. If the U.S. paper dollar is no longer honored at its face value, then we've got a much, much larger problem than the loss of our personal savings. If U.S. dollars are worthless, that means the U.S. government and financial system have completely collapsed. Only the most deeply pessimistic Y2K watchers believe such a worst-case scenario is even remotely possible—and such a scenario is simply not supported by the evidence currently available.

Similarly, some people who may not be familiar with the U.S. banking system voice concern that "you can't trust the banks" and believe that you should withdraw all of your money as the rollover approaches. This is poor advice, particularly because an irrational bank run could destabilize your otherwise perfectly healthy bank. Although it is wise to keep out some operating cash as insurance against temporary computer glitches, banks are still among the safest places to keep your hard-earned money over the long term. As noted in chapter 4, U.S. banks are preparing urgently for Y2K, are being held to an extremely high standard of disclosure and readiness by regulators, and are judged to be one of the most Y2K-ready sectors of our economy. That doesn't mean they won't encounter certain problems, but there is no reason to believe that we will encounter a massive breakdown of the entire banking system. Even if your bank were to *fail* because of Y2K (a very remote possibility), as long as the U.S. government is functioning, your deposits will be insured by the FDIC up to the legal limit of $100,000 per account. Therefore, if you have your money in the bank, do not pull out more cash than you anticipate needing for the disruption period itself. Banking authorities are preparing to have more cash in the system than normal, but no bank can withstand a mass run on deposits. As believers in a God of provision who tells us to support our civil authorities, we must encourage family and friends to deal in good faith with our financial institutions even while keeping some cash on hand for temporary disruptions.

The third good reason for ample liquidity is to *take advantage of the opportunities—financial or otherwise—that God might put in your path as a result of Y2K.* In a time of crisis, those who are prepared may have a tremendous opportunity to prosper even while helping those who aren't prepared.

Ron Blue advises clients to see how the biblical principles of living and working debt-free and being "prepared for anything" can work significantly to their advantage. As an illustration, he describes the choices faced by several of his clients—owners of thriving companies which could, in the current market, use additional loans to leverage dramatic expansion. These clients, however, have been considering paying off their companies' debt and increasing their liquidity in light of Y2K. Mr. Blue shared with me his advice to such a client:

> Consider your risk tolerance. Some companies are going to profit, instantly.... Perhaps you take your liquidity and pay off your business debt. The cost is obvious: it's lost opportunity. If you take a more conservative, cautious approach and use excess liquidity to pay off all your debt, you're going to give up some opportunity. But consider what you might be gaining on the other side.
>
> As a comparison, one of my clients in the early 1980s had a demolition business in Southern California. He got convicted about not needing all the money he had. I said, "Why don't you not kill the chicken, but give away the eggs? God has given you the ability to make money. So make money, then give it away!" And he caught the vision of what he could do to benefit others. As we looked at his financial situation, the first thing we recommended was that he get his business out of debt. From a worldly perspective, that made little sense...but he liked the counsel and did it. All of his competitors were leveraging up [going into debt to finance equipment and expansion] because everybody "knew" that...with all the capital coming in from Japan and Asia, there was no way Southern California was ever going to have a problem. So my client got rid of his debt while everyone else was leveraging up.
>
> When the bust in Southern California hit in the late '80s, he ended up having a significant amount of cash, and he bought every competitor out at a dime on the dollar—at *their* initiative. Then we had the earthquake in San Francisco, and he was the only one in California who could really do the demolition work. When the Los Angeles earthquake hit, he was still the only person in the business.
>
> So I tell businessmen, "You might give up some opportunity. And if it turns out that nothing happens with Y2K after all, the only thing that has happened is that you're less wealthy. But if Y2K does happen, and you're prepared, what you've really done is prepare yourself to take advantage of the situation." Christians, if they handle their finances correctly, should always be in a position to take advantage of any opportunity.

While this advice was given to a business owner, the same principle applies to households as well. Jim Lord notes in his presentations that, if an economic downturn does result from Y2K, individuals who are ready with cash may have the chance to buy a house or a business for pennies on the dollar. As we approach Year 2000, it only makes sense to maintain good liquidity.

3. Be Diversified

Diversification of assets is always sound fiscal advice, but it is even more important as we consider personal financial planning for Y2K.

At its most simple level, diversification means that you should (1) hold a variety of assets, and (2) be somewhat diversified even within an asset class as a hedge against negative Y2K impact on any single area. Here are some basic recommendations for your consideration:

- As previously mentioned, hold some actual cash outside your banking institution—an amount sufficient to cover your anticipated living expenses for several weeks to several months.
- Have a significant percentage of "safe" financial assets that you can liquidate fairly easily (such as certificates of deposit, money market accounts, treasury bills, etc.).
- If you have equity or debt investments (stocks or bonds), go for stability rather than growth (such as blue-chip companies or conservatively managed mutual funds).
- *If* the rest of your finances are in order (i.e. if you are out of debt and prudently liquid), consider holding some hard assets such as gold and silver as an additional level of diversification.
- Have "backup" financial arrangements such as accounts at two different banks or brokerage firms. If one institution is disrupted, the other might not be.

I want to emphasize that these are just starting points and cannot substitute for personalized advice from a Y2K-savvy financial planner. In particular, investment strategies in this climate could vary substantially depending on your age and general financial stability. Consider the advice on investment strategies from Larry Burkett:

> SCF: What would you advise your average $45,000 income family? Looking toward Y2K, do the normal, prudent rules of investing (buy and hold, invest long term, allocate certain percentages to stocks, bonds, government securities) need to be temporarily suspended?
>
> LB: I try to look at it from two perspectives. First, the vast majority who try to time the market don't do well. So the buy-and-hold theory, over the long run, makes a lot of sense. The 1987 stock market crash is a good example. If you sold your stocks right after the crash, you would have lost about 40 percent of your equity. Had you held the same stocks for a ten-year period of time [following that crash], you would have made a 200 percent return on it. So the long-term theory, generally, does hold true.
>
> However, that counsel varies based on your investment horizon. My advice is totally different for a seventy-year-old person than for a thirty-year-old. The advice gets harder as you approach ages forty, fifty, and sixty because these people have progressively shorter periods of time to hold their money before they need to access it. If it's a thirty-year-old and his money is in a 401(k), and the 401(k)

is invested in growth mutual funds, my counsel would probably be to sit and hold, and just do dollar-cost-averaging. So for the average investor, if he or she is thirty to forty years old, my counsel would be: Don't do anything different from what you're doing; just ride it out.

Now, I *hope* that's not all the money they have. I hope they have some surplus in cash or in a money market account or something liquid so they can pay their bills, buy food, and fix their cars. If not, they need to take some of that money out of the 401(k) and put it into something more liquid. Let's theorize an individual strategy: Suppose this is a forty-year-old couple and they've got a son about ready to go to college, and their intention was to borrow the money out of their 401(k) to pay for college. Well, they may want to take that money right now and park it in a money market fund or treasury bills, because you don't want to *have to sell* those stocks after the market falls. Let's assume they are in an index fund and it takes a 30- to 40-percent hit during the Y2K rollover: they don't want to have to sell those index stocks at the low price, effectively locking in their loss.

For the *majority* of young couples, I'd say ride the thing out. However, for older investors who will need their money within, say, ten years, I would not be in growth funds right now.... I think the propensity for the market to go down is much higher than for it to go up. I'd recommend moving from growth stocks or growth mutual funds to U.S. government bond funds or money market funds until we see how Y2K plays out. We just don't know how much impact Y2K will have on the market. It's probably going to go down, and I believe it will take a big hit. Now, if we're invested in good-quality companies and *they* don't recover, it won't matter what we have your money in. It won't matter if it is in T-bills!

SCF: That's an interesting perspective—a really good point that people don't think about. If the best-quality companies don't recover, then something much more fundamental will have gone wrong with our economy. It won't matter what our investment choices were because even the safest will be gone.

LB: Bottom line, if you are sixty or sixty-five, you have to choose asset protection as your strategy over asset growth. Protection of your principal is so much more important than maximizing profit. So for those people, common sense would say they should move out of the stock market. They should move over to bonds and T-bills. The problem is, senior citizens need their money in a short period of time; companies affected by Y2K could take a big hit and stay down for a period longer than seniors can afford to ride out. A seventy-year-old doesn't have ten years to ride this thing out. So for him, I'd say he has to protect himself no matter what. Unfortunately, most people of retirement age are still putting money *into* the market. In my opinion, that's been a wrong strategy for more than a year. Granted, they would have missed this last year of profits, but the risk of a market downturn now is just too high.

[Author's Note: This interview was conducted in June 1998, when the Dow was around 9100 and price-to-earnings ratios were approaching 30 for the S&P 500—nearly double the level of just a few years ago. In the fall of 1998, as this book went to

press, the financial markets were experiencing a strong "correction," or downturn, amid almost unprecedented daily volatility.]

SCF: How about allocation among different investments?

LB: I would focus on asset preservation rather than asset growth. I'd recommend 70–30: 70 percent to safer assets—CDs, bonds, treasury bills—and 30 percent to conservative stock index funds. Buy quality—if you're going to hold corporate stocks at all, you had better hold stocks of solid, quality companies.

In summary, move to safer, high-quality investments if possible, but realize that "buy and hold" is still the best investment strategy if you have a long-term horizon. If you're young, hold your investments and ride out the potential market turmoil, *unless* you are relying on investment funds in the near future to pay for a vital investment such as your child's college education. If you are at or near retirement age, you should move swiftly to safeguard your principal; move away from growth (i.e. more risky) investments and toward more secure holdings such as treasury bills and high-quality corporate bonds.

The next category of diversification involves hard assets such as gold, silver, and other precious metals. Larry Burkett and Ron Blue have slightly different approaches to this issue. Mr. Burkett recommends holding cash rather than gold, while Mr. Blue advises holding both—although he strongly discourages his clients from holding hard assets until they are out of debt, have good liquidity, and are otherwise financially stable.

Mr. Burkett notes that gold has not been a particularly good investment vehicle, and that its uses for financial commerce are limited: "Our U.S. currency is *not* going to collapse, there isn't enough gold to do trading, and gold coins are too expensive. What are you going to buy with gold coins? I would probably still hold actual dollar bills. They have been the standard of value in the world and they will continue to be. In the worst economy, they may be worth less, but they will still be the best standard of value. So I probably wouldn't buy hard assets."

Mr. Blue advises clients who are out of debt to consider diversifying into hard assets, although investing in gold is not on many radar screens these days. He notes, "Our younger investors didn't live through the '70s and '80s. They don't think hard assets. Those who lived through the late '70s, when hard assets were a big deal, may feel it wise to keep some on hand. If you are otherwise financially healthy, it may be prudent to buy some gold."

4. Don't Panic; Trust God and Be Generous

Proverbs 19:2 warns that "zeal without knowledge is not good; a person who moves too quickly may go the wrong way." One of the problems with Y2K is that its very uncertainties cause extreme nervousness among some Y2K watchers. Ron Blue notes that "right now, the fact that the depth of the Y2K problem is unknown, *is* the problem—because when we deal with the unknown we're always subject to fear and panic." Realistically, the potential does exist for actual panic if in fact the effects of the rollover are severe. Mr. Blue and his associate Calvin Edwards shared their thoughts on how Christians can help overcome Y2K nervousness and provide a positive witness to the world:

> RB: Believers should remember two things. In times of uncertainty—whatever they may be—Christians have an answer. It may not be an economic answer, but believers always have *THE* answer. And second, Christians always have an opportunity.
>
> During every time of uncertainty or crisis, Christians should be the ones to say, "Here is the answer" with confidence and without arrogance—because it is not their personal confidence, it is confidence in God. And if the more dire predictions come true, we should be able to say, "It's okay. I know who is in control. And yes, I lost my money in the stock market, but that's okay because God owned it all anyway."
>
> We also have an opportunity. It may be that we have to lose things in order to say, "Let me tell you why I'm not upset about this. It's the hope that's within me." Calvin lost his home to a tornado a few months ago—he didn't expect it, didn't ask for it, didn't desire it. But as a Christian, he was able to handle it and provide a witness to his neighbors, to our own staff, and to everyone else because of the hope that is in him. It's the same type of situation with Y2K—we can be calm, positive witnesses to the love and sovereignty of God. This is a principle that has to govern the way we think.
>
> Frankly, once we're in the middle of the problem, we'll learn to live with it. So I can't get my bank statements for a month? Well, okay, I can't get my bank statements. So my car doesn't work? Well, I'll get it fixed. I'll begin to gather facts specific to the problem, and take positive action. When the tornado hit Calvin's house, he and his family became *focused.*
>
> CE: Suddenly we had fifteen things on our to-do list. We knew exactly what they were, and they hadn't been there yesterday.
>
> RB: The people who were anticipating the tornado were wondering, "Is it going to hit us, and are people going to die, and am I going to survive it?" There's a sense of relief once the crisis actually arrives, because then we know what we're dealing with, and we just deal with it.
>
> CE: Human nature is very resilient, very creative. It bounces back to deal with the reality that occurs.
>
> RB: So when I think of the Y2K problem, I am not too concerned about it because I will be prepared and will have an answer no matter what. Right now all I can do is try to figure out how it may impact me and our business, and I can determine what I and my business can do to prepare. But I'll have a lot more information, and I'll be able to actually deal with it, once it happens.

Our role as Christians is to provide an example and an answer to the world during any time of crisis—including Y2K. As Calvin Edwards underscored above, God has gifted us with extraordinary resiliency. We *will* find a way to respond to the Y2K reality once it arrives. God promises to provide for his children; we must trust in and honor that promise.

You will note that, as we provided a list of expenditures earlier in this chapter, the tithe was purposely placed at the top of the list. During times of economic uncertainty, we may be tempted to cut back on our giving to God's kingdom. But if God is still providing us with income, I believe it vital—even nonoptional—that we continue expressing our faith and gratitude by giving at least a tenth of our income ("tithe" means *tenth*) back to him, from the top of our income. This is one area in which we truly show in whom (or in what) we place our trust—whether in money and things (in other words, in ourselves), or in our sovereign, loving, caring, providing, all-powerful God. More than anything else, what we do with our money shows where our love is: "For where your treasure is, there your heart will be also" (Matthew 6:21, NIV). And think about it: if the whole point of the Year 2000 problem is God's rebuke of our distrustful and wayward hearts, we had better demonstrate that we are listening!

4. MAINTAIN INFORMATION RECORDS

Even if you scoff at the idea that Y2K could possibly pose a serious problem (in which case I doubt you would have read this far), the one absolutely indisputable outcome of Y2K is that computerized records will experience some degree of mix-up.

If there is one thing every person in an industrialized nation should do, it is to obtain and file copies of every record of personal importance to them—as well as any record necessary to prove their financial status as of December 31, 1999. Examples of those records include house and car titles, birth and marriage certificates, loan status statements, bank account or brokerage statements, insurance records, important medical records, and so on.

Perhaps most important of all: obtain and save copies of your credit reports from all three major credit bureaus—TRW, Equifax, and TransUnion. Remember, Capers Jones predicts a *70 percent probability* that individual credit reports will have errors. Because credit reports are so vulnerable to Y2K corruption and are so critical to your ability to obtain a mortgage, apartment, loan, job, or insurance, you need to do everything you can to protect your credit history. People who have discovered incorrect credit reports can testify to how difficult these errors are to correct. (The problem is that the credit bureaus are essentially giant repositories for all the information fed to them daily by your creditors—your bank, credit card companies, utilities, insurance companies, etc.—so you'll need to prevent and correct errors with both the credit bureau and the creditor itself.)

Save copies of the dated letters in which you request credit reports as well as the postmarked envelopes in which they arrive. That may sound a bit odd, but it is commonly used as proof of the report's authenticity and "as of" date. Likewise, you should always correct a report *in writing* (via return-receipt certified mail) and, of course, save copies of every piece of correspondence.

As you prayerfully consider your personal preparations for Y2K, you may find yourself entering unfamiliar territory. To most of us, the steps outlined above may seem extreme, and we need to emphasize that the evidence for disruptions is strong enough to warrant some unusual measures of Y2K insurance. The wife of one well-known pastor recently told me:

> You know, we recently decided—somewhat to our surprise—to do all the things people are recommending. Store food, store water. We may get a generator for the church. It still seems somewhat odd to us, to lug gallon jugs of water downstairs while everything around us is perfectly normal. But no matter how we look at it, we can't get around one simple fact: This thing is going to happen.

CHAPTER ELEVEN

PREPARING YOUR CHURCH, BUSINESS, OR NONPROFIT ORGANIZATION

As noted throughout this book, there is a great need for the church body and other organizations to prepare to function properly in a Year 2000 environment.

This is particularly true for nonprofit organizations. During Y2K disruptions, most profit-seeking businesses face the risk that demand for their products and services will decrease. Every church pastor, ministry director, and charity manager, on the other hand, must recognize the fact that the demands on their organizations are likely to increase as Year 2000 begins to impact society. However, at the moment these organizations (and, more importantly, the people they serve) are among the least prepared for Y2K and the most vulnerable to the types of disruptions Y2K might bring.

While nonprofit organizations look very similar to regular businesses under normal operating conditions, they may suddenly find themselves moving in dramatically different directions in a time of turmoil or crisis. When the economy slows down, private sector (i.e. profit-seeking) businesses usually slow down as well. Demand for their products and services decreases and they can't keep employees busy and productive. Staff may be laid off to reduce expenses. By contrast, charitable nonprofits speed up when the economy slows down. Demand for their services (free food, low-cost medical care, crisis counseling, emergency lodging) increases and, as a result, their staffing needs and operating expenses increase. However, their main source of income—charitable donations—often drops off just as expenses go through the roof, creating potentially serious cash flow problems.

If churches and other nonprofits are to survive and minister in a Y2K environment, then they must not only *react* wisely to the effects of Y2K, but they must also be especially *proactive* in addressing possible problems before they occur.

Over the past few years, the Y2K work done in both the private and public sectors has yielded a successful process for addressing Year 2000 vulnerabilities—with a multitude of resources now available to help private businesses. However, few if any resources focus on the specific needs of churches or nonprofit organizations. Therefore, in this chapter we will adapt the proven framework for addressing Y2K to include unique issues faced by nonprofits. We will also examine an actual case study of how one large parachurch organization has addressed and prepared for Y2K's possible effects.

In general, churches and other nonprofit organizations must prepare:

- to respond to Y2K impacts on those served by the organization; and
- to prevent or mitigate Y2K impacts on the organization itself.

These purposes are addressed in the two sections below on (1) preparing the church as a body of members, and (2) preparing the organization itself. (Please note that the latter section, "Preparing Your Organization," is designed for the church pastor, ministry director, or small business owner who must help manage the actual process of Y2K remediation. While written for the layperson, it is more technical than the rest of this book.)

PREPARING THE BODY OF CHRIST

Whether you manage a church, a business, or a nonprofit organization, as a Christian you are first and foremost a member of the body of Christ. We are placed within a church "body" because there are things we cannot accomplish alone and because the body has need of each of its members: "A spiritual gift is given to each of us as a means of helping the entire church.... There are many parts, but only one body" (1 Corinthians 12:7, 20). With Christ as the head, the whole body is much, much more than the sum of its parts. Fundamentally, therefore, no matter what your specific Y2K concern—whether it is the potential impact on the members of your church, your industry, the elderly, the residents of inner cities, or the poor—the best way to respond is through helping to energize the body of Christ as a whole. As Larry Burkett notes:

> What we can't do individually, we can do collectively...what we can do within the churches is far more than we can do individually. We *can* store more food, we *can* store more water, we *can* buy a generator for the church. And you can have a place to sleep if your power's off. Because in the northern hemisphere, if Y2K happens, it's going to be in the middle of winter. If you have a woodstove and extra wood outside, it won't be a problem, but if you live in a small apartment somewhere, having no heat could really be a problem. So you've got to have an

alternative. Our alternative is collective. We need to get through Y2K together, as a body of Christ, within the local church.

Members Must Act

So what can we actually do, collectively, as a body of Christ? The following ideas and description of one church's actual response will provide a starting point for discussion. However, don't limit your ideas to what you read here—use them as a springboard to other, more community-specific ideas for your own church or Christian organization. Above all, do not wait for someone else to initiate action. If the Y2K issue resonates with you, *God may very well be calling you to join him in the work he wants to do through Y2K.* Henry Blackaby's *Experiencing God* workbook study points out that "you cannot know the activity of God unless He takes the initiative to reveal it to you" and that a heart in love with God will be "tender and sensitive [and] ready to respond to God at the slightest prompting." Blackaby notes that God always reveals what he is about to do to those he is calling to work with him, and that this revelation *itself* becomes the invitation to join him.[1]

Under the spiritual authority of your pastor and other church leaders, begin today to look for what God might be doing through Y2K where you are—and for ways you can join him in his work. As you adjust to his call and obey him by exercising your gifts, watch with anticipation to see the great things God will do through you! As Henry Blackaby says, "The record of the Bible is not the record of what people did with God, but what God did with people."

Larry Burkett offers some ideas and describes how one church is preparing for Y2K. This may spark some possible responses for your church:

> Do the same thing as a church that you would do individually. Put in enough food to feed half of your church families and half of the other families in the community. You could do that. To set up food and clothes closets and to buy a 50 kilowatt generator for the church are doable things for 200 people. Now, nobody with certainty can say that "on January 1, 2000, this is what will happen and this is how long it will last." So you have to take a balanced approach. Granted, it will cost you some money. Granted, you may be ridiculed if you clear out two rooms of your church to store food and then you don't need the food. But you know what? There are always hungry people—you will always be able to give the food away to people who need it.
>
> From a practical perspective, what do you do if you're the pastor of a church and you can't access any funds to pay your staff? What is your contingency plan? Most pastors don't have one; they don't even know the potential problem exists. If I were a leader in my community, I would initiate community meetings; I would bring in people who understand Y2K and do everything I could to make my community aware of the potential Year 2000 crisis. We don't know how bad Y2K will be, but people need to be aware and need to hold their officials accountable.

One church in Georgia determined which member lived on the highest hill in the area—he had five acres on the crest of a mountain. They erected a tower on that property and banded together to purchase a generator to generate power for that tower. They all bought cell phones that also work like walkie-talkies so they can communicate with each other no matter what.

They also found a member who is in a raw-grain business and bought soybeans, wheat, and other storable grains from him. They are grinding it up and storing and distributing it. The mechanic in the church researched generators to find what would be most affordable and appropriate to power the church plant. Not only are they getting physically prepared to care for their members and others in their community, but they are making this information available to everyone.

Most importantly, they are holding classes to train everyone to share their faith because they may be among the few who are ready to help others with light, heat, food, and communication. They believe people in need may come to them for help and ask, "How did you know about this?" And they're going to have an opportunity to witness like they've never had in their life.

Other Actionable Ideas

The following are some specific ideas for things you can do to help prepare your church and community for Year 2000.

- Offer to develop and lead all or part of your church's internal Y2K project in conjunction with your pastor(s)—duties such as storing food or water, researching and purchasing a generator, acquiring alternate sources of heat and light, etc.
- Offer to organize meetings for church leaders in your area, where leaders can discuss how churches can work together to prepare, respond, and be a blessing to others.
- Offer to organize a general awareness meeting for the members of your church. Bring in a speaker or show an instructional video (such as Jim Lord's video, videos from the Joseph Project 2000, or the *700 Club* specials on Y2K) to help people understand the issues, learn to prepare themselves, and invest in your church's vision for Y2K.
- Plan how you will physically and spiritually reach out to your family's neighborhood and your church's neighborhood, in the event gasoline distribution is disrupted and people must walk or bike to their destinations. Offer to help your local pastors develop a "neighborhood church" concept, whereby churches will welcome those who are unable to get to their regular house of worship.
- Provide important articles and factual material on Y2K to your church newsletter to keep church members up to date.

- Offer to help your church hold training sessions on how to witness and serve others during times of crisis.
- Develop a strategy for partnering sister churches in different neighborhoods, whereby communities that encounter problems can lean on those less affected. This can be particularly useful if a wealthier church already has a sister church in a less prosperous community.
- Similarly, develop a strategy to partner higher-risk households within or even outside your church (households such as the elderly, a family with many children, or a family in a higher-risk neighborhood) with those who might be at lower risk, so that these families can receive help and even safe shelter in the event of an emergency.

Note that every one of these ideas needs to be initiated *now,* so that the plan can be accepted, refined, resourced, and ready for activation in the event the contingency does occur.

Further suggestions—including ways to specifically prepare for the less fortunate among us—are discussed in chapter 12, "Preparing Your Community."

Leaders Must Lead

Those whom the Lord has placed in positions of leadership have a special responsibility to address the Year 2000 issue—both in the management of their organization and in their ministry to constituents. Some church and ministry leaders do not want to address Y2K for fear of seeming unduly alarmist or sparking fear in their congregation. However, as with so many things, silence is not necessarily neutral.

On Father's Day 1998, Johnny Crist, pastor of Atlanta Vineyard Christian Fellowship, noted that our children need to be "fathered," and that if we don't do it, something else will. He said, "They *will* be fathered by something.... If we don't spend the time with them, they will be fathered by TV, movies, our popular culture, or their peers." The same truth applies to preparing our churches and communities for Y2K. People will look for information and take their cues from *something.* Therefore, pastors and other individuals who have the attention of the Christian community must take the lead in addressing this critical issue—for if they do not, something else will. For similar reasons, Christians should prepare to sacrificially serve their communities as Y2K plays out. Jesus longs for his people to meet the deep human needs of his lost sheep so that they might be drawn to his kingdom rather than to a beneficent government agency or a compassionate but false cult.

Ernie Fitzpatrick, pastor of Liberty Revival Church in Houston, Texas, has created a helpful model for pastors to develop Y2K leadership within their churches, which I have adapted below:

1. Prepare yourself (Acts 20:28): Study the problem via books and the Internet, and tentatively decide upon your Y2K position (i.e., on the scale of 1 to 10, the severity for which you will/should prepare. This will be dynamic and likely to change over time).
2. Get agreement of your elders: Share information and get the elders' buy-in; set out a month-by-month battle plan for the remaining time you have left; determine a budget.
3. Educate your staff: Orient the church agenda and staff meetings toward Y2K, explain the battle plan, and ensure that church members see that the staff is following.
4. Lay Leadership/Deacon Support: Introduce and build upon the concept of your church's Y2K plan/goals until you get full buy-in; incorporate ideas.
5. Body Development: Distribute credible Y2K information to members, then begin to mention in sermons and introduce the Joseph Strategy for your church. Get the buy-in of the body and assess the special needs of individual congregants by having deacons, support pastors, or lay leadership meet with the entire body through their assigned members. Finally, set up a Y2K Hurricane storehouse.
6. Public Serving: (This topic is expanded upon in chapter 12.) Gather several churches together and bring in an expert to speak; develop a special Y2K section on your church Web site; have members go to their neighbors to prepare them; conduct events to inform and prepare the community.
7. Counting Down: Have weekly briefings for all members; develop and add to the list of necessary solutions and strategies (on Web site); and continue research.

(For further information on LRC's leadership strategy, see the church's Web site at www.liberty-revival.org/y2k/. For further information on the Joseph Project 2000's community service strategy see our Web site at www.josephproject2000.org.)

PREPARING YOUR ORGANIZATION

Business, government, and nonprofit organizations alike should use the well-tested process summarized below to assess and resolve their Y2K vulnerabilities.

Although on a much more technical level, the process is basically the same as the foundation of individual preparedness: *Determine what your organization can't live without and address those vulnerabilities.*

What is presented below is simply a summary. If you are a manager in any business or organization, please read through the full description of the strategic process provided in the appendix. Also, remember that the following process description is general and generic and must be tailored for each organization.

Your *most important mandate will be to start immediately,* if you haven't already. A well-respected research firm, Greenwich Mean Time, surveyed multiple businesses and determined that an average company with 500 employees needs a bare minimum of 467 days of full-time, full-speed-ahead work in order to adequately remedy their Y2K problems. (September 20, 1998, was the 467th day before the rollover.)

Outline Every Aspect of Your Operating Environment

Before going through the process of addressing your potential Y2K vulnerabilities, develop a flow chart of everything critical that your organization relies upon to function—including everything it interacts with externally. List and personalize the following parts of your entire operating environment (some people call this the organizational "food chain"):

- *Suppliers*—vendors, contractors, banks, utilities, product suppliers, service companies, maintenance firms, etc.
- *Systems*—computer and other systems: business computer systems, PCs, software, servers, mainframes, embedded chips, telecommunications, security
- *Facilities*—buildings, elevators, printers, fax machines, photocopiers, other office machinery, audio/visual equipment
- *Products*—anything provided or conducted (a good or service) by the organization related to its mission, such as widgets, preaching, counseling, education, hot meals, worship, conferences, arts and crafts, medical services
- *Constituents*—recipients or supporters of the organization's mission such as customers, donors, members, attendees, congregants

Apply the Six Steps to Y2K Readiness to the Food Chain

The following six steps should be conducted with regard to every aforementioned part of your organization's environment—every aspect of the food chain—including inputs and outputs as shown below. As you work through this process summary (described in more detail in the appendix), remember that "you are only as ready as those you do business with."

Y2K: SIX STEPS TO ORGANIZATIONAL READINESS

1. *Awareness.* Educate and involve all levels of your organization in solving the problem.

2. *Inventory.* Audit your organization and create your checklist toward Year 2000 readiness.

3. *Assessment.* Examine how severe and widespread the problem is in your organization and determine what needs to be fixed.

4. *Fixing and Testing.* Implement your readiness strategy and test the fix.

5. *Implementation.* Move your repaired or replaced system into your "live" operating environment.

6. *Control.* Don't allow your organization to be contaminated by less-ready entities.

Addressing Year 2000 Problems

Suppliers | Systems | Facilities | Products | Customers

- Awareness / Assemble Team
- Audits / Inventories
- Planning / Assessment
- Fixing and Testing
- Deployment / Implementation
- Control

Prepare Your Organization Financially

Managers of any organization must take careful note of financial Y2K vulnerabilities, but those managing nonprofit organizations have a special responsibility. History has demonstrated that during times of economic turmoil, the burden on nonprofit ministries and charities often increases just as income (i.e. giving) decreases. See the appendix for more detail on what you can and should be doing to ready your organization for possible Year 2000 crises.

PLAN TO THRIVE!

As we have stated, Year 2000 doesn't have to be doom and gloom. While it seems likely that most organizations will encounter some type of difficulty, some well-prepared organizations are nevertheless expected to *thrive* in a Y2K environment—much as Joseph's wise preparation enabled Egypt to prosper in the midst of famine. As noted in chapter 4, the Forrester Research Group estimates that 35 percent of Global 2000 companies will be prepared for potential disruptions and therefore will have a competitive advantage that translates into actual increases in sales, customer base, and profits.

While nonprofit organizations obviously face unique challenges, it is not unreasonable to expect that some nonprofits will thrive as well. Whether you are a small business, a church, a ministry, a charity, or some other nonprofit organization, look for ways in which God might seek to *bless* your organization through Y2K—whether through an increase in impact, an increase in donations or revenues, or even an increase in efficiency and effectiveness. Professionally, your organization can be in that 35 percent! If the Lord blesses you during this time, plan to turn it right back around and be an even greater blessing to others.

CASE STUDY

HOW ONE NATIONAL PARACHURCH MINISTRY IS PREPARING FOR Y2K

While there are dozens of books and other resources on the market that help businesses address their Y2K vulnerabilities, there is very little specific to nonprofit institutions. Therefore, it is hoped that the following case study (combined with additional material in the appendix) will serve as a helpful resource for any ministry director or church pastor leading a Y2K effort for their organization. This case study describes the Y2K effort of a large, nationally respected parachurch ministry. Because it contains significant proprietary information, the case study is anonymous; we will refer to the parachurch ministry as PCM.

DESCRIPTION OF ORGANIZATION

This large parachurch ministry is located in a city of about 250,000 residents. Under the leadership of its widely respected president, PCM employs 1,300 people and has a budget of approximately $100 million per year. The organization is complex, conducting more than seventy separate ministry efforts including ministries to pastors and single parents, a radio program, and multiple periodicals for different audiences. PCM intensively interacts with the public, receiving more than 5,000 phone calls and 5,000 letters per day.

REALIZATION OF THE POTENTIAL PROBLEM

Until mid-1997, PCM, like many organizations, had accepted the prevailing belief that a "magic bullet" to fix Y2K problems would provide a rather effortless solution. In early 1997, several members of the executive management team became increasingly concerned about the potential impact of Y2K on the organization and on society itself. They in turn raised the issue with other managers and members of the board of directors. In the summer of 1997 it became increasingly clear that no simple fix would be possible; PCM's president then ordered an organization-wide initiative to address and resolve its Y2K vulnerabilities.

Note: In order to truly address all Y2K risks, you must do a full sweep of an entire organization, from top to bottom (including all inputs and outputs). It will be extremely difficult to do an effective full sweep and release the manpower and resources necessary to resolve all critical Y2K problems, without the full support and buy-in of the organization's top leadership.

The Y2K Project began in August of 1997. A group of five senior officers from various parts of the ministry was assigned to guide the effort on a policy level. This project leadership team (or "steering team") consisted of the vice presidents of finance and ministry information systems (MIS), marketing, product development, human resources, and operations. Several project teams were also assembled from MIS and user-department staff members to work on the various project efforts. These assignments required the commitment of more than 50 percent of the information technology (IT) staff.

PCM recognized that they would encounter issues involving organizational change (e.g., "This monthly computer-generated management report is noncompliant—do we really need it anymore?") completely aside from the technical efforts necessary to fix actual Y2K problems. In order to allow the technical project to continue unimpeded by management-change questions, two "streams" of the project were formed.

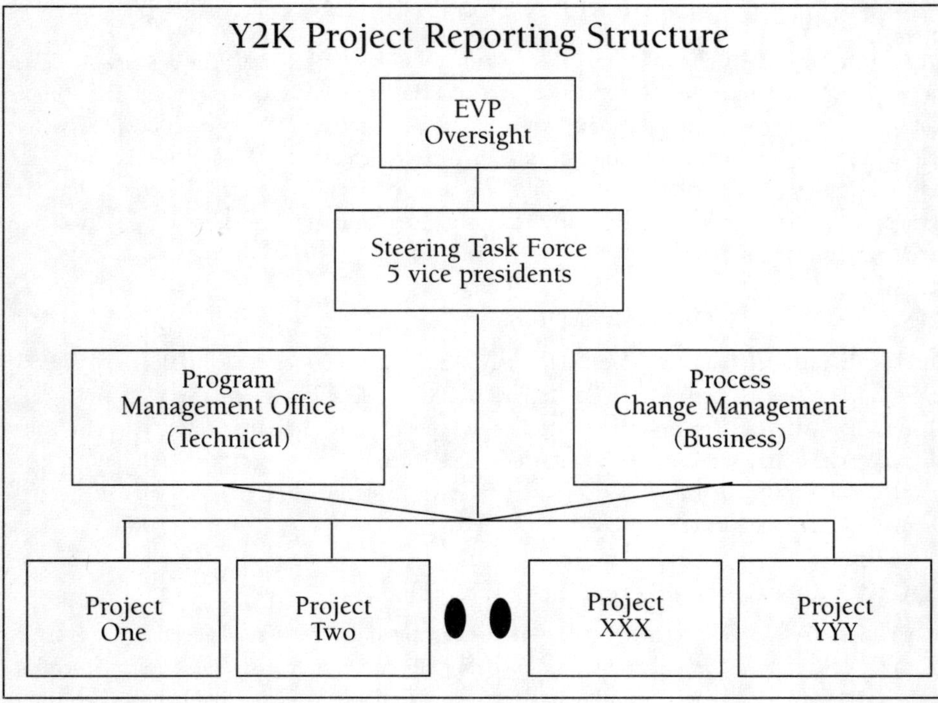

DETERMINATION OF STRATEGIC FOCUS

PCM determined that the Y2K Project's top priority would be to focus on mission-critical systems, services and items. The management team considered mission-critical to be "anything necessary to keep ministry activities functioning." They identified several important areas for strategic focus:

A. *Internal Operations*—everything internal to the daily operation of the ministry
B. *External Issues*—everything external that intersects PCM, from utilities to suppliers to constituents
C. *Financial Considerations*—the impact of Y2K on PCM's financial position
D. *Ministry Response*—how PCM as a Christian ministry would respond to Y2K
E. *Contingency Planning*—what PCM would do in the event of particular Y2K disruptions

Next, the management team made an executive decision: Y2K was important enough to deserve top priority treatment within the organization. Therefore, resolving Y2K problems would take precedence over all other organizational activities. The leadership team knew that the project would require significant amounts of time and resources, but as the vice president of operations noted, "We knew that the project would pay for itself within one day—one minute—if it prevented a Y2K problem that would otherwise shut down the organization."

A. Internal Operations

The Y2K Project staff, with the assistance of several contractors, conducted an audit and general inventory to determine what areas needed to be addressed. Then the leadership team broke the Y2K Project down into five subprojects, each of which would address a specific problem area, as follows:

- *Major Customer Service System*—database of all customer transactions;
- *Business System*—back-office system;
- *Ministry Information System*—support system, where all internal information needs reside;
- *Desktop Systems*—all desktop PCs and application software; and
- *Ancillary Systems*—other systems/machinery such as elevators, fax machines, and telephones.

PCM initially targeted a final completion date of February 1999 for the entire project and allocated a budget of more than $4,000,000 to address more than 1.6 million lines of custom computer code, 3700 custom AS400 programs, 801 Custom PC programs, 1100 personal computers, 143 servers, routers, etc., 395 PC software applications, 75 printers, and numerous other specialized ancillary systems. The strategy and status of the five subprojects are detailed below:

- *Major Customer Service System*. PCM's "Donor Accounting" (DA) database tracks every transaction with PCM; it includes all known customer history and all information that comes through their call center. This database is the most critical for PCM's ministry interaction with constituents and the general public. It had been built upon, customized, and gradually expanded since 1982, and houses an estimated 1.6 million lines of code. The system was riddled with date codes that allowed only two spaces for each year rather than four. PCM determined that if this application was not corrected the organization could not effectively interact and meet the needs of thousands of constituents each day—and be unable to process the donations that support that activity.

> *Note: Before undertaking a major effort to fix Y2K, determine what will happen if a certain system is not fixed. That way you can concentrate your first efforts on the highest-risk system, which in PCM's case was this main customer service database.*

Strategy:

In July 1997, PCM brought in several systems consultants to bid on remediation efforts for the main DA system. These bids were very high, averaging more than $2 million. As PCM management discussed this cost, the prevailing opinion was, "Why spend so much money just to make an old system compliant and get no new functionality? We'll eventually have to spend even *more* money to buy a whole new system in a year or two. Let's kill two birds with one stone by buying the new system *now* rather than fixing the old one. That way we get rid of our Y2K problems, get brand-new functionality, and save the expense of fixing the old code."

The old DA system had been highly customized, and PCM determined that they didn't really want to be in the "programming business." So in September 1997 they began conducting research to look for an off-the-shelf product that would meet their needs. They found one they thought might work and began a ninety-day trial of the new system in October 1997.

> *Note: This same logic is being applied by businesses all over the world. Instead of spending big money to fix an old system, they are preferring to upgrade to a whole new system. This entails researching either off-the-shelf packages or taking bids for customized systems. But note PCM's experience with this method below.*

During the three-month trial, PCM determined that the off-the-shelf product would require (like most systems) a great deal of customization. Furthermore, they realized that it would take significant effort to fully integrate the product with all of PCM's other systems required to run their seventy-two separate areas of ministry. They estimated that this customization and integration would take eighteen months *at a minimum,* leaving very little room for them to test the finished product or to correct errors in the implementation.

Thus, when the "replacement system" trial period ended, PCM management took a hard look at their situation. One vice president told me:

> *The whole purpose behind having a new system was to increase its "functionality"; in other words, it should allow us to do useful things we couldn't do with the old system. But we recognized that we had an immovable deadline for completion: December 31, 1999. We were in a Catch-22. If we insisted on all the functionality we wanted, we probably wouldn't have enough time to finish the customization by Year 2000. If we drove to complete on time, then we would need to compromise the functionality we wanted from the new system in the first place.*

Several senior officers of the organization, who had been responsible for information systems projects at major U.S. corporations, knew that software and hardware projects usually ran months late—even years. PCM's executive vice president said, "I used to work for General Motors, and I was involved with a lot of systems projects. None of them came in within a year of when they were scheduled to be finished." If the replacement system wasn't ready by the immovable deadline, PCM would be left with the old bug-ridden system and critical ministries might have to be discontinued for many months. They determined that, with twenty-three months left, they could not take the risk that their system would be noncompliant or nonoperational by December 31, 1999.

Therefore, in the interests of good stewardship, the management team decided to redirect their efforts and return to the basics: PCM would conduct Y2K remediation after all. The vice president of operations reported, "Under a fixed deadline, remediation was much more feasible because we didn't have to design a new system." That is, they would spend the $2 million-plus to fix the old code in the old DA system. But they would make the minimum investment, fixing *only mission-critical* Y2K problems. They would continue their search for replacement systems without the urgency of the December 1999 deadline.

In order to ensure that the remediation itself would be done in time, certain safeguards were put in place. First, as already noted, was the executive decision that management and staff would dedicate their first attention and resources to Y2K activities above everything else. Second, good project management practices were implemented as follows: the task was defined in detail, the right resources were involved, resource requirements were estimated, the task was broken into logical subunits, change management procedures were established, and (a critical step) success/completion criteria were defined. Third, the management review team committed to meeting each week for two to four hours to review progress and eliminate obstacles to progress.

> *Note: Defining success and completion criteria, and constant management monitoring of the process, are viewed as two critical linchpins in any effort to ready businesses and ministries for Y2K.*

As of mid-July 1998, PCM had been fixing code for six months, and had completed roughly 10 percent of the total task. The ministry hopes to have the code completely fixed by February 1999, leaving ten months for testing.

> *Estimated staff hours: 15,000 (in addition to contractor hours)*
>
> *Initial cost estimate: $2.3 million*
>
> *Revised cost estimate: $2.1 million*
>
> *Note: In late 1997 (when PCM's management team determined to fix the code after all), the Gartner Group was estimating the average cost to fix each line of code at $1.50 (although the estimate has more than doubled since then). Thus the strategy and efforts described above are in range with the typical experience. Further, unlike many organizations, PCM was able to lower its estimated cost by nearly 10 percent because of good project management, which included targeted assessment and concentration on genuine needs, and use of good automated tools such as Into2000.*

• *Business System.* The back-office system handles all of PCM's financial statements, inventory, accounts payable, payroll, and similar tasks. PCM had an earlier software release that was not Y2K-compliant. If this application were not fixed, PCM could again expect severe disruption to mission-critical activities such as accounts payable, general ledger accounting, inventory control, and accounts receivable.

Upon review, the easiest solution was to upgrade this application to a Y2K-compliant release. In order to accomplish this goal, many product customizations and interfaces needed review and correction prior to the cutover to the new release. PCM upgraded to the new version in July 1998, a process that took six months beginning February 1998.

Expected cost: $260,000

Estimated staff hours: 6,500

Note: Many businesses are finding the simplest method of Y2K compliance is a wholesale upgrade to a Y2K-compliant release, as long as their vendor is still in business and has a compliant version.

• *Ministry Information System.* The PCM ministry uses a specialized application to support staff information-and-research requirements necessary to meet constituent ministry needs; it also supports correspondence management. The system houses all letter prototypes, all research information, and huge amounts of supporting material. If this application were not made Y2K-compliant, PCM would have greater difficulty addressing people's informational needs and be far less efficient in responding to correspondence to the ministry.

Strategy:

The Y2K management team decided on another upgrade. PCM currently plans to change from the current version to a new, compliant version by February 1999.

Expected new cost: $110,000

Expected staff hours: 5,000

• *Desktop Systems.* As with many organizations, PC-based operating systems and applications (such as Windows and Microsoft software) are prolific throughout PCM. When the Y2K Project started, the organization had few uniform standards for hardware or applications. Numerous models of PCs were in use; many were running Windows 3.1 rather than a later version. Up to five versions or models of any type of software application were in use throughout the organization at any one time. Some of these applications were Y2K-compliant, but many were not. Management knew that if noncompliant PCs, operating systems, or applications were not fixed by the deadline, there would be significant disruption to the work of the staff as well as negative impact on the ministry's communication network.

Strategy:

PCM committed to replace noncompliant PCs and servers and take their operating system to a new release, upgrading the entire organization to Windows 95. In addition, PCM is evaluating how to standardize applications and upgrade to compliant releases where possible. A team of IT staff inventoried and reviewed all hardware and existing applications in use, interrelationships between applications, mission criticality of the use, and strategies for migration or correction.

Through checking hardware BIOS and other elements, noncompliant PCs were identified and upgraded to Pentium-level equipment. An assessment of PCM's Local Area Network found its software and hardware to be compliant. The Hewlett-Packard servers were less than three years old.

For each daily-use application such as word processing, spreadsheet, graphics, and time management, PCM's Y2K Project team plans to choose one appropriate, compliant program and switch all staff members over to that application. For example, all spreadsheet programs will be standardized; all staffers who don't already have it will be given a Y2K-compliant version. For the remaining applications, PCM's team will either make sure the current version is Y2K-compliant or acquire a compliant version. This process is expected to take nine months.

The team is validating Y2K compliance by calling or writing each vendor, asking them to certify in writing that their program would function properly after 1999. This has been a time-consuming and not entirely satisfactory process; many of the vendors assured PCM that their products would be Y2K-compliant, but most could not provide a written certification (many companies have been advised by their legal counsel not to make such statements). A vice president involved in this review said, "Although we cannot be totally confident in the vendors' assurances at this point, it doesn't hurt to start asking the questions. At this point we're just trying to get the mission-critical systems fixed, and *any* information is helpful. Ultimately, the solution is to have everything thoroughly tested."

Estimated new cost: $465,000

Estimated staff hours: Unknown

Note: Many organizations face the same frustration; they are not sure whether their applications will truly be Y2K-compliant, despite assurances from vendors and suppliers. The changing comments of Microsoft (from "We're all compliant" to admitting the need for some fixes) have altered the confidence level in the assurances of software companies in general. The key will be to test all "compliant" products, with sufficient time for replacement if necessary. When checking PCs and their software, most organizations are finding that addressing applications takes much more time than initially expected. On average, hardware and operating system software constitutes just over 2 percent of the overall problem, while application software makes up 21 percent and data and data sharing constitute 77 percent.

- *Ancillary Systems.* Because PCM is a large organization spread over multiple facilities, they have a number of ancillary systems such as elevators, all types of office machines, security

> systems, telecommunications systems, and climate control systems. Similarly, PCM has a large amount of critical hardware—such as radio broadcasting equipment and mail sortation and addressing machines—that is software-based, often with embedded systems. Most of these systems and machines are recent models and are supported through maintenance services from vendors/manufacturers.

PCM realizes that determining which ancillary systems need to be fixed will be difficult, time-consuming, and costly, entailing a great deal of contact with vendors and suppliers. In many cases, the information sought is simply not available and there is no clear way to test the system for compliance. PCM is relatively confident that they themselves will be Y2K-compliant in time, but a lingering concern is whether their vendors and suppliers will be compliant.

Strategy:

The leadership team's first action was to develop an inventory of ancillary systems and determine which to investigate. They realized that it would be simple to tell if certain items *were* date-sensitive (e.g., if they had LCD displays of the date), but that it would be difficult to rule out items that were *not* date-sensitive. Any electronically powered device could potentially have an embedded chip carrying a latent date functionality, even if the end user never realized it. Thus, the team decided that they had to take an inventory of *all* ancillary systems and equipment within PCM, regardless of whether those items seemed date-sensitive, then determine which listed items should be investigated for Y2K compliance.

> *Note: Because of the difficulty of "ruling out" date sensitivity, experts recommend that organizations check every truly critical item whether it seems date-sensitive or not. The probability of problems with this equipment may be low, but businesses have in fact found latent date-sensitivity—and Y2K problems—within seemingly benign equipment. Thus, if the survival of your organization depends on a particular piece of equipment, it is best to make the effort to check it regardless.*

PCM used an existing staff infrastructure to conduct the time-intensive process of pulling together an inventory. PCM already had staff members acting as "MIS facilitators" within their individual departments; these staff were go-betweens for the information technology people and the "normal" end user. Beginning in June 1998, these MIS facilitators were asked to draw up an inventory of critical ancillary systems by instructing each staff member, "If something has a plug or a battery and you can't do your job without it, put it on this list." This process required virtually full-time attention by the facilitators for two weeks; because preparing for Y2K was the organization's top priority, management approved temporary replacements or fill-ins for the facilitators' normal tasks while they completed Y2K-required activities.

> *Note: Because many Y2K projects are time-intensive, take advantage of existing staff groups or organizational infrastructure rather than creating new structures. Making Y2K the organization's top operational priority will allow the organization to reallocate staff resources to accommodate disruptions caused by the projects. If the priority is not clear, staff would otherwise feel torn by the need to do their "real jobs" as*

> *well—and the project may not receive the appropriate attention and intensity to assure timely resolution.*

The leadership team then went down the list and identified which ancillary systems and equipment items were truly mission-critical (e.g., a high-tech calculator was not, but radio broadcast equipment was). On all items deemed non-mission-critical, and where the probability of Y2K problems seemed low, PCM decided to simply wait until the rollover to address any problems. This weeding-out process reduced the list of to-be-checked ancillary systems to a manageable size. Such critical specialized systems included audio, mailing and shipping, mail addressing/sorting, lighting, HVAC, material handling systems (conveyors), elevators, security, telecommunications (telephone hardware and software), point-of-sale systems, satellite communication, publishing equipment, and some fax machines, printers, and photocopiers.

In July 1998, PCM began calling and sending letters to the vendor or manufacturer of the mission-critical items, asking for their perspective as to Y2K compliance. Ideally, the leadership team hopes the manufacturer will certify compliance, but they will settle for any information they can gather. The Y2K Project's goal was to complete the check of ancillary systems by September 1998.

The team also began to strategize contingency plans. Between July and October 1998, they developed a backup plan for any important ancillary systems that might fail unexpectedly, all checking/fixing to the contrary. See the section on contingency planning below for further detail.

B. External Issues

PCM management realized that, in addition to the external suppliers and vendors previously discussed, they needed to assess the Year 2000 readiness of other external organizations and individuals with whom the ministry regularly interacts. Any external entity that had a serious Y2K vulnerability could potentially impact PCM's ability to continue its ministry. They considered, for example:

- *Utilities*—power, water, telephone service (domestic and international), satellites, radio/TV signals, and networks;
- *Business services*—FedEx, UPS, mail delivery, building maintenance services, banking services, communications support;
- *Vendors and suppliers* of systems;
- *Contributors*—individual and corporate donors (i.e., Would Y2K disrupt donations?);
- *Clients/Constituents*—those in need of PCM's ministry (i.e., Would their needs increase?);
- *Customers*—commitments for which PCM might be liable if the ministry was unable to provide an agreed-upon service (e.g., if a scheduled conference was canceled by Y2K disruptions).

PCM has begun meetings with certain external entities to investigate their readiness. For example, in August 1998 they met with the public utilities of their city and were relatively satisfied with their plans. Although the power industry has been of particular concern to Y2K experts, PCM was somewhat reassured by that representative's statement that they had a huge incentive to be ready, as regulators were going to pull all noncompliant companies off the power grid in July 1999. Despite these reassurances, PCM management is proceeding with contingency planning (as addressed below).

C. Financial Considerations

Because PCM is a nonprofit organization and thus fairly dependent on a stable cash flow, the ministry's leadership was particularly interested in identifying the financial ramifications of the Year 2000 problem. Several considerations became apparent, including:

- whether the money necessary to fix the Y2K problem would be available;
- whether the money required for the fix would need to be diverted from ongoing or other desired ministry efforts;
- whether PCM should delay several large upcoming projects (such as buying a new building for staff expansion), given the uncertain effects of Y2K;
- whether donations would dwindle if Y2K had a negative financial impact on PCM donors;
- whether PCM would face difficulty bringing in necessary revenues while expenses remained constant (thus creating a cash-flow problem);
- whether PCM would be faced with expenses related to canceled or rescheduled events that were disrupted by Y2K problems;
- whether PCM could position itself to take advantage of all potential ministry opportunities resulting from Y2K.

The first two questions were resolved as PCM allocated the necessary funds from the general operating budget. This allowed PCM to continue operating and expanding their ministry programs as constituent needs required. PCM did briefly consider backing off a long-planned building program in light of Y2K uncertainties, but the board of directors decided the ministry was financially stable, the facilities were necessary, and the program should continue.

In July 1998, ministry management began the process of considering the remaining, longer-term issues in order to include them in a more comprehensive Y2K strategy scheduled for development in September 1998.

D. Ministry Response

PCM's president and management team believe that Y2K might afford tremendous opportunity for the ministry to expand the scope and impact of its services. They also believe PCM can be used to raise awareness about the importance of Y2K and how Christians can respond. They are prayerfully considering what the ministry might do to address both the issues and the needs of its constituency as well as those of the community at large. That process was starting at the time of this writing, so no specific details were available regarding this effort or its direction.

E. Contingency Planning

In 1995, PCM spent nine months developing a "disaster recovery plan" for the entire organization. This plan laid out high-level business responses to potential disruptions to PCM operations—everything from very localized problems (such as losing access to part of a building) to more widespread events (such as a power loss in the city in which they are located). This plan is a living document that changes as names, assignments, contacts, and vendors/suppliers change.

The plan has also been refined as actual events have occurred, such as a 1997 loss of power to the call center. PCM successfully deployed the plan's recommendations to work on the current problem (such as calling electrical service providers and maintenance crews to determine how to restore power gently under this particular type of situation), check possible resolution options, and determine when to implement contingency recommendations (such as moving call center personnel into other offices). During this power outage, they also learned of holes in the plan that needed to be filled. (For example, their backup generator didn't kick in and prevent the outage. Upon investigation, they found that the switch was not connected to the circuitry the generator supported!) PCM learned something from the outage that improved their ability to implement their disaster recovery plan.

The leadership team decided to attack the planning for Y2K-specific problems on two tracks:

Track 1: In the interest of using existing infrastructure and resources, the Disaster Recovery Group was asked in July 1998 to review PCM's plan in light of potential Y2K problems. Because the organization is not starting from scratch, they expect this process to take less time than it otherwise would.

Track 2: The leadership team began to consider responses to specific Y2K scenarios and develop policy for alternate plans, asking, "If we can't solve an identified problem immediately in Year 2000, what do we do? For example, how long do we wait before we implement backup plans?"

PCM's overall contingency planning is built around three different crisis profiles: (1) a *perceived* crisis, (2) a localized disruption or one of short duration, and (3) a more intense or widespread crisis. In order to determine appropriate action within their contingency plan, PCM management is considering how each profile might impact different aspects of the ministry and dividing them into three decreasingly serious areas of concern:

Level One (highest priority): Life and safety issues, the ability to support critical/urgent ministry needs (such as preventing suicides, violence, etc.), any functions necessary to support PCM's income stream (such as the ability to take donations and process deposits), any functions necessary to maintain primary communication with constituents (e.g., via radio broadcasts), and employee and family communication systems.

Level Two (moderate priority): Print communications to constituency, maintaining relationships and interaction with vendors (particularly for accounts payable), employee services (such as payroll), and the normal ministry needs of the organization.

Level Three (lower priority): Everything else PCM does as an organization that is not otherwise identified.

PCM's vice president of operations explained: "The contingency planning process has helped us determine who gets first cut at resource deployment *now* and helps us determine the priority of people to talk to. For example, our Level One list includes our ability to take and process donations to continue the ministry. So we have to ensure that our bank will be ready and plan how we will continue to process donations if something goes wrong."

CHAPTER TWELVE

PREPARING YOUR COMMUNITY

Community preparation for Year 2000 naturally brings together both individual and organizational preparation, for your community's Y2K readiness will greatly depend upon the level of synergy between individuals and organizations. Consider two fundamental purposes behind coming together as a geographic community:

- *Prevent problems and maintain community cohesion.* Many of the most likely Y2K impacts will be specific to a particular geographic area. Advance preparation and planning is incredibly important to head off some of the potential effects of Y2K and to maintain community cohesion if they do actually happen.
- *Help the less fortunate.* In every city there will be a multitude of people who are particularly vulnerable to the sorts of disruptions Y2K might bring. Paloma O'Riley, founder of the Cassandra Project, notes that "individual preparation is for people who *can.* Community preparation is for people who *can't.*" As Christians, those who are more physically and financially stable have a responsibility to help those whom the Lord has placed in their path (i.e., their geographic area).

LEADERSHIP, SERVICE, LOVE

As with Y2K preparation within a church, community readiness doesn't just happen; someone with the vision and heart for this issue must take the lead and coordinate the work. Obviously, Christians have a directive from our Lord to take that sort of responsibility. We also have, as Henry Blackaby describes, the infrastructure, support, and compassion to make something happen. Dr. Bill Hinson, president of the Haggai Institute (a global evangelism ministry) also notes that, historically, communities have tacitly looked to Christians for leadership:

The word *parson*—which today we consider to mean a church pastor—historically used to mean much, much more. In the 1700s, the parson was the local pastor and/or Christian leader in the community with responsibility for the library information, financial resources, and counsel that kept the community functioning smoothly. They would adjudicate disagreements, collect and distribute food and money to the poor, visit the sick, dispense wisdom when residents asked for it, and otherwise act as servant leaders on important issues within their town.

As noted before, whatever role God is calling you to, whether servant leadership or an anonymous roll-your-sleeves-up kind of service, he will be the one to make it happen. In order to be vessels in his hands, we must aim for three fundamental goals:

- *Become informed*—investigate and inform ourselves of the potential Y2K vulnerabilities in our geographic area, so that we have some idea of what issues to address.
- *Build relationships*—not only build a network of informational contacts to help our community preparation effort, but also build relationships with those the Lord has put in our path. The best way to be in a position to love someone in their time of need is to have built that kind of relationship with them before the need becomes evident.
- *Be submitted to God*—walk daily in an intimate personal relationship with the Lord, constantly open to his leading. This is by far the most important thing we can do.

Remember that God doesn't need a perfect person; all God needs is someone in wholehearted relationship with him whom *he* can make into a perfect tool in his hands.

Examples of this are Michael and Debra Goldstone, two friends of mine who are just ordinary people with an extraordinary heart for the Lord—and a gift for friendship. Whenever a new neighbor moves into their subdivision, they take over a plant, some food, or another housewarming gift. Out of their love for Jesus, their love for their neighbors is evident—they invite their new neighbor for a meal or coffee, offer to help with moving, and make it clear that they are there if the neighbor ever needs anything. While they will mention their faith, they want their neighbors to see Jesus through their lives—or in the words of Saint Francis, "Preach the gospel at all times, and if necessary, use words." They want to plant seeds that God can use to bear fruit, even in today's impersonal culture.

We all know that neighbors—especially in today's modern metropolitan subdivision—rarely interact with each other on a deep level. People establish contacts at work, or make acquaintances in church or through recreational pursuits, but rarely know the names of the people five houses down from them. Even in that impersonal climate, Debra describes how God can use a loving approach to bring forth fruit in his timing:

> A family moved in down the block last year, and we brought over a plant and said hello. We invited them over and I ended up having a nice lunch with the wife, Claudia, but we didn't particularly connect on a deep level. I mentioned that we went to church, but it was clear that they didn't, and we didn't go into anything further about that. Over the next four months, I would run into Claudia from time to time and I would stop and say hello and invite her to get together. She would smile and say thanks, but we never really connected. One night, out of the blue, I got a distraught phone call from her. Her husband had just left a note saying that he was leaving her and their three children. Claudia was devastated, obviously, and didn't know where to turn. She said she knew I was a Christian and asked me to pray for her. I went over right away, gave her a hug, and talked with her for several hours. One week later, she gave her life to the Lord. Her husband eventually returned and, after two years of seeking, he came to the Lord as well. At first, when her crisis started, I was surprised that Claudia would call me—a neighbor she hardly knew—but I guess I shouldn't be surprised by that. If we have God living in us, people will see *him,* not us—and that was who she was really running to.

If we truly have God living in us, people *will* see him and come to us in their time of need. All we need to do is plant ourselves in their lives and begin developing relationships *now*—to whatever extent we can—and let God do the rest. As we approach Y2K, God will work through us, using the seeds already sown in these relationships to draw people to himself.

PREPARING YOUR COMMUNITY

So what can we do to be servant leaders within our communities and help our areas prepare for Y2K? The following are several examples, but again are only starting points. Observe the specific situations around you, ask God what he would have you do personally, and use your God-given creativity to spring into helpful action.

Develop a Year 2000 Church Coalition for Your Area

First and foremost, the churches of a given geographic area should come together to discuss working as a team to prepare and respond. The power of the body of Christ working in unity will be so much more effective than that of lone rangers going it alone. Furthermore, when Year 2000 hits it is likely that a given church will *have* to depend on other area churches for something anyway; it is only prudent to set up those networks and relationships now.

There are several ways of gathering churches together. Some communities already have a formal or informal infrastructure of interdenominational cooperation, and this should be employed wherever possible. Recall the last time your church or pastor met in unity with the other believers or leaders in your geographic area—for example, the National Day of Prayer—and renew those contacts.

If your area doesn't have a usable network, you need to start one. All it takes is a few pastors to gather in agreement that Y2K is a serious issue—one that needs to be addressed in unity by the Christian community. This core group can easily send a simple flyer to every church in the area, inviting them to meet and plan how the church can respond to Y2K on a ministry level.

The churches in the area that eventually participate can form a loose coalition, serving as both springboard and spiritual authority over many of the efforts of their members (as discussed below). While most pastors are obviously too busy to take on more actual tasks, they, as the "CEOs" of their churches, need to take the lead in the vision and governance of this effort. The core group should select an appropriate steering team of respected pastors *before* the all-city meeting. This will ensure the meeting is productive and credible and that the group itself is under proper governance once its work gets underway.

The nonprofit organization I founded, Joseph Project 2000, exists in part to help these community-based, Christian-led groups get started. If you are interested in starting a Joseph Project 2000 group in your area, or in linking with an existing group, contact us at *info@josephproject2000.org.*

Organize Community Awareness Meetings

One of the most helpful tools for anyone dealing with the Y2K issue is knowledge—something many ordinary citizens don't have. A group of churches in a given city or town can easily organize a Y2K Community Awareness Event for their entire area (in cooperation with the Joseph Project, if desired), offering it free or at a low cost as a service to the community. This event should bring in a Y2K expert or show an informational video on the subject, bring in local municipal officials to explain issues specific to that community, and generally provide as much information as possible as to what the problem entails and how individuals can prepare. In order to make this as effective as possible, try to do this on as large a scale as you can to reach your whole city or regional area and avoid duplication of effort down the road. (See the case study at the end of this chapter for a great example.)

Develop Follow-Up Task Forces

The large community awareness event should be only the beginning, setting the stage and putting plans into place for follow-up action. Community working groups and task forces in each geographic location should be established, led by whoever has an interest in those subjects, to address specific areas of vulnerability and serve as a central resource within each county, city, or region. (Again, see the case study for specific ideas.)

Develop Plans for Your Neighborhood

Help your local neighborhood organization think through ways to draw neighbors together and serve your own small area. Think through both preparation and contingency planning. For example, you might work with your apartment complex to investigate whether the apartment heating units have date-sensitive embedded chips. For contingency planning, you could create and implement plans to enhance your Neighborhood Watch in case Y2K disruptions lead to a measure of social turmoil and crime.

On a personal level, be sure your individual preparation for Y2K includes a plan in which you and your family can serve others in your local community.

Partner with Municipal Officials

Groups of Christians with various areas of expertise can partner with municipal agencies to help address local Y2K problems. One of the most Y2K-vulnerable areas—one of the weakest links in the chain—may be the services provided by your local municipality. Municipal officials, while usually highly talented and dedicated, are often overworked and underpaid. With their limited local budgets and staff, they are able to focus on only the most crucial items before them. Very few municipalities in the country have resources necessary to effectively address Y2K concerns.

While it is important to urge our municipal officials to prepare, we must recognize that they may need our help, support, and time in order to investigate Y2K vulnerabilities and take preventive measures. It will do no good to vote a hard-working public official out of office *after* Y2K disrupts our essential city services. Instead, we must volunteer to work with our officials and actually help them address the issues, in order to be as sure as we can that disruptions will not happen.

Partner Programmers with Government and Nonprofit Groups

A recently developed partner program run by Alan Simpson of Adopt-a-Charity provides a model for how experienced businesses and programmers can make their resources and skills available to community organizations, churches, ministries, and other nonprofits. You can work with them or set up a similar system in your area to partner needy nonprofits with willing technical experts. (Contact Adopt-a-Charity at *www.asimpson.com/adopt/chmenu.htm*.)

Partner with Other Community Charities and Organizations

While church members may be most comfortable helping their own mercy ministries, evangelism programs, and education centers prepare for Y2K, it is important that we as Christians reach out to the charities run by secular organizations and people of other faiths. There are many wonderful programs out there that are not operated by the Christian community—everything from soup kitchens to homeless shelters to mentoring programs for at-risk youth. If an organization is compassionately meeting the human needs of any of God's children, we should be involved and try to help them, expecting nothing in return.

Furthermore, many secular organizations such as the Red Cross are in the business of specifically responding to crisis situations. Church groups in every city should partner with agencies such as the Red Cross and the Salvation Army to plan for the possible contingencies of Y2K.

Reach Out to Small Businesses

As noted in preceding chapters, the small businesses that are likely the cornerstone of your local economy are often the least prepared. Make an investment in the future health of your economy by helping them learn about and begin to address their Y2K problems. Most small businesses would be more than willing to address the issue if they realized the potential impact of the problem. You can get them started.

Think of small business owners you come into contact with regularly—as you take clothes to the dry cleaners, buy ice cream at the corner store, eat in a family restaurant, or get your hair done. Ask if they have heard of the Year 2000 problem and discuss it with them. Point out any machines you see that might be vulnerable to Y2K disruptions and should be checked. Explain that it is not just a problem affecting mainframe computers, but that it could even impact the tiny embedded computers in the machinery they rely on for their business. (Will the ice-cream freezer quit? Will the dry-cleaning equipment or credit-card reader malfunction?) Out of simple desire to help your neighbor, pass along the checklists from this book or resources from the Internet to small businesses in your area that may otherwise be completely unaware of the Y2K threat.

Again, think of it from the standpoint of "Love your neighbor as yourself." If Bob at the dry cleaners happened to notice that the wheel on your car appeared to be coming loose, wouldn't you want him to tell you? Likewise, if you were a small business owner who had invested your life savings and countless hours to build this little enterprise, wouldn't you want a compassionate customer to mention a potentially severe problem to *you?*

BE WILLING TO STEP OUT OF YOUR COMFORT ZONE

To do some of these things, we will have to overcome one of the tools the enemy wields in his battle against God's purposes on earth: namely, the Don't-get-involved, it's-none-of-my-business syndrome. Deuteronomy 22:1 instructs, "If you see your neighbor's ox or sheep wandering away, don't pretend not to see it. Take it back to its owner." The apostle Paul writes, "Look not only to your own interests, but also to the interests of others" (Philippians 2:4, NIV). If we see our brother's business at risk of Y2K disruption, we should show him a simple Y2K business guide. If we see our neighbors having no awareness of Year 2000, we should offer to show them a video on the subject. If we see that a retired friend's stockbroker is pouring their life savings into the stock market, we might want to pass along Larry Burkett's advice on investing in a Y2K environment. We don't have to be pushy or verbally assault them with statistics and quotes and speculation on an issue they may know little or nothing about, but there are many, many things we can do to gently, lovingly, and sincerely help others in our community.

CASE STUDY

Y2K COMMUNITY ACTION IN MEDFORD, OREGON

(Based on interviews with Liza Christian)

In May 1998, Medford, Oregon, was the first community in the nation to sponsor a mainstream Year 2000 Community Awareness Event for its region. It all started because one local investment broker, Will Reishman, a Christian, became increasingly concerned about the Year 2000 problem. He realized the potential impacts of Y2K and didn't want the community to be caught in an every-man-for-himself situation. Will asked Liza Christian and several other Christian friends to join him in organizing a seminar for ordinary citizens to learn about Y2K and how to prepare. His vision was to help individuals prepare themselves so they could then work to help their friends and neighbors, and then expand their reach to their community.

Fairly quickly, Will had a group of volunteers from all walks of life and philosophic outlooks working hard to stage the event. They found a local pastor, Charles Marsolini, who caught the vision and importance of what they were trying to do; he agreed to host the event at his large church, the First Church of the Nazarene. They asked two national Y2K experts, Jim Lord and Paloma O'Riley, to come to Medford and address both the facts of Y2K and how to prepare for it. Since the event had been pulled together so quickly it was not advertised particularly widely, and word was spread mostly by word of mouth and a few radio programs over the space of a few weeks. The organizers were hoping for perhaps 300 people to attend.

When the event actually occurred, the volume and diversity of interest caught everyone by surprise. Only 50,000 people live in the Medford area, but 700 showed up—a fairly high percentage of the adults in the area. A smaller meeting, where civic leaders were briefed by Jim Lord, was relatively disappointing in its turnout, but a few local government officials began to catch the vision for what they could do about Y2K. Afterward, Medford's *Mail Tribune* ran a letter to the editor from Jim Lord and Paloma O'Riley that read, in part:

> The most surprising aspect of the Medford meetings was the broad diversity of the attendees.... Young, Generation-X working couples and Social Security recipients sat side by side in the audience [to learn how Y2K would affect them].... For a day and a half, it was a magical manifestation of community togetherness. Political leaders across the country should take note of what took place in Medford. A powerful coalition for good is standing ready to take on the "Millennium Bug."

Because of the surprisingly high level of interest, the event's organizers admit that—in retrospect—they wish they had done a few things differently. Liza Christian, coordinator of the Rogue Valley Y2K Task Force, shares some advice for communities hosting a "Medford Model" event:

- Prepare a large amount of printed material, which all the Medford attendees were clamoring for, but which was not available in sufficient quantity or depth. Give all attendees a one-page flyer of referrals to other resources, and make other brochures, books, or informational packets available for purchase.
- Have two or three information tables staffed at all times by Y2K-knowledgeable people.
- Put a significant amount of effort into local advance advertising and publicity to increase awareness of the event. Get press releases to local newspapers, TV, and radio stations; follow up with phone calls to offer brief interviews. Take advantage of free public service "community calendar" announcements offered by the media. Write announcements or print flyers for churches to insert in their Sunday bulletins.
- Set up meetings with civic leaders to get their support for what you are trying to accomplish, since their buy-in will be needed both *at* the event and for all the local-area work to address Y2K *after* the event.

Most important, of course, is what resulted from the Medford event, as the community-wide seminar was only the beginning. The organizers asked prospective volunteers to sign up to help address the issue in more depth in their local communities (that area of Oregon is comprised of a string of smaller towns, each needing to address particular local issues). About one hundred people signed up, and fifty responded to a follow-up letter inviting them to the first task force meeting.

The following information about ongoing community action in that area comes from Liza Christian, who now works full time as a paid coordinator of several dozen highly active volunteers. Watching the path Medford has taken is valuable for any community seeking to both prevent and prepare for Y2K contingencies in their area, as Medford is at least six months ahead of any other community on this issue.

LEADERSHIP ADVICE

Ms. Christian provides the following advice for those taking the lead in their community:

- *Organize Your Leadership*. "You will probably need to find a local nonprofit organization or church willing to raise funds for a paid coordinator for Y2K action in the area, as coordinating all the volunteers, resources, fund-raising, committees, and community action on Y2K is an enormous job. Bring in people at the beginning with whom you would work well, and form a steering team—a dedicated group that can coordinate policymaking and guide the effort on a broad scale. Find people to chair the various specialty committees. In particular, if you're building a volunteer-based organization you need a special volunteer coordinator—someone dedicated just to organizing and managing the volunteers."
- *Organize Your Volunteers*. "Use a response form to specifically ask volunteers what their skills are, and give them some options to explain what they might do with those skills. Sign volunteers up for a three-month commitment to a committee or particular task force. That time frame is manageable for most people, and that way they can sign up for a second round if they are interested or politely step away if they have disagreements with the focus or approach of the overall effort."
- *Focus on the Essentials and Your Time Frame*. "Given our nonnegotiable deadline, you have to have a focus, announce it, and stick to it. Set all the extraneous things aside that tend to come up in committee discussions, since everyone has a different approach to Y2K. As an organizer and leader, say right up front that 'this is how these committees will be formed and how the leadership of this effort will function.'"
- *Do Triage*. "Focus on the most critical needs. Within each committee, invite experts from that area or industry to help assess the importance of the various issues. Prioritize the issues, then take the most important one or two and have everyone work on those first. Then go on to the next most critical thing."
- *Be Credible*. "Stick to a mainstream, credible approach and don't allow yourself to be sidetracked by (for example) all the likely philosophic discussions of the issue. Try *not* to make specific predictions, such as exactly how long Y2K disruptions will last or exactly how much cash every family should set aside. No one knows the answers to those questions. Instead, work toward preventing disruptions in your area and providing enough information so every family feels comfortable making an educated decision on exactly how much they need to prepare. To gain credibility, strive for excellence in your materials through quality control over the efforts of the volunteers."
- *Assess Donations vs. Fees*. "We have found that, in the early stages of people's learning curve, they usually don't want to straightforwardly pay for something—but they are sometimes willing to make a small donation. We have wanted to make information available for free so everyone will see it. We produced a brochure and were reluctant to charge for it, so we just asked for a donation. We are starting to think about charging or formally asking for donations for events."

COMMUNITY FOLLOW-UP

The Medford area initiated a significant amount of community action after the awareness event. Committees in several critical areas were created, and more are started every few weeks as new volunteers with additional interests arrive. At this writing, the following six committees exist—each chaired by a member of the steering team:

- *Utilities and Critical Infrastructure.* Investigates status of public utilities and infrastructure (such as transportation) on behalf of area residents and potential ways volunteers can assist utilities' preparation;
- *Health Care.* Investigates reliability and develops contingency strategies for the medical system; identifies local institutions (such as community nursing homes) that volunteers could help;
- *Food, Water, and Other Basic Supplies.* Investigates information on purchase and storage of food, water, and other critical supplies, and related issues such as refuse disposal;
- *Government Committee.* Seeks information and works with local government agencies such as the National Guard, FEMA, schools, fire and police, municipal Neighborhood Watches, social services, etc.;
- *Faith Communities and Service Organizations.* Interfaces with churches, synagogues, civic clubs, etc., to help coordinate their preparation efforts, largely on behalf of the less fortunate in the community; and
- *Education.* Takes information from all other committees and disseminates it via the Internet, video, and live presentations to generate awareness with subsequent action.

CHAPTER THIRTEEN

PREPARING SPIRITUALLY

As Christians anticipating Year 2000, it is important that we look for the work God wants to accomplish through Y2K so we might be instruments in his hands. Dr. Henry Blackaby and his assistant, Kerry Skinner, were asked how believers might join God in his work. Dr. Blackaby outlines three ways we must respond: by turning our hearts fully toward the Lord, by adjusting to him in readiness, and by obeying his call.

SCF: When considering what the Lord could be doing through Y2K, how do we join him in his work?

HB: Number one, it has to start in the heart. God says, "The one thing I want is not activity: I want you to love me with all of your heart, and mind, and soul, and strength." And that begins with your relationship to his cross. That's where his love overwhelms us. And that turns us back to him, with the release of our own ideas, our own lives. And we are his servants. If we do not begin there, he will never have an opportunity to speak to us, because we will never be listening. God always listens and is always ready to respond. The great indictment against the church of Ephesus was that they were doing all the religious activities, they were spiritually orthodox, but they had left their first love. And that's a problem today.

What would happen if God's people came back to their homes, their marriages? The joy in our families would reach out to the world and give hope and draw them, and the world would want to be there. So to begin, the people of God need to return to the love relationship.

SCF: Okay, what's the next step?

HB: When we return to him, we need to make the major adjustments that are required for God to be God of our churches, our lives, our workplaces. You deal with the problems and get to the root source of those problems. And in the love relationship with the Lord, you now see things as he does.

KS: So, for example, if you saw the Y2K problem coming, it would be helpful to prepare other communities. You don't know what the answer is, but you know you're ready to respond to God.

SCF: It seems that there may be some major adjustments necessary in regard to the Year 2000 situation—can you talk about them for a moment?

HB: Many do not see the problem. They see this as a technological situation, not a spiritual one. And I have been astounded at how God's people systematically leave God out of everything. Almost anything can happen, and the average Christian never includes God in the conversation.... There has never been a time in history when God let his leaders know what he was about to do that didn't require a lot of prayer and very specific practical adjustments. Whether it was the Exodus, or Abraham leaving his country, or the disciples leaving their work and homes and following Jesus.

And this is the third thing we must do: we must obey. The early church was obedient; they spontaneously responded to God's call. But that would never have happened had they not had an intimate relationship with him first. With that intimate relationship intact, it didn't matter what happened—they immediately responded, spontaneously, whether it was a physical or practical problem. But their first adjustment was a heart adjustment. Then they saw the problem as part of God's plan and responded instantly. So we've got to get our hearts ready for this spontaneous response, and to look for how Jesus would respond.

If I had a model scenario, I'd give you the Texas Baptist Men, a group of men from all livelihoods who network to help those in need. Those men got their hearts right with God, then they made themselves unconditionally available to God. They give no thought about what it will cost. They just believe that when God calls them to do something, he will also provide. So when the earthquake struck Mexico, they were there. When North Korea needed 100,000 blankets, they were there. Immediately, *snap,* just like that, they see a need and they go. It doesn't matter where the disaster is.

But it started with getting their hearts right. That meant they then adjusted their lives to God. Every assignment they sensed they were getting from God was way beyond their resources, but it never crossed their mind that God would not provide. It was theirs to obey and God's to provide. He's provided millions of dollars' worth of medicines; he's provided airplanes; he's provided blankets, and many other items the men were praying for. These men have seen miracle after miracle.

They now see as they have never seen before: they see as God sees. So they saw that these weren't just tragedies to pray for, but chances to come alongside God. They've built a whole network of doctors that will drop everything in a heartbeat and just go. They have lawyers, they have builders. They have a network of ministers and laypeople who affirm that "where there is a need, we will go."

KS *(laughing):* Bob Dixon, the director, has told his men, "If you don't have your passports up to date and all your shots to go anywhere in the world in a given moment, you're not right with God."

SCF: What would you say to encourage the average Joe and Mary Christian that they could be used to help reach the world during the Year 2000 crisis?

HB: Scripture. Jesus says, "If you continue in my word, then are you my disciples indeed. Then you will know the truth and the truth will set you free." So the Texas Baptist Men are Scripture-driven.

SCF: And these are just ordinary men...

HB: Ordinary men. Thousands of them. They understand that they are not their own, that they belong to God. And they have yielded their lives to him, absolutely and completely.

SCF: There are a lot of average believers who are just trying to make the mortgage payment, just trying to handle their two or three kids and their job, who just think, *This is a huge problem and I can't do anything about the fact that the Department of Defense isn't going to be ready for Y2K. I can't do anything about the fact that the IRS might not be able to process my tax refund. So I'll just pray and the Lord will take care of it.* How do you encourage those people?

HB: Use Scripture. They need to remember how God works. They feel limited. That might be so, but God isn't limited! God has the answer, so no matter how deep the problem, he is encouraging you to believe and trust him. I think that is one of the most important things for all of us to keep in mind.

Second Corinthians 6 tells us, "As God's fellow workers, we urge you not to receive God's grace in vain, for he says, 'In the time of my favor, I have heard you and in the day of salvation I helped you.'" If there was ever a golden opportunity to work together with God for his kingdom, that time is now. If you are one of God's children, this is your *responsibility.* God never expects you to function all alone; you are part of a larger picture of God's people in your local church. Where one lacks, the other makes it up. When one is weak the other is strong. But when you put that together, the weakest part of the body is a participant in the greatest effort of God.

Right now, when you release your life to God where he's put you, you can participate with him, and with his people, in one of the greatest moments in our history.

IN CONCLUSION...

In this book you have encountered a whirlwind of facts and statistics, possibilities and probabilities, emotional scenarios and hard advice on the Year 2000 computer problem. My prayer is that this has both sobered and encouraged you—and provided practical insight into ways we can respond positively as we draw closer and closer to the rollover.

Hopefully, as you have read this book you have been challenged to consider both your physical and spiritual readiness for the events of the Year 2000. It's possible that in your life, Christianity has been tied largely to church attendance and other outward aspects of religion. Even when you pray, you may still sense a void, an emptiness inside. You may feel as if you are carrying the weight of the world on your shoulders. You may feel distant from or "too bad" for God, but you want desperately to feel the tender, forgiving love he has for you. You may believe all the stories of the Bible and believe that Jesus is the Son of God who died for us and rose again, but you don't understand (or you secretly envy) the fervor some Christians have in their hearts toward him.

If this describes you—if you are not certain that Jesus is your Savior and Lord of your life, I invite you to reach out to him today. In the quiet of your own heart, set aside all the external aspects of religion, talk to Jesus, and ask him to come into your life as your Lord and Savior. In this way, enter into a deep and intimate relationship with God who loves you so much that he was willing to die for you. Accept his forgiveness and what he has done for you. Don't keep him at arm's length anymore.

Two thousand years ago, Jesus Christ looked through time, saw you and your need for him, and said to you: "Come to me, you who are weary and burdened, and I will give you rest. Take my yoke upon you and learn from me...for my yoke is easy and my burden is light" (Matthew 11:28–30, NIV). He also said he has been standing at the door of your heart and knocking and knocking, yearning for you to invite him in (Revelation 3:20). If you've never consciously thanked Jesus for his great love and sacrifice for you, if you have never consciously given yourself to him fully, do it today. Please don't wait. In your own words, run to him and tell him what is on your mind, and ask him into your heart.

If you are praying this prayer for the first time, or renewing your love for the Lord after a long time apart from him, please tell a Christian friend. Read the Bible (perhaps starting with the Gospel of John). Get hooked up with the many wonderful Christian resources out there—from the vibrant churches in your area, to Christian Internet communities like Christianity Online (www.christianity.net), Charisma (www.charismamag.com), or the Willow Creek Association (www.willowcreek.org). Any of those online sites can help you find a good church near you. And enjoy the most precious gift of all—new life!

As we conclude our time together, I leave you with the wisdom of three trusted Christian leaders on how every believer should respond to the Year 2000 computer problem:

- "The question in my mind is whether God's people are willing to listen. We know that unbelievers are probably not going to listen until it's too late, but are God's people willing to listen? The church is our element: that is a vehicle through which God can work."—*Larry Burkett*
- "Right now, when you release your life to God where he's put you, you can participate with him, and with his people, in one of the greatest moments in our history."—*Dr. Henry Blackaby*

- "While no one knows how the Y2K problem will develop, I'm inclined to believe it could be quite disruptive to the social order. At the least, it seems likely to produce an economic downturn with worldwide implications. But I would urge Christians not to panic or despair, regardless of the circumstances. God often uses hard times to accomplish his purposes. If chaotic times come, our responsibility will be to remain faithful to him and to spread the gospel of Jesus Christ in the circumstances with which we are presented."—*Dr. James C. Dobson*

Way back in the prologue I stated that this book was merely a launching pad to get you started. As you finish, you are at T-minus ten minutes, and counting.

It's time to get started.

Godspeed.

So will I save you, and you will be a blessing.
Do not be afraid, but let your hands be strong.
Zechariah 8:13, NIV

AFTERWORD

HOW THIS BOOK CAME TO BE

Let each generation tell its children of your mighty acts. I will meditate on your majestic, glorious splendor and your wonderful miracles. Your awe-inspiring deeds will be on every tongue; I will proclaim your greatness. Everyone will share the story of your wonderful goodness; they will sing with joy of your righteousness.... All of your works will thank you, LORD, and your faithful followers will bless you. They will talk together about the glory of your kingdom; they will celebrate examples of your power.... I will praise the LORD, and everyone on earth will bless his holy name forever and forever. (Psalm 145:4–7, 10–11, 21)

I think it important that every reader know the story behind this book. It is a story not about a nervous first-time author, but about the Author of all things; not about the works of human hands, but the work of One who flung the stars into motion. This brief section is just a note from me to you, that you might see and be encouraged about what God is doing in this world; that you might seek and join him in his work. This story describes just a small part of how God is working in the midst of the Year 2000 problem. May the world "bless His holy name forever and forever..."

A GOD-SIZED WORK

I first became familiar with the Y2K problem when I worked on Wall Street in the mid-1990s. I began researching Y2K as a hobby in 1995, but nothing really came of it at the time—nor did I expect it to. My expertise and training were primarily in risk analysis, which allowed me to recognize the seriousness of the problem early on, but in my perception, only "computer jocks" (which I wasn't) could really be involved in the race to fix the Millennium Bug.

Fast-forward—through a few years and a job change—to early 1998. My husband, Jeff, and I had recently moved to Atlanta. Through a combination of factors, the ministry I directed disbanded and I was left in a brand-new city wondering where God would place me next. Little did I know at the time that God was setting the stage for a truly God-sized work. While I considered full-time job options, I pursued independent business and financial consulting projects and continued my sporadic habit of Y2K-watching. I sent out résumés, made contacts, and prayed for the Lord's direction.

Over Easter, a group of friends and alumni from the Harvard Law School Christian Fellowship got together for a retreat, and Li-ann Thio, a Singaporean friend from the group, stayed in our home the following week. Li-ann began questioning me about my job path. We mused whether I should return to finance or stay in the ministry arena, and I found myself explaining to my friend that I was also somewhat interested in the Year 2000 issue. Given her many advanced degrees and attention to world affairs, I expected her to be fully aware of the Y2K problem, but she had never heard of it.

As we talked, she grew more and more concerned that no one in the Christian arena was focusing on the issue. She observed that, in the Bible, when Joseph was warned of the coming famine he was able to "save up" and not only protect himself and his country, but also bless the surrounding areas. Her point resonated with me, but I still didn't see what I could do about it. Li-ann urged me to write an article for *Christianity Today* on the subject; when I hesitated she refused to let the matter drop—even after she had returned home. (Those who know Li-ann will attest to her tenacity.)

It wasn't that I was averse to writing such an article; it just didn't click for me. I was experienced in writing but not in publishing, and I knew how hard it was to publish an unsolicited article in a major magazine. Driving in the car one day, I prayed, "Lord, the problem is that a *CT* article wouldn't be enough. There need to be tons of articles in Christian magazines and tons of stories on Christian radio and TV—but that sort of attention to one issue doesn't usually happen unless, say, somebody writes a book."

I know it sounds strange (it *felt* strange), but the very moment I prayed this there came the utmost certainty that this was what I was supposed to do: write a book on the Christian response to the Y2K problem.

Now hopefully I'm as logical and skeptical as the next person—I knew perfectly well how impossible it is for first-time authors to get published (statistically, the big Christian publishers publish just *one-third of one percent* of book ideas from first-time authors). But this feeling was so strong that I went home, pulled out three years' research on Y2K, and began writing. I had recently started Henry Blackaby and Claude King's excellent Bible study, *Experiencing God: Knowing and Doing the Will of God,* so I decided to accept their challenge that—once God invited me to join him where he is working in the world—I could trust God to actually, practically, guide me day by day. I didn't know anything about publishing, but if this crazy idea was from the Lord, then I knew he would do all the work to bring it about.

MIRACLE AFTER MIRACLE

You really should be careful about what you pray for. I saw more miracles in the next three months than I had seen in my whole life as a Christian.

Not long after I began writing, I went to a job interview at a Christian-led financial planning firm. I mentioned to the human resources director, Dianne Reisinger, that since I was in the midst of a "project" I wasn't sure of my availability. After Dianne asked me about the project, she promptly introduced me to Calvin Edwards, an executive at the firm who had spent years in the Christian publishing arena. Calvin was, understandably, wary when he heard I was writing a book (publishing people get approached all the time for help), but he was quickly taken aback when I told him the book was about Y2K. Just a few days before, he had been talking with a Christian publisher about their desire to publish a Christian response to Year 2000. After hearing my perspective, Calvin offered to serve as my book agent.

When he called the publisher (Multnomah), they were immediately interested and asked for a book proposal. Within three weeks, they decided to publish the book. In another it-could-only-be-God twist, Multnomah was one of the few publishers with the flexibility to produce a book quickly enough; they committed to having it on bookshelves by fall of 1998.

While this was going on, I felt a strong impression that I should interview several respected Christian leaders and include their insight and wisdom regarding the Christian response to Y2K.

Again, I thought this was crazy since I did not know any of these people. But I started making phone calls and trying to network my way in through friends of friends. Nothing happened; I wasn't getting anywhere. During a time of prayer I sensed the Lord gently pulling me back, as if he were saying, "Shaunti, a few weeks ago all you had was this crazy idea that you were supposed to write a book; now you have a book agent and a potential publisher. Let *me* handle this, okay? The glory for this entire work will accrue to *me*." For the second time I had to consciously give control of the project back to God, trusting him to show me, and open doors to, appropriate Christian leaders. Within days I was pointed toward Pat Robertson and Larry Burkett as individuals already interested in Y2K; after nothing more than a letter from me, they graciously agreed to interviews. Similar things happened with other leaders, including several who just "happened" to be coming through the Atlanta area as soon as I found out about them.

Simultaneously, as I kept writing and continued daily in the *Experiencing God* study, I felt a growing certainty that my book wasn't to be the end of this project. I wanted to do more to help individuals, churches, ministries, and communities prepare for Year 2000. I had been praying, *Lord, you seem to be calling Christians to preparation and leadership with Y2K, much as you called Joseph to prepare Egypt. What should that Christian service and leadership look like on this issue?*

One day, in my normal research, I ran across an article about the first-ever Year 2000 community awareness event in Medford, Oregon, a town of 50,000 people. The article described how a few ordinary citizens had organized a free seminar for residents and were thrilled by the huge turnout of 700 people and the diversity of interest. It was a very mainstream event, and they had brought in a nationally recognized Y2K expert to teach the community. As I read, it became clear to me that this was a model to be applied: churches could organize such events in their communities. I copied the article, but since the event had been held across the country in Oregon—and the article contained no contact information on the organizers—I put the idea on the back burner.

Two days later, I received an excited call from Jim Greer, a church friend who was also interested in Y2K. "Shaunti, you have to call Michael and Debra Goldstone [mutual friends from church]. They have some people vacationing with them this week in Atlanta who apparently just organized some sort of Y2K community awareness event in their home town of Medford, Oregon." At this point, as you can imagine, I started to literally quake. It was becoming increasingly clear to me that *God cares about Y2K!*

Upon meeting these Medford folks, Liza Christian and her fiancé, Jeff Sherman, I discovered that the entire Medford event had been sparked by Christians who just wanted to serve their community. These dear people had even brought videotapes of the seminar with them (who brings videotapes on vacation?) and gave me a whole day of their vacation. It seemed that I was being pressed to not only put this sort of model in the book, but to step out in faith and organize a similar event for Atlanta. Within a week, I had the same nationally recognized speaker—Jim Lord—lined up to conduct an Atlanta Y2K community awareness event. Shortly thereafter, Larry Burkett and the chief information officer of the state of Georgia also agreed to speak at the event.

Stepping out in faith, I asked my husband (an attorney at Bird and Associates, specializing in nonprofit organizations) to incorporate the Joseph Project 2000 as a nonprofit organization to generate Christian leadership for Y2K—an endeavor that would include just this sort of community event.

Of course, this posed the problem of who would do the legwork to organize the event, as I needed to concentrate on finishing the book. That same week, my husband found a reference to a panel of national Y2K experts that was being held that weekend in—guess where?—Atlanta. The organizers of the panel—a group called Y2KNet—were all Christians, and they agreed to announce the Joseph Project 2000 and the upcoming Atlanta Y2K Awareness Event from the podium.

After the panel, a few people came up to me to volunteer their help. Three stood out: a pastor named Dan Baker, and a couple, Mel and Harriett Guinn. I felt that the Lord might be tapping the Guinns to lead the effort, but since I still didn't have a real group of volunteers for them to lead I didn't bring this up. A few days later, when Dan Baker asked me to speak to his church, I suspected that the Lord would use that to raise up a group to organize the Atlanta Event—and he did! Out of the blue, Mel Guinn called, repeating his offer of help. Dan Baker offered the names of Kate and Greg Allen, a couple at his church whom he felt would also be good leaders. After I spoke in Dan Baker's church, a group of fifteen responded as volunteers and the Guinns and Allens agreed to take the lead. Strikingly—and a key factor I could never have anticipated—both couples had unusual job situations that allowed them to work on the Event during normal working hours. The Allens, for example, were between jobs and were willing to trust the Lord and work nearly *full time* on the legwork for the Event—without pay. (Kate soon became the Joseph Project's full-time executive director on a volunteer basis.) Shortly thereafter, friends from graduate school who were in Atlanta, Vernadette and Kevin Broyles, became very involved, and Vernadette's law firm adopted the Joseph Project 2000 as an official *pro bono* client. I was in awe as God brought the perfect people across my path, and excited to see how he would bless these faithful leadership couples and the rest of the volunteers.

As all this was happening, I had been updating my pastor, Johnny Crist. He felt that Y2K could be a God-given opportunity to bring the churches of Atlanta together in service to their community. He hosted a roundtable discussion and another conference for dozens of Atlanta pastors, who agreed to become the spiritual authority over the Atlanta Event and began to discuss how Atlanta Christians could prepare for service and outreach if Y2K indeed caused difficulties.

While it was exciting to watch the Atlanta effort unfold, I began to think that God wanted us to do more: to set up the Joseph model through churches across the country. Of course, this seemed impossible as our plate was more than full with arranging the Atlanta event, and we didn't have contacts elsewhere. We laid it before the Lord. Suddenly, we started to get phone calls and e-mails from Christians all over the country, asking how they could do what we were doing in their area. Again, we were in awe.

On September 12, after only three weeks of publicity, nearly 3000 people gathered at the New Birth Missionary Baptist Church for the Atlanta Y2K Community Awareness Event. God pulled the day together without a hitch, and at the end of the day 100 people volunteered to carry forward the work of the Joseph Project in Atlanta.

I could go on and on about what has happened—things so miraculous only God could have orchestrated them. Given his track record, I fully expect to see many more miracles in the coming months. It all convinces me that God wants to use this time of uncertainty to prepare his people, that he wants to be honored and glorified in the way Christians prepare for and respond to the potential societal problems of the Y2K rollover. May we be living examples of his sufficiency. May we be ready to share his love and his Good News. *"I will proclaim your greatness, Lord!"*

Acknowledgments

Thank You…

To Calvin Edwards, my miracle book agent, who listened to God's quiet voice.

To Ronald Blue, Larry Burkett, Dean Webb, Pat Robertson, Ken Klein, Henry Blackaby, Kerry Skinner, Tim Keller, Bill Hinson, Richard Scurry, John Houghton, Kelly Monroe, James Dobson, Betsy Neuenschwander, Victor Porlier, and Bill Merrell—the Christian leaders I interviewed (or who provided me with comments) for this book. Your time and insight are precious, and you gave it generously to me. Ron, Larry, and Calvin, your willing counsel and advice have helped to shape this book in ways you'll never know.

To the dedicated staff at Multnomah who worked so diligently to produce this book in such a short time frame—especially Steve Curley, Jennifer Curley, Steve Shepherd, Michele Tennesen, Chris Sundquist, Bob Keffer, Rod Morris, and my wonderful editor, Dan Benson.

To Jim Lord and Victor Porlier, who vetted this book for technical content. Thank you for willingly sharing your knowledge and time, and for supporting the work of the Joseph Project 2000.

To Focus on the Family, especially Tom Mason, Stan John, and David Jones. You became an unexpected and delightful answer to prayer.

To Liza Christian in Medford, Oregon. I am eternally grateful for your willingness to share from your experience for many long hours on the phone, and for your friendship as a sister in Christ.

To Dale and Janell Moseley in Bend, Oregon. Thank you for showing us how to adapt to Y2K your model of service and witness in crisis.

To Drew Parkhill and Chris Mitchell, CBN's Y2K czars, who patiently fielded my frantic last-minute phone calls asking for technical content and provided many fruitful contacts. Your help and friendship have been both invaluable and a great joy. May God bless your work.

To all those I depended on for technical advice and professional insight: Jim Duggan at Gartner Group, Eric Greenburg at AMA, Capers Jones at SPR, Ed Yourdon, Joseph Slife at CFC, Wendy at the city of Williamsburg, David Bradshaw at Y2KNet, Bruce Webster at the Washington, D.C., Y2K Group, Karen Anderson at Y2K Women, Paloma O'Riley at the Cassandra Project, Dean Harbry and Fran Lamatina at RBC, John Zachman, Nick Allen at Forrester Research Group, Ollie Davidson, Jon Shirek at Channel 11/NBC Atlanta, Brad Slutsky at King and Spalding, Sylvia Ronsville at Empty Tomb, Joel Ackerman at Rx2000, J. I. Packer, and Mike Hyatt.

To my friends and former colleagues at the New York Fed and ELIC who laid a great professional foundation and provided insight during this process—especially Gerard Dages and Ken Wendling, who held me to high standards and brought out the best in me.

To my precious friends who so willingly spent hours (often last-minute!) helping me meet my various deadlines: Alison Lambert and Kyleen Deanda, who researched all my permissions and helped me edit; David Treadwell and Margaret Carroway, who edited my chapters until the wee hours the day before my deadline; Kevin Broyles, who cross-checked facts and prepared citations; Michael, Debra, and Florie Goldstone, who provided a quiet writing retreat just when we needed it; David and Nancy French, Damon Preston, and Susan and Phil Rodenberg, who read and commented on the very first chapters and encouraged the beginning of this project; Marvin Goodwin, Anna Afshar, Kevin and Becky Loechel, Rishi Arora, Kerrin and Joe Kostelic, Tom Walsh, Ruth and Tadé Okediji, Tim and Audrey Lambert, D.J. Snell, Mary Ann and Jon Alger, Liz Tucci, and my many other friends who pitched in enthusiastically to support me with technical information and friendship through this process. I am especially grateful to Keith Lee, who may not realize that by convincing me to do the *Experiencing God* study he was laying the spiritual foundation for this book.

To Li-ann Thio, who started the whole thing, would not let it go, and first brought up the "Joseph model"; and to Mark and Annabelle Robertson, who told me about the Puritans during the great plague and who live that same sacrificial love every day.

To my God-given prayer team, who covered this book in prayer from day one and willingly fielded dozens of e-mail and phone prayer requests for everything from inspiration to interviews: Alison Lambert, John and Lisa Nagle, Debra and Michael Goldstone, Lara Johnson, Hilary Gettman, Steve and Deb Blum, Betsy Beinhocker, Tom and Michelle Jennings, John and Missy Bigham, Kathryn and Bjorn Lindstrom, Lilliana Colgate, and Judy "Mom" Hitson. You have upheld me in the most beautiful of ways, and I pray that God richly blesses your faithfulness.

To Kate and Greg Allen, Mel and Harriett Guinn, Lilliana Colgate, Vernadette Broyles, Jim Greer, Peter Erbele, Sheila Busby, Marge Chadwick, William Fisher, Ray Pate, and all the other tireless Joseph Project 2000 volunteers. You truly are the vigorous body of Christ—eyes, ears, hands, feet…and knees.

To Dr. Bill Hinson, who held me biblically accountable by reading my manuscript. We never did talk about China, but your wisdom on Y2K and this book are a gift from God.

To Johnny Crist, my pastor at the Atlanta Vineyard Christian Fellowship, who dealt patiently with this Y2K whirlwind that was suddenly added to his church. Thank you for your vision, your prayers, your reading of my manuscript, and your authority. Jeff and I thank God for your and Anne's friendship.

To my family: You may be a world away but you are ever near to my heart. To Rick, Canny, and Carrie Reidinger in Singapore. Rick, thank you for your friendship. All that writing you did years ago must have inspired me. Canny, welcome to the family.

To my parents: I miss you, but I am so excited for your joint adventure in China. God used your tender, loving care to "train me up" to give this message. I love you. To Grandpa Bob and Grandma Dorothy, Aunt Glenys, Bob and Rob, Carolyn and Steve and young Carrie, and all the rest of my extended family and Feldhahn in-laws—we may not see each other as often as we would like, but "I always thank God for you, remembering you in my prayers." I pray that this book touches you.

To my husband: You exhorted me, "*Please* don't say something sappy like 'You are the wind beneath my wings,'" so I won't. Just let me publicly acknowledge that you are the most loving, giving, Christlike man I've ever known. This book would not have been possible without your daily actions of love. You anguished in prayer so that I would be covered and protected. You encouraged me beyond my stress and self-doubt so I would remember that "he who began it is faithful to complete it." You read through books looking for one dimly remembered quote so that I could keep writing. You cheered me through long days and nights of typing at the keyboard as the deadline loomed. We are one. This book is yours, too.

To my Lord: I have come to know you in a way more deep, more beautiful, more intimate than ever before. You are *Jehovah Jireh,* my Provider for a task that was far beyond my abilities. If the words on these pages touch hearts, it is only because of you. You are Jesus, my Friend. ("Who am I, that you should regard me?") "Here is my heart, Lord, take and seal it; seal it for thy courts above." O Lord, give me the strength and the love to live the words within these pages. Amen.

APPENDIX

CHECKLISTS AND OTHER RESOURCES

Guide to this appendix (in order):

A. Setting up a Joseph Project 2000 group in your area

B. Resources for further investigation

C. Checking your personal computer

D. Preparing your organization

E. Preparing yourself and your family

A. SETTING UP A JOSEPH PROJECT 2000 GROUP IN YOUR AREA

To organize a Joseph Project 2000 group in your area or to contribute to the work of the Joseph Project 2000 nationally, contact the Joseph Project 2000 at 6409 Bells Ferry Road, Woodstock, GA 30189. Phone 678-445-5512; fax 678-445-5503. E-mail: *info@josephproject2000.org;* Web site: *www.josephproject2000.org.*

B. RESOURCES FOR FURTHER INVESTIGATION

From Shaunti Feldhahn:

Newsletter: *Y2K Countdown* monthly newsletter, see *www.josephproject2000.org* or e-mail *info@josephproject2000.org.* Also see subscription card in the back of this book.

Regular, free column on "Y2K and Charities" for Westergaard's online Y2K resource: *www.y2ktimebomb.com/Industry/NPO/sf9833.htm.*

From Jim Lord, P.O. Box 84910, Phoenix, AZ 85071, 1-888-Y2K-2555:

Book: *A Survival Guide for the Year 2000 Problem: Consumer Solutions,* $32.97 (consumer focused)

Newsletter: *Jim Lord's Year 2000 Survival Newsletter,* $104/year; book is free with subscription

From Michael Hyatt, 1-888-Y2K-PREP, *www.michaelhyatt.com*:

Book: *The Millennium Bug,* $24.95 (focuses on potential problems, personal preparation)

Resource Manual and Tape Series: *Countdown to Chaos,* David Dunham, editor, $89 complete set, $59 for the resource manual alone.

From Michael Fletcher, HighSpin Corporation, P.O. Box 2201 Station D, Ottawa ON K1P 5W4, phone 613-692-0752, fax 613-692-5033:

Book: *Computer Crisis 2000* (focuses on the needs of small business)

Online free column entitled "Y2K on the Job" that provides useful examples of potential impacts to different types of jobs: *www.y2ktimebomb.com*

From Alice and Eddie Smith, U.S. Prayer Track, 1-888-772-9872:

Book: *Y2KAOS!* (focuses on physical and spiritual preparation and how Christians can pray for Y2K)

From the Christian Broadcasting Network:

Video: Excellent one-hour specials on Y2K; combine documentary style with helpful studio interviews. *Y2K and the World* (aired July 10) and *Y2K and the Church* (aired August 7). Phone 1-800-777-8398. If you are looking for a resource to show your pastor, both of these are helpful.

Fact Sheets: Excellent compilation of relevant information about Y2K, targeted to the issue behind each TV special. FREE at 1-800-716-3228.

From Ed Yourdon and Jennifer Yourdon:

Book: *Time Bomb 2000* (focuses on industry-by-industry impacts. An excellent all-around resource in its second edition. *New York Times* bestseller in bookstores everywhere)

From Ronald Blue, 1-800-987-2987, *www.ronblue.com:*

Book: *Storm Shelter: How to Survive in Uncertain Economic Times.* Gives counsel on protecting personal finances. Available in Christian bookstores and on RBC Web site.

From Dynamic Solutions, 500 Trombley Bay Lane, Lawrenceville, GA 30044, 770-979-9792:

Video: *Getting Ready for Y2K.* Excellent presentation on how the average person with average resources can prepare for Y2K-related disruptions. Extensive resource guide included. $34.95.

From Jubilee Christian Fellowship, L&S Resources, P.O. Box 2494, Clackamas, OR, 97015, 1-800-510-6456:

Booklet: *Y2K and Other Unsettling Scenarios—Peace in the Midst of the Storm.* A 13-page booklet on using Y2K to build faith and bring God's church together. Also available for bulk distribution in churches and ministries (at $2.50/per or less). By George La Du, pastor.

From the Web:

It is ironic that the very technology we are worried about with Y2K is also the most useful tool for doing personal Y2K research. If you do not yet have an Internet service provider, you should make every effort to get Internet access to facilitate this process. Following are the Web sites I use in my daily research of Y2K, and which I believe are the most credible. As you investigate your industry and your area, you will be led to others.

www.year2000.com—Managed by Peter de Jager, the leading Y2K expert. Credible and extensive. If you have to pick just one Web site to check out, this is it.

www.y2ktimebomb.com—Westergaard's Y2K resource. Columns by recognized industry experts on telecommunications, power, banking, etc. Also check out Michael Fletcher's "Y2K on the Job," Jim Lord's "Tip of the Week," and my column on "Y2K and Charities."

www.y2kinsights.com—Christian Broadcasting Network. Good information and insights for the Christian community.

www.cfcministry.org—Christian Financial Concepts. Position paper and other Y2K information from Larry Burkett's financial ministry; advice on financial preparation.

www.ronblue.com—Ronald Blue & Co. Provides high-end personal financial, estate, and investment counsel; gearing up to provide "fiscal check-ups" in advance of Y2K.

www.sba.gov/y2k/cdc2.html—The Small Business Administration. Includes a primer on how to address Y2K vulnerabilities in organizations, as well as how to test your personal computer for Y2K problems.

www.millennia-bcs.com—The Cassandra Project, dedicated to helping individuals and communities prepare. Extensive and understandable. Highly practical information.

www.itpolicy.gsa.gov/mks/yr2000/usgovt.htm—Links to U.S. government Y2K sites.

www.worldbank.org/infodev/y2klinks.htm—Links to other countries' Y2K sites.

www.senate.gov/~bennett/y2k.html—Site of Senator Bennett, chairman of U.S. Senate Y2K Committee.

www.house.gov/reform/gmit—Site of Congressman Horn, chairman of House Y2K Committee.

www.itpolicy.gsa.gov/mks/yr2000/state.htm—Y2K links for different states.

www.y2kwomen.com—Well-regarded site for women on Y2K preparation; particularly targeted to interests of homemakers.

www.y2knews.com—Comprehensive coverage of breaking news on Y2K globally. Great source for personal research as 1999 progresses.

www.yardeni.com—Comprehensive and highly factual coverage of Y2K (and other) issues from respected Wall Street economist Edward Yardeni.

www.asimpson.com/adopt/chmenu.htm—Adopt-a-Charity. Helpful resource for nonprofits that need professional Y2K help.

www.rx2000.org—Y2K issues in medical industry.

www.euy2k.com—Y2K issues in power industry. Web site of Rick Cowles, electric utility industry representative.

www.gmt-2000.com—Greenwich Mean Time research firm. Y2K issues in personal computers.

www.y2kwatch.com—Balanced information to help individuals prepare "spiritually, physically and financially."

www.itaa.org/year2000.htm—Information Technology Association of America. Good source of technical but accessible information, including congressional testimony.

www.iee.org.uk/2000risk/guide/home.htm—Great report on the facts of the embedded systems problem from the Institute of Electrical Engineers.

www.christiany2k.com—"Information to guide a credible Christian witness."

churches.net/y2k/—Very good Y2K links from a network of churches.

C. CHECKING YOUR PERSONAL COMPUTER

How do you check a personal computer for Year 2000 readiness? Jim Lord warns that "setting the clock ahead on a PC is an incomplete test that does not adequately measure hardware compliance. It is also a dangerous test because it could corrupt or delete data files and could cause software licenses to expire for some types of commercial, specialty software." Lord also warns that 98 percent of PC Y2K problems come from applications or data, rather than from hardware or the operating system. Therefore, proceed with caution and be sure to allocate sufficient time for checking the former items. The following steps come directly from a Small Business Administration brochure (available from SBA's Web site at *www.sba.gov/y2k/cdc2.html*):

> The test presented here requires a bootable DOS floppy diskette. This is a safer method to test your PC's system clock because it leaves the data and programs on your PC's hard disk unaffected. If you boot to your C: drive, you may end up loading Windows or Windows 95 and other applications from your startup routine. Using a bootable diskette will ensure the integrity of the data and programs on your PC's hard disks. The test script presented here will check your PC's ability to transition to Year 2000 and recognize it as a leap year. Do not perform the tests by changing your system's BIOS Setup screen.

1. Create a bootable test diskette. Insert a blank floppy diskette into the PC's A: drive. From a DOS prompt, type FORMAT A: /S. Or from Windows File Manager, click on DISK/FORMAT and check MAKE SYSTEM DISK.

2. With the bootable diskette created in Step 1 still in your PC's floppy drive, shut down your system (close Windows) and turn off the power to your PC. Don't just hit the reset button or warmboot (CTL-ALT-DEL).

3. Turn the power on and allow the PC to boot from the diskette.

4. After bootup, DOS automatically shows the current date. Make sure the correct date is displayed. Otherwise, you may have to set the correct date on your PC's BIOS.

5. At the *Enter New Date (mm-dd-yy):* prompt, type *12-31-1999*. After changing the date, the current time will be displayed. At the *Enter New Time:* prompt, type *23:55:00*.

6. Turn the PC's power off and wait at least ten minutes. If you don't, DOS will appear to transition correctly to the year 2000. However, once you reboot the PC, it will display the incorrect date if your system's RTC has the flaw described above.

7. Turn the power back on and wait for the boot process to complete.

8. Type in date at the *Ready* prompt. If *Sat 01-01-2000* is displayed, your PC's BIOS passes the test.

9. At the *Enter New Date (mm-dd-yy):* prompt, type *02-28-2000*. This will test your system's ability to recognize A.D. 2000 as a leap year.

10. After changing the date, the current time will be displayed. At the *Enter New Time:* prompt, type *23:55:00*.

11. Power off your PC again and wait at least ten minutes.

12. Turn the power back on. Type in date at the *Ready* prompt. If *Tue 02-29-2000* is displayed, your PC's BIOS passes the leap year test.

13. To conclude testing, at the *Enter New Date (mm-dd-yy):* prompt, enter the correct date, e.g. *12-20-1998*.

14. After changing the date, the current time will be displayed. At the *Enter New Time:* prompt, type correct time, e.g. *06:00:00*.

15. Remove the bootable diskette from the floppy drive and power off your PC.

PC Checking Software

Greenwich Mean Time, one of the principal companies researching the effects of Y2K on individual PCs, sells a $75 software package that checks your PC for problems and offers other tips. Contact them at *http://www.gmt-2000.com/ck2000pc.htm*.

Several additional Web sites purport to offer free PC testing software and other tips, although the author cannot guarantee that these products will actually be effective, or even that they will not damage your PC:

- Mitre *http://www.mitre.org* (recommended by Jim Lord);
- Ymark 2000 *http://www.nstl.com*;
- Test 2000 *http://www.rightime.com*;
- Survive 2000 *http://www.patssb.com*.

D. PREPARING YOUR ORGANIZATION

Business, government, and nonprofit organizations alike should use the well-tested process summarized below to assess and resolve their Y2K vulnerabilities. The following information is drawn directly from the Small Business Administration's Y2K resources, which can be viewed free online under "Checklist for Small Businesses" at *www.sba.gov/y2k/*. Remember that this information is just a starting point for further investigation, and that it must be tailored for each organization.

The following six steps should be conducted with regard to every part of the organization's environment—every aspect of the "food chain." These steps are generally accepted by all experts working to resolve Y2K problems in organizations of all kinds. This section cannot provide the level of detail sufficient for full development of a Y2K strategy and is no substitute for a full professional assessment—it is meant simply to provide an overview of the primary issues.

1. Awareness

Educate and involve all levels of your organization in solving the problem. Assemble a team to address Year 2000 problems, create an organization-wide communication strategy (most especially with and among management), and develop an internal standard for Y2K readiness.

2. Inventory

Audit your organization and create your checklist toward Year 2000 readiness. Identify and list all of your computer-based systems, components (such as in-house developed systems, purchased software, computers, and associated hardware), service providers, and hardware that contain microchips that support your business. Each entry on your list should be ranked by how critical it is to your business. You may decide to put off addressing non-mission-critical, low-risk items. Record vendor and release number where appropriate. Assign a person who will be responsible for assessing that item and preparing for Year 2000. (Remember that some systems will begin failing before the rollover. This "time horizon to failure" should be listed on the inventory.)

3. Assessment

Examine how severe and widespread the problem is in your business and determine what needs to be fixed. Starting with the most critical items on the inventory and those with an imminent time horizon to failure, determine which systems are date-sensitive and may fail when the century changes. A date-sensitive system is one that manipulates or works with dates, or operates differently based upon the date. Remember that it may not be possible to determine whether some systems or items have hidden date sensitivity, so you should assess anything that is critical to the functioning of your organization.

For example, date-sensitive systems include those that perform any kind of forecasting or projections through time, such as calculating interest on a loan or projecting inventory levels. Date-sensitive systems may retrieve records based on a date (such as invoices) or sort items by date (such as accounting or inventory systems). Examples of date-sensitive hardware include lighting systems that switch on automatically on weekdays, manufacturing control systems, and scanners or card readers that read ID badges or credit/debit cards. (For a good checklist, see Figure 4 from the excellent report entitled "Year 2000 Problems in Machinery" by the Institute of Electrical Engineers, available by calling their office in Great Britain: 44-1438-313311 (or fax to 44-1438-742792).

There are several ways to assess your critical inventory:

- Look at the computer code and follow the logic.
- Contact the vendor, supplier, or manufacturer and ask for an assessment of Y2K compliance. Ideally, this should be a written guarantee that the item will work properly after 1999, but many suppliers resist providing such blanket assurances. In the absence of a guarantee, any credible information will be helpful.
- Test the system (this is *not* recommended for many systems!) by running it as if it were already A.D. 2000. Such testing may require resetting the system date, which may involve serious risks for the machinery. Therefore, each organization should evaluate the impact of this sort of testing on their organization. The Institute of Electrical Engineers advises organizations *not* to test complex systems by resetting dates, unless there is no other means of deciding the item's readiness and the item is critical to the business.
- For some specialized systems, such as building or manufacturing control systems, or systems with embedded microchips, you may need to have the vendor work with your staff to test and assess the system.

Once you have determined the state of readiness for each system and component listed in your inventory, you should develop a strategy for dealing with those systems that have to be fixed. There are only three possible strategies: repair, replace, or retire the system. In addition, you should develop a strategy to "work around" any possible problems that might still occur in spite of all your efforts.

• *Repair*. If you decide to repair a computer system, there are basically two possible approaches: windowing (interpreting whether a given year falls into the 20th or 21st centuries before performing calculations) or date expansion (expanding all two-digit year fields to four digits). You will need to investigate the appropriate approach for your business. If you are repairing items with embedded chips, you will likely need to go through the manufacturer or vendor.

• *Replace*. To replace a nonready system, you can build the replacement in-house (with or without contractors), purchase a replacement system from a vendor (after ensuring it is Y2K-ready!), or you can outsource that particular line of business to a compliant service bureau or other outside service provider. It is very important to determine when the replacement will be ready. If the replacement won't be tested and installed until after the time horizon to failure, you may be forced into a repair strategy.

No business systems operate in isolation. Most interface with other systems—both inside and outside your organization—to exchange data. Your strategy for nonready systems should take into account their interfaces with other internal and external systems. You should develop a chart that shows the systems with interfaces, what those interfaces are, and when they occur.

When you find that a system is not Year 2000-ready, determine how critical that system is to your business. For example, if the system prints an invalid date on an internally used report, you may decide that this problem is not significant enough to address. If, however, the system loses track of inventory data or fails to forecast properly, you will probably want to fix it.

4. Fixing and Testing

Implement your readiness strategy and test the fix. Testing is one of the most critical aspects of a Year 2000 project and consumes roughly half the time of the total Y2K project. Testing verifies that the repaired or replaced system and its functions operate properly when the date changes, and verifies that interfacing systems are not adversely affected. You should not confine your testing efforts solely to computer programs. Other systems (including network operating systems, vendor-supplied software, building infrastructure systems, PCs, and components with embedded microchips) should be tested to ensure they will not fail when the century changes.

You should perform several critical tests once you change or replace a system to see if it is truly ready for Year 2000.

The best way is to test the system as if it were already A.D. 2000. Test that the system will operate correctly after the date has rolled over from 12/31/1999 to 1/1/2000, and for other key dates, such as 2/29/2000, since the year 2000 is a leap year. However, please note that rolling dates forward on computers can be risky. (For example, if your system tracks the last time a user accessed it, it may revoke or inactivate that user's password if it thinks the user has been "gone" a year.) Data sets that should be retained may be marked as expired and could be written over. With leased software packages, rolling the date past the end of the lease may cause the software package to freeze up or generate error messages.

There are several other tests that you may want to carry out, depending on the functions your system supports. If your system does end-of-month processing, for example, you should test that the system will forecast and retrieve data properly. Set the date to December 1999 and check that the system will forecast into the next century. Further, set the system to any date after the rollover, and test that it will retrieve historical data from before 12/31/1999.

Whenever possible, testing should be carried out in a test environment to minimize the chance of corrupting the production systems. Also, be careful of changing historical or backup files if you choose date expansion. You may lose an important audit trail, so consult with auditors/lawyers before changing historical or backup files. Further, you should test changed systems in an environment that is ready for Year 2000. Work with your vendors to determine when their hardware platforms will be compliant and use those dates to build your test plans. If your vendor cannot supply the platform to meet your schedule, you should be aware of the risks involved and be prepared to retest your changed systems once the platform is ready.

Embedded systems pose unique problems during both the assessment and testing process. Victor Porlier, a Y2K consultant, passes along some useful insight shared by a CalTrans representative at a

May 1998 conference: "The problem is compounded because you can't duplicate the embedded system environment for testing like you can a software application; for many devices you can't roll the date forward without destroying the equipment.... We are finding it is taking us about four hours per device to test out after getting them on our inventory."

5. Implementation

Move your repaired or replaced system into your "live" operating environment. Before you install your replacement or repaired system, you should develop an installation plan and contingency plans. The installation plan lists all the files and programs that need to be moved into production, and all the steps to make your changed system work. Your installation plan may include testing in production to ensure that the installed systems are working as expected. Contingency plans list the possible problems that you can foresee and what steps you will take if these problems occur.

You may want to make backups of the production files from the old system. If possible, you may want to install the ready system and run it in parallel with the old system and compare results. Your contingency plans should not include reverting to the old system. The old system is not ready for Year 2000; otherwise you would not be replacing or repairing it.

Important note: You must ensure that your system for backing up files, data, etc., is Year 2000-ready itself. It would be disastrous if your primary system fails in January 2000 and you discover that you can't restore your lost data because your backup system is inoperable as well.

6. Control

Once you have repaired your systems and made them Year 2000-compliant, you should take steps to make sure that subsequent changes do not contaminate those systems with Y2K bugs. As you replace and upgrade old computers, packages, and other hardware, ensure that the new equipment is Year 2000-ready. Make sure your programmers don't make changes to a repaired system that inadvertently change the logic handling the century change.

Retest the Year 2000 changes as part of any subsequent system modification effort. Save the test data and test cases that were used to test the original changes and use them whenever you test other changes to that system. All new releases of vendor-supplied packages should also be Year 2000 tested, regardless of the vendor's assurances of compliance.

Applying These Steps to the Food Chain

When considering the above steps, remember the adage that "you are only as ready as those you do business with." The outline above principally addresses the systems and facilities portion of your organization's operating environment, but you also need to consider the Y2K vulnerabilities of your suppliers, your products and services, and your constituents. Their vulnerabilities could become yours.

For example, if your bank is somewhat disrupted and you cannot access your bank account, you won't be able to pay yourself or your employees. If your city's power grid goes out, it won't matter how compliant your computers are. If the distribution system for medicines goes haywire, your free medical ministry services will be curtailed. If 15 percent of your congregation loses their jobs, your donations may drop off dramatically. Your entire chain of vulnerabilities needs to be considered and addressed directly. You will need to develop good contingency plans for what to do under varying Y2K scenarios.

The Small Business Administration offers the following four tips as examples for how to protect your organization within this chain:

- *Vendor-supplied products*. Many software vendors were caught by surprise by the Y2K problem and some will not be able to make their products ready. Others may make their products ready but won't be able to deliver until late 1999. Some vendors may no longer support your particular product or may have gone out of business entirely. For date-sensitive systems, contact the vendors to find out their readiness plans. If a vendor will not give you information about the readiness status of a package, or if a ready version will not be available until late 1999, you should investigate an alternate system. Even if a vendor insists its product can handle the century date change, you still should test and certify his product to your satisfaction. If the vendor insists that an upgraded version of a program package is ready, that package still must be tested since the vendor may have a different definition of readiness.
- *Data processing service bureaus*. If you use a service bureau for your data processing needs, ask for its plans for Year 2000 readiness. Make a list of all the services provided by your service bureau, ranking them according to how critical they are to you, and then contact the bureau in writing about each service. If a service bureau says it is ready for Year 2000, ask it to provide test results demonstrating this. If possible, test the service for yourself. If it is ready for certain services but not for others, you should determine what this means to your organization. Decide if there is a "work around" you can implement. If the service bureau says it will have a Year 2000 version in the future, you need to assess what that means to your business. A date late in 1999 may be too risky.
- *Utilities and services*. If your local utility fails to provide you with water, gas, or electricity, your buildings will not be usable and your business will suffer. You should also contact other companies that provide essential services such as janitorial, repair, delivery, etc. You should contact all of your suppliers to discuss the state of their Year 2000 readiness and make contingency plans.
- *Record storage/retention firms*. You may use such a firm to store critical legal documents and backup tapes off-site. These firms should be contacted to determine their state of readiness. It could be disastrous if you have an emergency and discover that your off-site storage firm can't find or operate your backups.

Financial Vulnerabilities

The assessment of external vulnerabilities must include an evaluation of financial prospects in the Year 2000 environment. The last economic slump in the U.S. came during the real estate and banking crisis of 1989–1991. Statistics from the Independent Sector, a coalition of corporations, foundations, and charitable organizations, demonstrate that charitable and especially religious giving dropped off dramatically during that time. Consider the following table:

	Changes in Total Charitable Giving (constant $)	Change in Total Religious Giving (constant $)	Change in Annual Household Income (constant $, U.S. Census Bureau)	Change in Population (U.S. Census Bureau)
1987–1989	20%	17%	3%	1.8%
1989–1991	-19%	-21%	-5.5%	2.1%
1991–1993	-7%	-8%	3%	2.2%

During the last period of economic difficulty, average household income dropped only 5 percent but total charitable giving dropped nearly 20 percent. Of greater concern for churches, religious giving (the bulk of which was directly to churches) dipped even more than the general trend. However, an empirical study of church giving by Empty Tomb, Inc., documented inconsistencies with this data. Their research posited that periodic reductions in giving are actually more highly correlated with other factors, such as increasing "consumer" attitudes among church members (i.e., "Church is about what I get out of it") and declines in a proactive church agenda for dealing with affluence. These findings aren't necessarily reassuring in light of Y2K, as they closely track our current societal situation. In the end, disproportionate reductions in donations during past economic downturns are also supported by the anecdotal accounts of ministry directors.

Furthermore, nonprofits face all the other quandaries of regular businesses in that they are exposed to the risk of external disruption of the financial system (e.g., that banks will be unable to grant immediate access to deposits in order to pay employees or fund ministry needs).

As Year 2000 approaches, nonprofit organizations—especially churches and other ministries—need to develop plans to deal with the simultaneous possibility of increased demands and decreased financial income. There are at least three primary means of dealing with these potential pressures:

- *Prepare the organization financially.* Ministries with a healthy flow of donations, for example, might decide to delay the start of a new program in order to increase their reserve fund. Diversify financial holdings into two different banks, increase savings, and increase cash on hand in the same way a household should.
- *Prepare constituents.* A church or ministry should consider addressing the issue directly, perhaps making an appeal for contributions to a "Y2K reserve fund" that will prepare that particular church body to serve the community during any serious Y2K disruptions.
- *Pray.* Begin a serious intercessory effort over the church's financial strength and its ability to meet both regular obligations and any increase in demand.

E. PREPARING YOURSELF AND YOUR FAMILY

The following condensed checklists are used by permission of Paloma O'Riley, founder of the Cassandra Project. For complete details, go to *http://millennia-bcs.com/prep.htm.*

Long-Term Food and Basic Supplies (Courtesy of FEMA)

At least three or four months in advance, store large amounts of staples along with a variety of canned and dried foods (canned goods should be rotated periodically) and other basic supplies such as toiletries. Bulk quantities of wheat, corn, beans, and salt are inexpensive and have nearly unlimited shelf life. From a sporting or camping equipment store, you may consider purchasing commercially packaged, freeze-dried or air-dried foods (which are costly but might be your best form of stored meat). FEMA recommends stocking the following amounts of bulk food staples per person, per month:

> wheat—20 pounds; powdered milk (for babies and infants)*—20 pounds; corn—20 pounds; iodized salt—1 pound; soybeans—10 pounds; vitamin C**—15 grams. (* Buy in nitrogen-packed cans; ** Rotate every two years.)

Also include other foods such as ready-to-eat canned meats, fruits, and vegetables; canned juices, milk, soup; staples such as sugar and pepper; vitamins; ready-to-eat cereals; vegetable oils; baking powder; beans; white rice; dry pasta.

Store basic supplies such as plastic plates/utensils, flashlights and batteries, matches, toilet paper, baby supplies, feminine products, soap, and garbage bags in large, covered plastic storage bins. A basic first-aid kit should include a first-aid manual, bandages and gauze pads, adhesive tape, scissors, tweezers, needles, towelettes, antiseptic, thermometer, petroleum jelly or other lubricant, safety pins, soap, nonprescription drugs (such as pain reliever, antidiarrhea medication, antacid, laxative), syrup of ipecac (use to induce vomiting if advised by the Poison Control Center), activated charcoal (use if advised by the Poison Control Center). Be sure to see the Cassandra Project's Web site for the complete lists.

Food Storage

In case of power shortages, store prepackaged food that won't spoil until opened, or canned foods that don't require cooking, water, or special preparation. Survival rations can usually be bought at an army surplus store and camp rations at a camping supply store. Milk may be purchased in cans, vacuum-packed, or in powder form. Powdered eggs can be used in a pinch. Baby formula is usually canned or powdered. Be sure your canned perishables are sized for use—you won't be able to store opened cans of milk, etc., without risking food poisoning. Store wheat, corn, and beans in sealed cans or plastic buckets. Buy powdered milk in nitrogen-packed cans. And leave salt and vitamin C in their original packages. For favorite perishables such as strawberries, bananas, etc., you might consider purchasing far in advance and dehydrating. Today's dehydrators are simple to use and very effective. Storage can be as simple as Ziploc bags or vacuum-sealed jars. Keep all stored food in the driest and coolest spot in the house—a dark area if possible—and covered or sealed at all times. Be sure you inspect all food containers for signs of spoilage before use.

Food Preparation

A propane or kerosene stove works just fine for most stovetop cooking. The only problem is having enough fuel, proper ventilation, and fire prevention (keep ABC-type extinguishers handy). Other options are outdoor charcoal or propane grills and wood-burning fireplaces. You can also heat food with candle warmers, chafing dishes, and fondue pots. Camping supply stores have many cooking devices—from solar stoves to the old sterno cans. Make any purchases well in advance, because prices are bound to rise and availability fall as Year 2000 approaches.

To avoid serious digestive problems, you'll need to grind the corn and wheat into flour and cook them, as well as boil the beans, before eating. Many health food stores sell hand-cranked grain and corn mills. You can also grind grain by filling a large can with whole grain one inch deep, holding the can on the ground between your feet and pounding the grain with a pipe.

Storing Water

A normally active person needs to drink at least two quarts of water each day. Hot environments and intense physical activity can double that amount. Children, nursing mothers, and ill people need more. Store one gallon of water per person per day (two quarts for drinking, two quarts for food preparation and personal hygiene).

Before storing water, you will need to treat it with a preservative such as chlorine bleach to prevent the growth of microorganisms. Use liquid bleach that contains 5.25 percent sodium hypochlorite and no soap. (Some containers warn, "Not For Personal Use." You can disregard these warnings if the label states sodium hypochlorite is the only active ingredient and if you use only the small quantities in these instructions.) Add four drops of bleach per quart of water (or two scant teaspoons per ten gallons) and stir. Seal containers tightly, label them, and store them in a cool, dark place. You may also want to consider boiling your storage water, for boiling is the safest method of water purification. Bring water to a rolling boil for ten minutes, keeping in mind that some water will evaporate.

Store water in thoroughly washed plastic or fiberglass containers, or enamel-lined metal containers. Never use a container that has held toxic substances, because trace amounts may remain in the pores of the container. Sturdy, unbreakable plastic containers, such as soft drink bottles, are good. You can also purchase food-grade plastic buckets or large drums (drums are perhaps the best method for volume storage, but be sure you also purchase a siphon to get the water out as you need it). You can purchase large containers of drinking water at your grocery store or simply fill containers from your own tap. Again, always treat water before storing it long term.

NOTES

Unless otherwise noted, multiple comments from Christian leaders and Y2K experts are referenced as follows:

- *Henry Blackaby.* Author's interview, July 15, 1998, Rex, Georgia
- *Ronald Blue.* Author's interviews, RBC headquarters, June 26 and July 9, 1998, Atlanta, Georgia
- *Larry Burkett.* Author's interview, CFC headquarters, June 16, 1988, Gainesville, Georgia
- *James Dobson.* Written comments provided to author, September 1998
- *William Hinson.* Author's meeting, Haggai Institute headquarters, June 2, 1998, Atlanta, Georgia
- *Tim Keller.* Author's telephone interview, June 29, 1998
- *Jim Lord.* Author's interviews and correspondence in person and via telephone and e-mail, June through September 1998
- *Kelly Monroe.* Author's telephone interview, July 9, 1998
- *Victor Porlier.* Author's telephone interviews and e-mail correspondence, September 1998.
- *Pat Robertson.* Author's interview, CBN headquarters, June 8, 1998, Virginia Beach, Virginia

CHAPTER TWO

1. From a speech by Senator Bennett before the National Press Club, Washington, D.C., July 15, 1989.
2. General Accounting Office, *Year 2000 Computing Crisis: Potential for Widespread Disruption Calls for Strong Federal Leadership,* GAO/AIMD-98-85 (April 30, 1998) at Letters 1 and 3.
3. GAO, Letter 3.
4. Author's telephone interview with Jim Duggan, Gartner Group, July 31, 1998.
5. Edward Yourdon and Jennifer Yourdon, *Time Bomb 2000* (New Jersey: Prentice Hall PTR, 1998), 381.
6. From a presentation at SPG's Year 2000 Conference and Expo, New York, March 1998. As reported by Scott Kirsner in *CIO Magazine,* July 1, 1998; www.cio.com/archive/070198_y2k_content.html.

CHAPTER FOUR

1. Author's telephone interview with Bill Merrell, July 9, 1998.
2. Testimony before the Senate Special Committee on the Year 2000 Technology Problem, July 6, 1998.
3. Capers Jones, *The Global Economic Impact of the Year 2000 Software Problem* (Software Productivity Research Group, 1997), available online at www.spr.com/html/year_2000_problem.htm.
4. Robert Samuelson, "Computer Doomsday?" *Washington Post,* May 6, 1998.

5. From a speech by George Colony, "Blunt Talk About Year 2000," Forrester Research, Inc., before the Securities Industry Association, New York City, January 15, 1998.
6. *Summary Report: Small Business and the Year 2000 Problem,* prepared by NFIB Education Foundation, sponsored by Wells Fargo Bank, April 1998.
7. *Summary Report,* Wells Fargo.
8. Author's telephone interview with Richard Scurry, July 22, 1998.
9. Peter de Jager, appearing on the *700 Club* special "Y2K and the World," July 10, 1998.
10. "Readiness for the Upcoming Solar Maximum," White Paper (National Academy of Sciences, National Academy Press, Washington, D.C., 1998); www.nas.edu/ssb/maxmenu.htm.
11. Jim Lord, Westergaard "Tip of the Week," 8 December 1997, www.y2ktimebomb.com/Tip/Lord/lord9749.htm.
12. Senator Bennett, July 15, 1989.
13. Jim Seymour, "Y2K...Time for Triage," *PC Magazine,* June 30, 1998.
14. *Atlanta Business Chronicle,* April 20, 1998.
15. Bruce Webster, "The Estimated Impact of the Year 2000 Problem in the United States," survey released April 21, 1998; www.bfwa.com/bwebster/y2k.
16. Author's telephone interview with Joel Ackerman, Executive Director Rx2000, July 24, 1998.
17. As reported on CNN, June 5, 1997; (cnnfn.com/hotstories/bizbuzz/9706/05/smith_barney/)
18. Calvin Woodward, "Government Faces Computer Dilemma," Associated Press, May 26, 1998.
19. Michael Mandel, "Zap! How the Year 2000 Bug Will Hurt the Economy," *Business Week,* March 2, 1998, 95.
20. Confidential information from the personal contacts of a respected Christian leader.
21. "Hong Kong Airport Chaos Shows How Y2K Bug May Pan Out," *Bloomberg News,* July 13, 1998.
22. Genevieve Buck, "New Century Means a New Problem," *Chicago Tribune,* June 19, 1998.
23. Senator Bennett; July 15, 1989.
24. Senator Bennett; July 15, 1989.
25. Report Cards are periodically released by Subcommittee Chairman Horn, Subcommittee on Government Management, Information and Technology; www.house.gov/reform/gmit.
26. Capers Jones, *Probabilities of Year 2000 Damages,* Table 3 (Software Productivity Research, February 27, 1998).

CHAPTER FIVE

1. Rich Mullins and Steven Robert Cudworth, IF I STAND, © 1988 BMG Songs, Inc. (ASCAP), All Rights reserved. Used By Permission.

CHAPTER SIX

1. Larry Burkett, *Money Matters*, Issue 245, June 1998; Christian Financial Concepts.
2. Motto posted on Paloma O'Riley's Web site, the Cassandra Project; www.millennia-bcs.com.
3. Rodney Stark, *The Rise of Christianity* (New Jersey, HarperCollins, 1997).
4. Rodney Stark, "Live Longer, Healthier and Better," *Christian History Magazine* (online version), Issue 57; www2.christianity.net/christianhistory/, a publication of the Christianity Today family.

5. Stark, *The Rise of Christianity,* 82.
6. Ibid., 212.
7. Ibid., 94.
8. Henry Blackaby and Claude King, *Experiencing God: Knowing and Doing the Will of God* (Nashville, LifeWay Press, 1990).
9. Taken from Elizabeth Dole's essay "Crisis and Faith" appearing in the book *Finding God at Harvard,* edited by Kelly Monroe. Copyright 1996 by Kelly K. Monroe. Used by permission of Zondervan Publishing House.
10. "Prologue" from the musical *Les Miserables* by Alain Boublil and Claude-Michel Schonberg. Music by Claude-Michel Schonberg. Lyrics by Alain Boublil and Herbert Kretzmer. Copyright Alain Boublil Music Ltd (ASCAP). Used by permission.
11. Drs. Mark and Betsy Neuenschwander, from their essay "Watch the Window Open Wider," appearing in the book *Windowatchman II* (compiled and edited by Beverly Pegues, Christian Information Network, Colorado Springs, 1997).

CHAPTER EIGHT

1. From Dr. Michael Youssef's pastoral letter appearing in *Apostles News,* Newsletter of the Church of the Apostles, Volume XI, Number 7, July 1998. Used by permission.

CHAPTER TEN

1. Yourdon and Yourdon, 292.

CHAPTER ELEVEN

1. Blackaby and King, 52, 66, 71.